14.99

Seasons of Devotion

Seasons of Devotion

365 Bible readings and prayers
to guide you through the year

Compiled by

PHILIP LAW

continuum

Continuum
The Tower Building, 11 York Road, London SE1 7NX
15 East 26th Street, Suite 1703, New York, NY 10010

www.continuumbooks.com

This abridgement copyright © Philip J. Law 2005, taken from the text of the
Revised English Bible originally published by Oxford University Press and
Cambridge University Press in 1989.

This abridged edition is published with the permission of the Syndicate of the Press of the
University of Cambridge, Cambridge, England.

© Oxford University Press and Cambridge University Press, 1989.

Selection and arrangement of Bible readings and prayers copyright © Philip J. Law, 2005

British Library Cataloguing-in-Publication Data
A catalogue record for this book is available from the British Library

ISBN 0-8264-8045-4 (hardback)

Designed and typeset by Kenneth Burnley
Printed on acid-free paper in Great Britain by MPG Books Ltd, Cornwall

CONTENTS

A Season for Everything

For everything its season,
and for every activity under heaven its time:

a time to be born and a time to die;
a time to plant and a time to uproot;

a time to kill and a time to heal;
a time to break down and a time to build up;

a time to weep and a time to laugh;
a time for mourning and a time for dancing;

a time to scatter stones and a time to gather them;
a time to embrace and a time to abstain from embracing;

a time to seek and a time to lose;
a time to keep and a time to discard;

a time to tear and a time to mend;
a time for silence and a time for speech;

a time to love and a time to hate;
a time for war and a time for peace.

PART ONE

Meditations on God

WEEK 1

God's Creation

Day 1

The Beginning

IN THE BEGINNING God created the heavens and the earth. The earth was a vast waste, darkness covered the deep, and the spirit of God hovered over the surface of the water. God said, 'Let there be light,' and there was light; and God saw the light was good, and he separated light from darkness. He called the light day, and the darkness night.

God said, 'Let there be a vault between the waters, to separate water from water.' So God made the vault, and separated the water under the vault from the water above it, and so it was; and God called the vault the heavens.

God said, 'Let the water under the heavens be gathered into one place, so that dry land may appear'; and so it was. God called the dry land earth, and the gathering of the water he called sea; and God saw that it was good.

Then God said, 'Let the earth produce growing things; let there be on the earth plants that bear seed, and trees bearing fruit each with its own kind of seed.' So it was; the earth produced growing things: plants bearing their own kind of seed and trees bearing fruit, each with its own kind of seed; and God saw that it was good.

God said, 'Let there be lights in the vault of the heavens to separate day from night, and let them serve as signs both for festivals and for seasons and years. Let them also shine in the heavens to give light on earth.' So it was; God made two great lights, the greater to govern the day and the lesser to govern the night; he also made the stars. God put these lights in the vault of the heavens to give light on earth, to govern day and night, and to separate light from darkness; and God saw that it was good.

O God, we thank thee for this universe, our great home; for its vastness and its riches, and for the manifoldness of the life which teems upon it and of which we are a part. Grant us, we pray thee, a heart wide open to all this joy and beauty.

Walter Rauschenbusch, 1861–1918

Day 2

Crown of Creation

G OD SAID, 'Let the water teem with living creatures, and let birds fly above the earth across the vault of the heavens.' God then created the great sea-beasts and all living creatures that move and swarm in the water, according to their various kinds, and every kind of bird; and God saw that it was good. He blessed them and said, 'Be fruitful and increase; fill the water of the sea, and let the birds increase on the land.' Evening came, and morning came, the fifth day.

God said, 'Let the earth bring forth living creatures, according to their various kinds: cattle, creeping things, and wild animals, all according to their various kinds.' So it was; God made wild animals, cattle, and every creeping thing, all according to their various kinds; and he saw that it was good. Then God said, 'Let us make human beings in our image, after our likeness, to have dominion over the fish in the sea, the birds of the air, the cattle, all wild animals on land, and everything that creeps on the earth.'

> God created human beings in his own image;
> in the image of God he created them;
> male and female he created them.

God blessed them and said to them, 'Be fruitful and increase, fill the earth and subdue it, have dominion over the fish in the sea, the birds of the air, and every living thing that moves on the earth.' So it was; and God saw all that he had made, and it was very good.

> *Lord, since you exist, we exist. Since you are beautiful, we are beautiful. Since you are good, we are good. By our existence we honour you. By our beauty we glorify you. By our goodness we love you.*
>
> *Lord, through your power all things were made. Through your wisdom all things are governed. Through your grace all things are sustained.*

Edmund Rich, c.1120–1240

Day 3

The Voice of Wisdom

Hear how wisdom calls
and understanding lifts her voice.

'The Lord created me the first of his works
long ago, before all else that he made.
I was formed in earliest times,
at the beginning, before earth itself.
I was born when there was yet no ocean,
when there were no springs brimming with water.
Before the mountains were settled in their place,
before the hills I was born,
when as yet he had made neither land nor streams
nor the mass of the earth's soil.
When he set the heavens in place I was there,
when he girdled the ocean with the horizon,
when he fixed the canopy of clouds overhead
and confined the springs of the deep,
when he prescribed limits for the sea
so that the waters do not transgress his command,
when he made earth's foundations firm.
Then I was at his side each day,
his darling and delight,
playing in his presence continually,
playing over his whole world,
while my delight was in mankind.'

O Creator past all telling,
you have so beautifully set out all parts of the universe;
you are the true fount of wisdom
and the noble origin of all things.
Be pleased to shed on the darkness of my mind
the beam and warmth of your light
to dispel my ignorance and sin.

Thomas Aquinas, 1225–74

Day 4

Where Were You?

Where were you when I laid the earth's foundations?
Tell me, if you know and understand.
Who fixed its dimensions? Surely you know!
Who stretched a measuring line over it?
On what do its supporting pillars rest?
Who set its corner-stone in place,
while the morning stars sang in chorus
and the sons of God all shouted for joy?

Who supported the sea at its birth,
when it burst in flood from the womb –
when I wrapped it in a blanket of cloud
and swaddled it in dense fog,
when I established its bounds,
set its barred doors in place,
and said, 'Thus far may you come but no farther;
here your surging waves must halt'?

Have you gone down to the springs of the sea
or walked in the unfathomable deep?
Have the portals of death been revealed to you?
Have you seen the door-keepers of the place of darkness?
Have you comprehended the vast expanse of the world?
Tell me all this, if you know.

Which is the way to the home of light,
and where does darkness dwell?
Does the rain have a father?
Who sired the drops of dew?
Whose womb gave birth to the ice,
and who was the mother of the hoar-frost in the skies,
which lays a stony cover over the waters
and freezes the surface of the deep?

Almighty God, whose glory the heavens are telling, the earth his power, and the seas his might, and whose greatness all feeling and thinking creatures everywhere herald; to you belong glory, honour, might, greatness and magnificence now and for ever, to the ages of ages, through Jesus Christ our Lord.

Liturgy of St James

Day 5

Silent Witnesses

The heavens tell out the glory of God,
heaven's vault makes known his handiwork.
One day speaks to another,
night to night imparts knowledge,
and this without speech or language
or sound of any voice.
Their sign shines forth on all the earth,
their message to the ends of the world.
In the heavens an abode is fixed for the sun,
which comes out like a bridegroom from the bridal chamber,
rejoicing like a strong man to run his course.
Its rising is at one end of the heavens,
its circuit reaches from one end to the other,
and nothing is hidden from its heat.

You alone are unutterable,
from the time you created all things
that can be spoken of.
You alone are unknowable,
from the time you created all things
that can be known.
All things cry out about you;
those which speak,
and those which cannot speak.
All things honour you;
those which think,
and those which cannot think.

In you, the One, all things abide,
and all things endlessly run to you
who are the end of all.

Gregory of Nazianzus, 329–89

Day 6

The Eternal King

Lord, you have been our refuge
throughout all generations.
Before the mountains were brought forth
or the earth and the world were born,
from age to age you are God.

You turn mortals back to dust,
saying, 'Turn back, you children of mortals,'
for in your sight a thousand years
are as the passing of one day
or as a watch in the night.

You cut them off;
they are asleep in death.
They are like grass which shoots up;
though in the morning it flourishes and shoots up,
by evening it droops and withers.

Seventy years is the span of our life,
eighty if our strength holds;
at their best they are but toil and sorrow,
for they pass quickly and we vanish.
Who feels the power of your anger,
who feels your wrath like those who fear you?

So make us know how few are our days,
that our minds may learn wisdom.

Eternal King! Thy throne is established and immovable from everlasting, and will continue so throughout all the ages of eternity. Before the mountains were brought forth, before thou hadst formed the earth and the world, even from everlasting to everlasting, thou art God. All things that exist, whether visible or invisible, derive from thee their being, and all that they possess: and they all, from the least to the greatest, are subservient to thy purposes, who art their supreme King and Father.
Robert Leighton, 1611–84

Day 7

Lord of Creation

Bless the Lord, my soul.
Lord my God, you are very great,
clothed in majesty and splendour,
and enfolded in a robe of light.
You have spread out the heavens like a tent,
and laid the beams of your dwelling on the waters;
you take the clouds for your chariot,
riding on the wings of the wind;
you make grass grow for the cattle
and plants for the use of mortals,
producing grain from the earth,
food to sustain their strength,
wine to gladden the hearts of the people,
and oil to make their faces shine.

You bring darkness, and it is night,
when all the beasts of the forest go prowling;
the young lions roar for prey,
seeking their food from God;
when the sun rises, they slink away
and seek rest in their lairs.
Man goes out to his work
and his labours until evening.

Countless are the things you have made, Lord;
by your wisdom you have made them all;
the earth is full of your creatures.

My God, I thank thee, who has made
the earth so bright:
so full of splendour and of joy,
of grace and light;
so many glorious things are here,
of truth and right.

Adelaide A. Procter, 1825–64

WEEK 2
God's Fatherhood

Day 1

He Remembers We are Dust

The Lord is compassionate and gracious,
long-suffering and ever faithful;
he will not always accuse
or nurse his anger for ever.
He has not treated us as our sins deserve
or repaid us according to our misdeeds.
As the heavens tower high above the earth,
so outstanding is his love towards those who fear him.
As far as east is from west,
so far from us has he put away our offences.
As a father has compassion on his children,
so the Lord has compassion on those who fear him;
for he knows how we were made,
he remembers that we are but dust.

*Guide me, O Lord, in all the changes and varieties of the world; that in all
things that shall happen, I may have an evenness and tranquillity of spirit;
that my soul may be wholly resigned to thy divinest will and pleasure,
never murmuring at thy gentle chastisements and fatherly correction.*

Jeremy Taylor, 1613–67

Day 2

Father of All

I am the Lord, and there is none other;
apart from me there is no god.
Though you have not known me I shall strengthen you,
so that from east to west
all may know there is none besides me:
I am the Lord, and there is none other.

I make the light, I create the darkness;
author alike of wellbeing and woe,
I, the Lord, do all these things.
Will the child say to his father, 'What are you begetting?'
or to his mother, 'What are you bringing to birth?'

Thus says the Lord, Israel's Holy One, his Maker:
Would you dare question me concerning my children,
or instruct me in my handiwork?
I alone made the earth
and created mankind upon it.
With my own hands I stretched out the heavens
and directed all their host.

Be kind, dear Teacher, to us your children. You are our Father, Defender of Israel; God the Son and God the Father, united as one Lord. Grant to us who obey your commands that we may become more perfectly like you, and know you to the utmost of our ability as a good God and a tolerant judge.

Clement of Alexandria, c.150–c.215

Day 3

You are our Father

Look down from heaven and see
from the heights where you dwell holy and glorious.
Where is your zeal, your valour,
your burning and tender love?
Do not stand aloof, for you are our Father.

Though Abraham were not to know us
nor Israel to acknowledge us,
you, Lord, are our Father;
our Redeemer from of old is your name.

Why, Lord, do you let us wander from your ways
and harden our hearts until we cease to fear you?
We all became like something unclean
and all our righteous deeds were like a filthy rag;
we have all withered like leaves
and our iniquities carry us away like the wind.

There is no one who invokes you by name
or rouses himself to hold fast to you;
for you have hidden your face from us
and left us in the grip of our iniquities.

Yet, Lord, you are our Father;
we are the clay, you the potter,
and all of us are your handiwork.
Do not let your anger pass all bounds, Lord,
and do not remember iniquity for ever.

*I rejoice in your essential glory and blessedness. I rejoice in my relation to
you, that you are my Father, my Lord and my God. I thank you that you
have brought me so far. I will beware of despairing of your mercy for the
time which is yet to come, and will give you the glory of your free grace.*

Susanna Wesley, 1669–1742

Day 4

God's Adopted Children

YOU LIVE BY the Spirit, since God's Spirit dwells in you; and anyone who does not possess the Spirit of Christ does not belong to Christ. But if Christ is in you, then although the body is dead because of sin, yet the Spirit is your life because you have been justified. Moreover, if the Spirit of him who raised Jesus from the dead dwells in you, then the God who raised Christ Jesus from the dead will also give new life to your mortal bodies through his indwelling Spirit.

It follows, my friends, that our old nature has no claim on us; we are not obliged to live in that way. If you do so, you must die. But if by the Spirit you put to death the base pursuits of the body, then you will live.

For all who are led by the Spirit of God are sons of God. The Spirit you have received is not a Spirit of slavery, leading you back into a life of fear, but a Spirit of adoption, enabling us to cry Abba! Father! The Spirit of God affirms to our spirit that we are God's children; and if children, then heirs, heirs of God and fellow-heirs with Christ; but we must share his sufferings if we are also to share his glory.

Most great and glorious Lord God, accept my imperfect repentance, and send your Spirit of adoption into my heart, that I may again be owned by you, call you Father, and share in the blessings of your children.

John Wesley, 1703–91

Day 5

No Longer a Slave

IT IS THROUGH faith that you are all sons of God in union with Christ Jesus. Baptized into union with him, you have all put on Christ like a garment. There is no such thing as Jew and Greek, slave and freeman, male and female; for you are all one person in Christ Jesus. So if you belong to Christ, you are the issue of Abraham and heirs by virtue of the promise.

This is what I mean: so long as the heir is a minor, he is no better off than a slave, even though the whole estate is his; he is subject to guardians and trustees until the date set by his father. So it was with us: during our minority we were slaves, subject to the elemental spirits of the universe, but when the appointed time came, God sent his Son, born of a woman, born under the law, to buy freedom for those who were under the law, in order that we might attain the status of sons.

To prove that you are sons, God has sent into our hearts the Spirit of his Son, crying Abba, Father! You are therefore no longer a slave but a son, and if a son, an heir by God's own act.

> *Is there a thing beneath the sun*
> *That strives with thee my heart to share?*
> *Ah, tear it thence, and reign alone,*
> *The Lord of every motion there!*
> *Then shall my heart from pain be free,*
> *When it hath found repose in thee.*
>
> *O Lord! thy sovereign aid impart*
> *To save me from low-thoughted care;*
> *Chase this self-will through all my heart,*
> *Through all its latent mazes there;*
> *Make me duteous child, that I*
> *Ceaseless may 'Abba Father', cry!*

Gerhard Tersteegen, 1697–1769

Day 6

The Discipline of the Lord

THINK of him who submitted to such opposition from sinners: that will
help you not to lose heart and grow faint. In the struggle against sin, you
have not yet resisted to the point of shedding your blood. You have forgotten
the exhortation which addresses you as sons:

> My son, do not think lightly of the Lord's discipline,
> or be discouraged when he corrects you;
> for whom the Lord loves he disciplines;
> he chastises every son whom he acknowledges.

You must endure it as discipline: God is treating you as sons. Can anyone be a
son and not be disciplined by his father? If you escape the discipline in which
all sons share, you must be illegitimate and not true sons. Again, we paid due
respect to our human fathers who disciplined us; should we not submit even
more readily to our spiritual Father, and so attain life? They disciplined us for a
short time as they thought best; but he does so for our true welfare, so that we
may share his holiness. Discipline, to be sure, is never pleasant; at the time it
seems painful, but afterwards those who have been trained by it reap the
harvest of a peaceful and upright life.

> *Hear me, O God!*
> *A broken heart*
> *Is my best part;*
> *Use still thy rod,*
> *That I may prove*
> *Therein, thy Love.*
>
> *If thou hadst not*
> *Been stern to me,*
> *But let me free,*
> *I had forgot*
> *My self and thee.*
>
> *Fair sin's so sweet*
> *As minds ill bent*
> *Rarely repent,*
> *Until they meet*
> *Their punishment.*

Ben Johnson, 1572–1637

Day 7

The Divine Seed

CONSIDER HOW GREAT is the love which the Father has bestowed on us in calling us his children! For that is what we are. The reason why the world does not recognize us is that it has not known him. Dear friends, we are now God's children; what we shall be has not yet been disclosed, but we know that when Christ appears we shall be like him, because we shall see him as he is. As he is pure, everyone who has grasped this hope makes himself pure.

Children, do not be misled: anyone who does what is right is righteous, just as Christ is righteous; anyone who sins is a child of the devil, for the devil has been a sinner from the first; and the Son of God appeared for the very purpose of undoing the devil's work. No child of God commits sin, because the divine seed remains in him; indeed because he is God's child he cannot sin. This is what shows who are God's children and who are the devil's: anyone who fails to do what is right or love his fellow-Christians is not a child of God.

Lord God, heavenly Father, we know that we are dear children of yours and that you are our beloved Father, not because we deserve it, nor ever could merit it, but because our dear Lord, your only-begotten Son, Jesus Christ, will to be our brother, and of his own accord offers and makes this blessing known to us. Since we may consider ourselves his brothers and sisters and he regards us as such, you will permit us to become and remain your children for ever.

Martin Luther, 1483–1546

WEEK 3

God's Word

Day 1

Word of Creation

Shout for joy in the Lord, you that are righteous;
praise comes well from the upright.
Give thanks to the Lord on the lyre;
make music to him on the ten-stringed harp.
Sing to him a new song;
strike up with all your skill and shout in triumph,
for the word of the Lord holds true,
and all his work endures.
He is a lover of righteousness and justice;
the earth is filled with the Lord's unfailing love.

The word of the Lord created the heavens;
all the host of heaven was formed at his command.
He gathered into a heap the waters of the sea,
he laid up the deeps in his store-chambers.
Let the whole world fear the Lord
and all earth's inhabitants stand in awe of him.
For he spoke, and it was;
he commanded, and there it stood.

Oh God, we stand in awe of your creative power, and give thanks for all that your Word has brought forth. May your Word hold true, in our world and in our hearts, for ever.

Philip Law

Day 2

The Ten Words

M OSES brought the people out from the camp to meet God, and they took their stand at the foot of the mountain. The Lord came down on the top of Mount Sinai and summoned Moses up to the mountaintop.

God spoke all these words:

I am the Lord your God who brought you out of Egypt, out of the land of slavery.

You must have no other god besides me.

You must not make a carved image for yourself, nor the likeness of anything in the heavens above, or on the earth below, or in the waters under the earth.

You must not bow down to them in worship; for I, the Lord your God, am a jealous God.

You must not make wrong use of the name of the Lord your God; the Lord will not leave unpunished anyone who misuses his name.

Remember to keep the sabbath day holy. You have six days to labour and do all your work; but the seventh day is a sabbath of the Lord your God; that day you must not do any work.

Honour your father and your mother, so that you may enjoy long life in the land which the Lord your God is giving you.

Do not commit murder.

Do not commit adultery.

Do not steal.

Do not give false evidence against your neighbour.

Do not covet your neighbour's household: you must not covet your neighbour's wife, his slave, his slave-girl, his ox, his donkey, or anything that belongs to him.

Open our hearts, O Lord, and enlighten our minds by the grace of your Holy Spirit, that we may seek what is well-pleasing to your will; and so order our doings after your commandments, that we may be found fit to enter into your everlasting joy, through Jesus Christ our Lord.

Bede, c.672–735

Day 3

Word of Enlightenment

Your word is a lamp to my feet,
a light on my path;
I have bound myself by oath and solemn vow
to keep your just decrees.

I am cruelly afflicted;
Lord, revive me as you have promised.
Accept, Lord, the willing tribute of my lips,
and teach me your decrees.

Every day I take my life in my hands,
yet I never forget your law.
The wicked have set a trap for me,
but I do not stray from your precepts.

Your instruction is my everlasting heritage;
it is the joy of my heart.
I am resolved to fulfil your statutes;
they are a reward that never fails.

I hate those who are not single-minded,
but I love your law.
You are my hiding-place and my shield;
in your word I put my hope.

Lord, you have given us your word for a light to shine on our path. Inspire us to meditate on that word, and follow its teaching, that we may find in it the light which shines more and more until it is perfect day; through Jesus Christ our Lord.

Jerome, c.342–420

Day 4

Word of Promise

As the rain and snow come down from the heavens
and do not return there without watering the earth,
making it produce grain
to give seed for sowing and bread to eat,
so is it with my word issuing from my mouth;
it will not return to me empty
without accomplishing my purpose
and succeeding in the task for which I sent it.
You will go out with joy
and be led forth in peace.
Before you mountains and hills will break into cries of joy,
and all the trees in the countryside will clap their hands.

*Christ our God, who art thyself the fulfilment of the law and the prophets,
and didst fulfil all the ordered purpose of the Father, always fill our hearts
with joy and gladness, now and for ever, world without end.*

Liturgy of St John Chrysostom and Basil the Great

Day 5

Word of Nourishment

Now that you have purified your souls by obedience to the truth until you feel sincere affection towards your fellow-Christians, love one another wholeheartedly with all your strength. You have been born again, not of mortal but of immortal parentage, through the living and enduring word of God. As scripture says:

> All mortals are like grass;
> all their glory like the flower of the field;
> the grass withers, the flower falls;
> but the word of the Lord endures for evermore.

And this word is the gospel which was preached to you.

Then away with all wickedness and deceit, hypocrisy and jealousy and malicious talk of any kind! Like the newborn infants you are, you should be craving for pure spiritual milk so that you may thrive on it and be saved; for surely you have tasted that the Lord is good.

O heavenly Father, which art the fountain and full of treasure of all goodness, we beseech thee to show thy mercies upon us thy children, so that hereby we may acknowledge thee to be the author and giver of all good things; and, above all, that we may remember continually to seek the spiritual food of thy word, wherewith our souls may be nourished.

John Knox, c.1513–72

Day 6

Word of Life

IT WAS THERE from the beginning; we have heard it; we have seen it with our own eyes; we looked upon it, and felt it with our own hands: our theme is the word which gives life. This life was made visible; we have seen it and bear our testimony; we declare to you the eternal life which was with the Father and was made visible to us. It is this which we have seen and heard that we declare to you also, in order that you may share with us in a common life, that life which we share with the Father and his Son Jesus Christ. We are writing this in order that our joy may be complete.

Here is the message we have heard from him and pass on to you: God is light, and in him there is no darkness at all. If we claim to be sharing in his life while we go on living in darkness, our words and our lives are a lie. But if we live in the light as he himself is in the light, then we share a common life, and the blood of Jesus his Son cleanses us from all sin.

If we claim to be sinless, we are self-deceived and the truth is not in us. If we confess our sins, he is just and may be trusted to forgive our sins and cleanse us from every kind of wrongdoing. If we say we have committed no sin, we make him out to be a liar and his word has no place in us.

O God, you are both the light and the guide of those who put their trust in you. Grant us in all our doubts and uncertainties the grace to ask what you would have us do; that the Spirit of wisdom may save us from all false choices, and that in your light we may see light; through Jesus Christ our Lord.

William Bright, 1824–1901

Day 7

Word of God

In the beginning the Word already was.
The Word was in God's presence,
and what God was, the Word was.
He was with God at the beginning,
and through him all things came to be;
without him no created thing came into being.
In him was life,
and that life was the light of mankind.
The light shines in the darkness,
and the darkness has never mastered it.

The true light which gives light to everyone
was even then coming into the world.
He was in the world;
but the world, though it owed its being to him,
did not recognize him.
He came to his own,
and his own people would not accept him.
But to all who did accept him,
to those who put their trust in him,
he gave the right to become children of God,
born not of human stock,
by the physical desire of a human father,
but of God.

So the Word became flesh;
he made his home among us,
and we saw his glory,
such glory as befits the Father's only Son,
full of grace and truth.

We give you thanks, O God, through your beloved Servant, Jesus Christ. It is he whom you have sent in these last times to save us and redeem us, and be the messenger of your will. He is your Word, inseparable from you, through whom you made all things and in whom you take delight. You sent him from heaven into the Virgin's womb, where he was conceived, and took flesh. Born of the Holy Spirit and the Virgin, he was revealed as your Son.

Hippolytus, c.170–236

God's Spirit

Day 1

The Giver of Life

Countless are the things you have made, Lord;
by your wisdom you have made them all;
the earth is full of your creatures.

Here is the vast immeasurable sea,
in which move crawling things beyond number,
living creatures great and small.
Here ships sail to and fro;
here is Leviathan which you have made to sport there.

All of them look to you in hope
to give them their food when it is due.
What you give them they gather up;
when you open your hand, they eat their fill of good things.
When you hide your face, they are dismayed.
When you take away their spirit, they die
and return to the dust from which they came.
When you send forth your Spirit, they are created,
and you give new life to the earth.

May the glory of the Lord stand for ever,
and may the Lord rejoice in his works!

Your Spirit, Lord, is around me
in the air I breathe,
your glory, Lord, touches me
in the light that I see
and the fruitfulness of the earth
and the joys of its creatures.
  John Ruskin, 1819–1900, adapted

Day 2

Guided by the Spirit

I shall recount the Lord's unfailing love,
the prowess of the Lord,
according to all he has done for us,
his great goodness to the house of Israel,
what he has done for them in his tenderness
and by his many acts of faithful love.

He said, 'Surely they are my people,
children who will not play me false';
and he became their deliverer
in all their troubles.
No envoy, no angel, but he himself delivered them,
redeemed them in his love and pity;
he lifted them up and carried them
through all the days of old.

Yet they rebelled and grieved his Holy Spirit;
so he turned hostile to them
and himself fought against them.
Then they recalled days long past
and him who drew out his people:
where is he who brought up from the Nile
the shepherd of his flock?
Where is he who put within him
his Holy Spirit,
who sent his glorious power
to walk at Moses' right hand?
Where is he who divided the waters before them,
to win for himself everlasting renown,
who brought them through the deep
sure-footed as horses in open country,
like cattle moving down into a valley
guided by the Spirit of the Lord?

O God, by whom the world is governed and preserved, enable us to resist all evil, and dispose us to follow the guidance of the good Spirit, not trusting in our own strength or wisdom, but looking to thee to establish us in every good word and work; through Christ our lord.

Charles James Blomfield, 1786–1857

Day 3

God Within

JESUS SAID, 'If you love me you will obey my commands; and I will ask the Father, and he will give you another to be your advocate, who will be with you for ever, the Spirit of truth. The world cannot accept him, because the world neither sees nor knows him; but you know him, because he dwells with you and will be in you. I will not leave you bereft; I am coming back to you. In a little while the world will see me no longer, but you will see me; because I live, you too will live. When that day comes you will know that I am in my Father, and you in me and I in you. Anyone who has received my commands and obeys them – he it is who loves me; and he who loves me will be loved by my Father; and I will love him and disclose myself to him.'

Judas said, the other Judas, not Iscariot, 'Lord, how has it come about that you mean to disclose yourself to us and not to the world?' Jesus replied, 'Anyone who loves me will heed what I say; then my Father will love him, and we will come to him and make our dwelling with him.'

> *O consuming Fire, Spirit of Love,*
> *descend within me*
> *and reproduce in me, as it were,*
> *an incarnation of the word,*
> *that I may be to him*
> *another humanity*
> *wherein he renews his mystery.*
> Elizabeth of the Trinity, d. 1184

Day 4

The Spirit of Truth

I F THE WORLD hates you, it hated me first, as you know well. If you belonged to the world, the world would love its own; but you do not belong to the world, now that I have chosen you out of the world, and for that reason the world hates you. Remember what I said: "A servant is not greater than his master."

'When the advocate has come, whom I shall send you from the Father – the Spirit of truth that issues from the Father – he will bear witness to me. When he comes, he will prove the world wrong about sin, justice, and judgement: about sin, because they refuse to believe in me; about justice, because I go to the Father when I pass from your sight; about judgement, because the prince of this world stands condemned.

'There is much more that I could say to you, but the burden would be too great for you now. However, when the Spirit of truth comes, he will guide you into all the truth; for he will not speak on his own authority, but will speak only what he hears; and he will make known to you what is to come. He will glorify me, for he will take what is mine and make it known to you. All that the Father has is mine, and that is why I said, he will take what is mine and make it known to you.'

O heavenly Father, Author and fountain of all truth, the bottomless sea of all true understanding; send down, we beseech thee, thy Spirit into our hearts, and lighten our understandings with the beams of thy heavenly grace. We ask this, O merciful Father, not in respect of our deserts, but for thy dear Son our Saviour Jesus Christ's sake.

Nicholas Ridley, 1500–55

Day 5

Pentecost

THE DAY OF Pentecost had come, and they were all together in one place. Suddenly there came from the sky what sounded like a strong, driving wind, a noise which filled the whole house where they were sitting. And there appeared to them flames like tongues of fire distributed among them and coming to rest on each one. They were all filled with the Holy Spirit and began to talk in other tongues, as the Spirit gave them power of utterance.

Now there were staying in Jerusalem devout Jews drawn from every nation under heaven. At this sound a crowd of them gathered, and were bewildered because each one heard his own language spoken; they were amazed and in astonishment exclaimed, 'Surely these people who are speaking are all Galileans! How is it that each of us can hear them in his own native language? Parthians, Medes, Elamites; inhabitants of Mesopotamia, of Judaea and Cappadocia, of Pontus and Asia, of Phrygia and Pamphylia, of Egypt and the districts of Libya around Cyrene; visitors from Rome, both Jews and proselytes; Cretans and Arabs – all of us hear them telling in our own tongues the great things God has done.' They were all amazed and perplexed, saying to one another, 'What can this mean?' Others said contemptuously, 'They have been drinking!'

But Peter stood up with the eleven, and in a loud voice addressed the crowd: 'Fellow Jews, and all who live in Jerusalem, listen and take note of what I say. These people are not drunk, as you suppose; it is only nine in the morning! No, this is what the prophet Joel spoke of: "In the last days, says God, I will pour out my Spirit on all mankind; and your sons and daughters shall prophesy; your young men shall see visions, and your old men shall dream dreams."'

O God, we pray that as the Holy Spirit came in wind and fire to the apostles, so he may come to us, breathing life into our souls and kindling in our hearts the flame of love; through Jesus Christ our Lord.

J. W. C. Masterton

Day 6

The Ministry of the Spirit

THERE IS NO question of our having sufficient power in ourselves: we cannot claim anything as our own. The power we have comes from God; it is he who has empowered us as ministers of a new covenant, not written but spiritual; for the written law condemns to death, but the Spirit gives life.

The ministry that brought death, and that was engraved in written form on stone, was inaugurated with such glory that the Israelites could not keep their eyes on Moses, even though the glory on his face was soon to fade. How much greater, then, must be the glory of the ministry of the Spirit!

With such a hope as this we speak out boldly; it is not for us to do as Moses did: he put a veil over his face to keep the Israelites from gazing at the end of what was fading away. In any case their minds had become closed, for that same veil is there to this very day when the lesson is read from the old covenant; and it is never lifted, because only in Christ is it taken away. Indeed to this very day, every time the law of Moses is read, a veil lies over the mind of the hearer. But, as scripture says, 'Whenever he turns to the Lord the veil is removed.' Now the Lord of whom this passage speaks is the Spirit; and where the Spirit of the Lord is, there is liberty. And because for us there is no veil over the face, we all see as in a mirror the glory of the Lord, and we are being transformed into his likeness with ever-increasing glory, through the power of the Lord who is the Spirit.

O God, who madest me for thyself, to show forth thy goodness in me: manifest, I humbly beseech thee, the life-giving power of thy holy nature within me; help me to such a true and living faith in thee, such strength of hunger and thirst after the birth, and spirit of thy holy Jesus in my soul, that all that is within me, may be turned from every inward thought or outward work that is not thee, thy holy Jesus, and heavenly working in my soul.

William Law, 1686–1761

Day 7

Led by the Spirit

Y OU, MY FRIENDS, were called to be free; only beware of turning your freedom into licence for your unspiritual nature. Instead, serve one another in love; for the whole law is summed up in a single commandment: Love your neighbour as yourself. But if you go on fighting one another, tooth and nail, all you can expect is mutual destruction.

What I mean is this: be guided by the Spirit and you will not gratify the desires of your unspiritual nature. That nature sets its desires against the Spirit, while the Spirit fights against it. They are in conflict with one another so that you cannot do what you want. But if you are led by the Spirit, you are not subject to law.

Anyone can see the behaviour that belongs to the unspiritual nature: fornication, indecency, and debauchery; idolatry and sorcery; quarrels, a contentious temper, envy, fits of rage, selfish ambitions, dissensions, party intrigues, and jealousies; drinking bouts, orgies, and the like. I warn you, as I warned you before, that no one who behaves like that will ever inherit the kingdom of God.

But the harvest of the Spirit is love, joy, peace, patience, kindness, goodness, fidelity, gentleness, and self-control. Against such things there is no law. Those who belong to Christ Jesus have crucified the old nature with its passions and desires. If the Spirit is the source of our life, let the Spirit also direct its course.

May your Spirit guide my mind,
which is so often dull and empty.
Let my thoughts always be on you,
and let me see you in all things.

May your Spirit quicken my soul,
which is so often listless and lethargic.
Let my soul be awake to your presence,
and let me know you in all things.

May your Spirit melt my heart,
which is so often cold and indifferent.
Let my heart me warmed by your love,
and let me feel you in all things.

Johann Freylinghausen, 1670–1739

God's Hiddenness

Day 1

A Meditation on Mortality

Every being born of woman is short-lived and full of trouble.

He blossoms like a flower and withers away;
fleeting as a shadow, he does not endure;
he is like a wineskin that perishes
or a garment that moths have eaten.

If a tree is cut down,
there is hope that it will sprout again
and fresh shoots will not fail.
Though its root becomes old in the earth,
its stump dying in the ground,
yet when it scents water it may break into bud
and make new growth like a young plant.

But when a human being dies all his power vanishes;
he expires, and where is he then?
As the waters of a lake dwindle,
or as a river shrinks and runs dry,
so mortal man lies down, never to rise
until the very sky splits open.

O Lord, my God! The amazing horrors of darkness were gathered round me, and covered me all over, and I saw no way to go forth; I felt the depth and extent of the misery of my fellow-creatures separated from the divine harmony, and it was heavier than I could bear, and I was crushed down under it; I lifted up my hand, I stretched out my arm, but there was none to help me; I looked round about, and was amazed.

In the depths of misery, O lord, I remembered that thou art omnipotent; that I had called thee Father; and I felt that I loved thee, and I was made quiet in my will, and I waited for deliverance from thee.

John Woolman, 1720–72

Day 2

Embracing the Mystery

Even today my thoughts are embittered,
for God's hand is heavy on me in my trouble.
If only I knew how to reach him,
how to enter his court,
I should state my case before him
and set out my arguments in full;
then I should learn what answer he would give
and understand what he had to say to me.

If I go to the east, he is not there;
if west, I cannot find him;
when I turn north, I do not descry him;
I face south, but he is not to be seen.
Yet he knows me in action and at rest;
when he tests me, I shall emerge like gold.

My feet have kept to the path he has set me;
without deviating I have kept to his way.
I do not neglect the commands he issues,
I have treasured in my heart all he says.
When he decides, who can turn him from his purpose?
What he desires, he does.

Whatever he determines for me, that he carries out;
his mind is full of plans like these.
That is why I am fearful of meeting him;
when I think about it, I am afraid;
it is God who makes me faint-hearted,
the Almighty who fills me with fear,
yet I am not reduced to silence by the darkness
or by the mystery which hides him.

*O supreme and unapproachable light! O whole and blessed truth! How far
are you from me, who am so near to you! Everywhere you are wholly
present, yet I do not see you. In you I move, and in you I have my being,
and cannot come to you; you are within me and around me, and I do not
feel you.*

Anselm, 1033–1108

Day 3

The Treachery of the Wicked

Why stand far off, Lord?
Why hide away in times of trouble?
The wicked in their arrogance hunt down the afflicted:
may their crafty schemes prove their undoing!
The wicked boast of the desires they harbour;
in their greed they curse and revile the Lord.
The wicked in their pride do not seek God;
there is no place for God in any of their schemes.
Their ways are always devious;
your judgements are beyond their grasp,
and they scoff at all their adversaries.

Because they escape misfortune,
they think they will never be shaken.
The wicked person's mouth is full of cursing, deceit, and violence;
mischief and wickedness are under his tongue.
He lurks in ambush near settlements
and murders the innocent by stealth.
Ever on the watch for some unfortunate wretch,
he seizes him and drags him away in his net.
He crouches stealthily, like a lion in its lair
crouching to seize its victim;
he strikes and lays him low.
Unfortunate wretches fall into his toils.
He says to himself, 'God has forgotten;
he has hidden his face and seen nothing.'

Arise, Lord, set your hand to the task;
God, do not forget the afflicted.
Why have the wicked rejected you, God,
and said that you will not call them to account?

God of love, whose compassion never fails; we bring before thee the troubles and perils of people and nations, the sighing of prisoners and captives, the sorrows of the bereaved, the necessities of strangers, the helplessness of the weak, the despondency of the weary, the failing powers of the aged. O Lord, draw near to each; for the sake of Jesus Christ our Lord.

Anselm, 1033–1109

Day 4

A Cry of Abandonment

My God, my God, why have you forsaken me?
Why are you so far from saving me,
so far from heeding my groans?
My God, by day I cry to you, but there is no answer;
in the night I cry with no respite.

You, the praise of Israel,
are enthroned in the sanctuary.
In you our fathers put their trust;
they trusted, and you rescued them.
To you they cried and were delivered;
in you they trusted and were not discomfited.

But I am a worm, not a man,
abused by everyone, scorned by the people.
All who see me jeer at me,
grimace at me, and wag their heads:
'He threw himself on the Lord for rescue;
let the Lord deliver him, for he holds him dear!'

But you are he who brought me from the womb,
who laid me at my mother's breast.
To your care I was entrusted at birth;
from my mother's womb you have been my God.
Do not remain far from me,
for trouble is near and I have no helper.

How long will you be absent? For ever? Oh Lord! have you forgotten to be gracious, and have you shut up your loving kindness in displeasure? Will you be no more entreated? Is your mercy clean gone for ever, and your promise come utterly to an end for ever? Why do you wait for so long? Shall I despair of your mercy? Oh, God! Far be that from me, for you know better that I what is good for me. Therefore do with me in all things what you will.

Lady Jane Grey, 1537–54

Day 5

A Cry for Help

Lord, hear my prayer
and let my cry for help come to you.
Do not hide your face from me
when I am in dire straits.
Listen to my prayer
and, when I call, be swift to reply;
for my days vanish like smoke,
my body is burnt up as in an oven.

I am stricken, withered like grass;
I neglect to eat my food.
I groan aloud;
I am just skin and bone.
I am like a desert-owl in the wilderness,
like an owl that lives among ruins.
I lie awake and have become like a bird
solitary on a rooftop.
My days decline like shadows lengthening;
I wither away like grass.

But you, Lord, are enthroned for ever;
your fame will endure to all generations.
Long ago you laid earth's foundations,
and the heavens were your handiwork.
They will pass away, but you remain;
like clothes they will all wear out;
you will cast them off like a cloak
and they will vanish.
But you are the same and your years will have no end.

*Lord, our heavenly Father, who orderest all things for our eternal good,
mercifully enlighten our minds, and give us a firm and abiding trust in thy
love and care. Silence our murmurings, quieten our fears, and dispel our
doubts, that rising above our afflictions and our anxieties, we may rest on
thee, the rock of everlasting strength.*
New Church Book of Worship, 1876

Day 6

The Futility of It All

THERE IS A futile thing found on earth: sometimes the just person gets what is due to the unjust, and the unjust what is due to the just. I maintain that this too is futility.

So I commend enjoyment, since there is nothing good for anyone to do here under the sun but to eat and drink and enjoy himself; this is all that will remain with him to reward his toil throughout the span of life which God grants him here under the sun.

I applied my mind to acquire wisdom and to observe the tasks undertaken on earth, when mortal eyes are never closed in sleep day or night; and always I perceived that God has so ordered it that no human being should be able to discover what is happening here under the sun. However hard he may try, he will not find out; the wise may think they know, but they cannot find the truth of it.

To all this I applied my mind, and I understood – that the righteous and the wise and whatever they do are under God's control; but whether they will earn love or hatred they have no way of knowing. Everything that confronts them, everything is futile, since one and the same fate comes to all, just and unjust alike, good and bad, ritually clean and unclean, to the one who offers sacrifice and to the one who does not. The good and the sinner fare alike, he who can take an oath and he who dares not.

This is what is wrong in all that is done here under the sun: that one and the same fate befalls everyone. The minds of mortals are full of evil; there is madness in their minds throughout their lives, and afterwards they go down to join the dead.

O my dear God and most merciful Father, who has not only directed, but encouraged me in all my troubles to call upon thee; hear, I beseech thee, the complaints that I now make, and the prayers which I pour forth in the anguish and bitterness of my spirit; for thou hast shown me heavy things, O God.

Bryan Duppa, 1588–1662

Day 7

How Long, Lord?

How long, Lord, will you be deaf to my plea?
'Violence!' I cry out to you,
but you do not come to the rescue.
Why do you let me look on such wickedness,
why let me see such wrongdoing?
Havoc and violence confront me,
strife breaks out, discord arises.
Therefore law becomes ineffective,
and justice is defeated;
the wicked hem in the righteous,
so that justice is perverted.

Your eyes are too pure to look on evil;
you cannot countenance wrongdoing.
Why then do you countenance the treachery of the wicked?
Why keep silent when they devour those who are more righteous?

The fig tree has no buds,
the vines bear no harvest,
the olive crop fails,
the orchards yield no food,
the fold is bereft of its flock,
and there are no cattle in the stalls.
Even so I shall exult in the Lord
and rejoice in the God who saves me.
The Lord God is my strength;
he makes me as sure-footed as a hind
and sets my feet on the heights.

Give us, O Lord God, a deep sense of thy holiness; how thou art of purer eyes than to behold the iniquity, and canst not overlook or pass by that which is evil. Give us no less, O Lord, a deep sense of thy wonderful love towards us; how thou wouldest not let us alone in our ruin, but didst come after us, in the person of thy Son Jesus Christ to bring us back to our true home with thee.

Charles John Vaughan, 1816–97

WEEK 6

God's Presence

Day 1

Fullness of Joy

Keep me, God, for in you have I found refuge.
I have said to the Lord, 'You are my Lord;
from you alone comes the good I enjoy.
The lines fall for me in pleasant places;
I am well content with my inheritance.'

I shall bless the Lord who has given me counsel:
in the night he imparts wisdom to my inmost being.
I have set the Lord before me at all times:
with him at my right hand I cannot be shaken.

Therefore my heart is glad
and my spirit rejoices,
my body too rests unafraid;
for you will not abandon me to Sheol
or suffer your faithful servant to see the pit.
You will show me the path of life;
in your presence is the fullness of joy,
at your right hand are pleasures for evermore.

It is well and good, Lord, if all things change, provided we are rooted in you. If I go everywhere with you, my God, everywhere things will happen for your sake; that is what I desire.

John of the Cross, 1542–91

Day 2

A Pure Heart

Turn away your face from my sins
and wipe out all my iniquity.
God, create a pure heart for me,
and give me a new and steadfast spirit.
Do not drive me from your presence
or take your Holy Spirit from me.
Restore to me the joy of your deliverance
and grant me a willing spirit to uphold me.

O my dearest Saviour, thou hast now entered my soul, never let my sins remove thee thence. Give me a clean heart, and renew a right spirit within me. And having thus fitted me for thy self, tarry with me, reign in me, guide and direct me, watch over me for good, preserve me in all trials and temptations, and never leave me, nor forsake me, till thou shalt have brought me to thy heavenly kingdom.

Susanna Hopton, 1627–1709

Day 3

Near to God

Assuredly God is good to the upright,
to those who are pure in heart!
My feet had almost slipped,
my foothold had all but given way,
My mind was embittered,
and I was pierced to the heart.
I was too brutish to understand,
in your sight, God, no better than a beast.
Yet I am always with you;
you hold my right hand.
You guide me by your counsel
and afterwards you will receive me with glory.

Whom have I in heaven but you?
And having you, I desire nothing else on earth.
Though heart and body fail,
yet God is the rock of my heart, my portion for ever.

O Lord our God, grant us grace to desire you with a whole heart, so that desiring you we may seek and find you; and so finding you, may love you; and loving you, may hate those sins which separate us from you, for the sake of Jesus Christ.

Anselm, 1033–1109

Day 4

God Is Everywhere

Lord, you have examined me and you know me.
You know me at rest and in action;
you discern my thoughts from afar.
You trace my journeying and my resting-places,
and are familiar with all the paths I take.

Where can I escape from your spirit,
where flee from your presence?
If I climb up to heaven, you are there;
if I make my bed in Sheol, you are there.
If I travel to the limits of the east,
or dwell at the bounds of the western sea,
even there your hand will be guiding me,
your right hand holding me fast.
If I say, 'Surely darkness will steal over me,
and the day around me turn to night,'
darkness is not too dark for you
and night is as light as day;
to you both dark and light are one.

How mysterious, God, are your thoughts to me,
how vast in number they are!
Were I to try counting them,
they would be more than the grains of sand;
to finish the count, my years must equal yours.

O Lord, thou hast searched and known me.
Thou know'st my sitting down
and rising up. Yea all my thoughts
afar to thee are known.

My soul, praise, praise the Lord!
O God, thou art great:
in fathomless works
thyself thou dost hide.
Before thy dark wisdom
and power uncreate,
man's mind, that dare praise thee,
in fear must abide.

Robert Bridges, 1844–1930, based on Psalm 139

Day 5

Awe in his Presence

I HAVE SEEN THE task that God has given to mortals to keep them occupied. He has made everything to suit its time; moreover he has given mankind a sense of past and future, but no comprehension of God's work from beginning to end.

I know that there is nothing good for anyone except to be happy and live the best life he can while he is alive.

Indeed, that everyone should eat and drink and enjoy himself, in return for all his labours, is a gift of God.

I know that whatever God does lasts for ever; there is no adding to it, no taking away. And he has done it all in such a way that everyone must feel awe in his presence.

> *O everlasting essence of things beyond space and time, and yet within them; you transcend yet pervade all things: manifest yourself to us, who feel after you, seeking you in the shadows of our ignorance. Stretch forth your hand to help us, for we cannot come to you without your aid. Reveal yourself to us, for we seek nothing but you; through Jesus Christ our Lord.*
>
> John Scotus Eriugena, c.810–c.877

Day 6

The Divine Indwelling

J ESUS REPLIED, 'I am the way, the truth, and the life; no one comes to the Father except by me. If you knew me you would know my Father too. From now on you do know him; you have seen him.' Philip said to him, 'Lord, show us the Father; we ask no more.' Jesus answered, 'Have I been all this time with you, Philip, and still you do not know me? Anyone who has seen me has seen the Father. Then how can you say, "Show us the Father?" Do you not believe that I am in the Father, and the Father in me? I am not myself the source of the words I speak to you: it is the Father who dwells in me doing his own work. Believe me when I say that I am in the Father and the Father in me; or else accept the evidence of the deeds themselves. In very truth I tell you, whoever has faith in me will do what I am doing; indeed he will do greater things still because I am going to the Father. Anything you ask in my name I will do, so that the Father may be glorified in the Son. If you ask anything in my name I will do it.

'If you love me you will obey my commands; and I will ask the Father, and he will give you another to be your advocate, who will be with you for ever, the Spirit of truth. The world cannot accept him, because the world neither sees nor knows him; but you know him, because he dwells with you and will be in you. I will not leave you bereft; I am coming back to you. In a little while the world will see me no longer, but you will see me; because I live, you too will live. When that day comes you will know that I am in my Father, and you in me and I in you. Anyone who has received my commands and obeys them – he it is who loves me; and he who loves me will be loved by my Father; and I will love him and disclose myself to him.'

Judas said, the other Judas, not Iscariot, 'Lord, how has it come about that you mean to disclose yourself to us and not to the world?' Jesus replied, 'Anyone who loves me will heed what I say; then my Father will love him, and we will come to him and make our dwelling with him.'

Lord Jesus Christ, you said that you are the Way, the Truth, and the Life; let us never stray from you, who are the Truth; nor rest in any other but you, who are the Life, beyond whom there is nothing to be desired, either in heaven or on earth. We ask it for your name's sake.

Erasmus, 1466–1536

Day 7

In God We Exist

PAUL STOOD UP before the Council of the Areopagus and began: 'Men of Athens, I see that in everything that concerns religion you are uncommonly scrupulous. As I was going round looking at the objects of your worship, I noticed among other things an altar bearing the inscription *To an Unknown God*. What you worship but do not know – this is what I now proclaim.

'The God who created the world and everything in it, and who is Lord of heaven and earth, does not live in shrines made by human hands. It is not because he lacks anything that he accepts service at our hands, for he is himself the universal giver of life and breath – indeed of everything. He created from one stock every nation of men to inhabit the whole earth's surface. He determined their eras in history and the limits of their territory. They were to seek God in the hope that, groping after him, they might find him; though indeed he is not far from each one of us, for in him we live and move, in him we exist; as some of your own poets have said, "We are also his offspring." Being God's offspring, then, we ought not to suppose that the deity is like an image in gold or silver or stone, shaped by human craftsmanship and design. God has overlooked the age of ignorance; but now he commands men and women everywhere to repent, because he has fixed the day on which he will have the world judged, and justly judged, by a man whom he has designated; of this he has given assurance to all by raising him from the dead.'

When they heard about the raising of the dead, some scoffed; others said, 'We will hear you on this subject some other time.'

O Lord God, in whom we live and move and have our being, open our eyes that we may behold thy fatherly presence ever with us. Draw our hearts to thee with the power of thy love. Teach us to be anxious for nothing, and when we have done what thou givest us to do, help us, O God our Saviour, to leave the issue to thy wisdom. Take from us all doubt and mistrust. Lift our hearts up to thee in heaven, and make us to know that all things are possible to us through thy Son our Redeemer.

Brooke Foss Westcott, 1825–1901

WEEK 7

God's Protection

Day 1

The Baby Moses

A CERTAIN MAN, a descendant of Levi, married a Levite woman. She conceived and bore a son, and when she saw what a fine child he was, she kept him hidden for three months. Unable to conceal him any longer, she got a rush basket for him, made it watertight with pitch and tar, laid him in it, and placed it among the reeds by the bank of the Nile. The child's sister stood some distance away to see what would happen to him.

Pharaoh's daughter came down to bathe in the river, while her ladies-in-waiting walked on the bank. She noticed the basket among the reeds and sent her slave-girl to bring it. When she opened it, there was the baby; it was crying, and she was moved with pity for it. 'This must be one of the Hebrew children,' she said. At this the sister approached Pharaoh's daughter: 'Shall I go and fetch you one of the Hebrew women to act as a wet-nurse for the child?' When Pharaoh's daughter told her to do so, she went and called the baby's mother. Pharaoh's daughter said to her, 'Take the child, nurse him for me, and I shall pay you for it.' She took the child and nursed him at her breast. Then, when he was old enough, she brought him to Pharaoh's daughter, who adopted him and called him Moses, 'Because,' said she, 'I drew him out of the water.'

> *O Lord my God, shed the light of your love on my child. Keep him safe from all illness and all injury. Enter his tiny soul, and comfort him with your peace and joy.*
>
> *Let him as a child learn the way of your commandments. As an adult let him live the full span of life, serving your kingdom on earth. And finally in his old age, let him die in the sure and certain knowledge of your salvation.*
>
> *Dear Lord, smile upon him.*
>
> Johann Starck, 1680–1756

Day 2

Daniel in the Lion Pit

I T PLEASED DARIUS to appoint three chief ministers; of these three ministers, Daniel was one. Daniel outshone the other ministers because of his
exceptional ability, and it was the king's intention to appoint him over the
whole kingdom. Then the ministers began to look round for some pretext to
attack Daniel's administration of the kingdom.

These ministers, having watched for an opportunity to approach the king,
said to him, 'Long live King Darius! We, the ministers of the kingdom, have
taken counsel and all are agreed that the king should issue an edict to the effect
that whoever presents a petition to any god or human being other than the
king during the next thirty days is to be thrown into the lion-pit.' Accordingly
the edict was signed by King Darius.

When Daniel learnt that this decree had been issued, he went into his house
and offered prayers and praises to his God as was his custom. His enemies, on
the watch for an opportunity to catch him, found Daniel at his prayers making
supplication to his God. They then went into the king's presence and reminded
him of the edict. 'Your majesty,' they said, 'Daniel, one of the Jewish exiles, has
disregarded both your majesty and the edict, and is making petition to his God
three times a day.' When the king heard this, he was greatly distressed; he tried
to think of a way to save Daniel, and continued his efforts till sunset.

Then the king gave the order for Daniel to be brought and thrown into the
lion-pit; but he said to Daniel, 'Your God whom you serve at all times, may he
save you.' A stone was brought and put over the mouth of the pit..

The king went to his palace and spent the night fasting. He was greatly agi-
tated and, at the first light of dawn, he rose and went to the lion-pit. When he
came near he called anxiously, 'Daniel, servant of the living God, has your God
whom you serve continually been able to save you from the lions?' Daniel
answered, 'Long live the king! My God sent his angel to shut the lions' mouths
and they have not injured me.' The king was overjoyed and gave orders that
Daniel should be taken up out of the pit.

O Lord, to be turned from you is to fall, to turn to you is to rise, and to
stand in your presence is to live for ever. Grant us in all our duties your
help, in all our perplexities your guidance, in all our dangers your protec-
tion, and in all our sorrows your peace, through Jesus Christ our Lord.

Augustine of Hippo, 354–430, adapted

Day 3

Lead and Protect Me

Listen to my words, Lord,
consider my inmost thoughts;
heed my cry for help, my King and God.

When I pray to you, Lord,
in the morning you will hear me.
I shall prepare a morning sacrifice
and keep watch.
For you are not a God who welcomes wickedness;
evil can be no guest of yours.
The arrogant will not stand in your presence;
you hate all evildoers,
you make an end of liars.
The Lord abhors those who are violent and deceitful.

But through your great love I may come into your house,
and at your holy temple bow down in awe.
Lead me and protect me, Lord,
because I am beset by enemies;
give me a straight path to follow.
Let all who take refuge in you rejoice,
let them for ever shout for joy;
shelter those who love your name,
that they may exult in you.
For you, Lord, will bless the righteous;
you will surround them with favour as with a shield.

We give you thanks,
yes more than thanks, O Lord our God,
the Father of our Lord and God and Saviour Jesus Christ,
for all your goodness
at all times and in all places,
because you have shielded, rescued, helped,
and guided us all the days of our lives,
and brought us to this hour.

Liturgy of St James

Day 4

Defend and Deliver Me

Lord, for the honour of your name
forgive my wickedness, great though it is.
Whoever fears the Lord
will be shown the path he should choose.

He will enjoy lasting prosperity,
and his descendants will inherit the land.
The Lord confides his purposes to those who fear him;
his covenant is for their instruction.

My eyes are ever on the Lord,
who alone can free my feet from the net.
Turn to me and show me your favour,
for I am lonely and oppressed.

Relieve the troubles of my heart
and lead me out of my distress.
Look on my affliction and misery
and forgive me every sin.

Look at my enemies, see how many they are,
how violent their hatred of me.
Defend me and deliver me;
let me not be put to shame, for in you I find refuge.

Let integrity and uprightness protect me;
in you, Lord, I put my hope.

Almighty God, my maker and protector, who hast graciously sent me into this world to work out my salvation; enable me, by the assistance of thy Holy Spirit, to root out all such unquiet and perplexing thoughts as may mislead or hinder me in the practice of those duties which thou hast required. When I behold the works of thy hands, and consider the course of thy providence, give me grace to always remember that thy thoughts are not my thoughts, nor thy ways my ways.

John Henry Hobart, 1774–1830

Day 5

The Lord Will Guard You

If I lift up my eyes to the hills,
where shall I find help?
My help comes only from the Lord,
maker of heaven and earth.

He will not let your foot stumble;
he who guards you will not sleep.
The guardian of Israel
never slumbers, never sleeps.

The Lord is your guardian,
your protector at your right hand;
the sun will not strike you by day
nor the moon by night.

The Lord will guard you against all harm;
he will guard your life.
The Lord will guard you as you come and go,
now and for evermore.

Grant me, gracious Lord, a pure intention of my heart, and a steadfast regard to thy glory in all my actions. Possess my mind continually with thy presence, and ravish it with thy love, that my only delight may be, to be embraced in the arms of thy protection.

John Cosin, 1594–1672

Day 6

Safe in Christ

I N VERY TRUTH I tell you, the man who does not enter the sheepfold by the door, but climbs in some other way, is nothing but a thief and a robber. He who enters by the door is the shepherd in charge of the sheep. The door-keeper admits him, and the sheep hear his voice; he calls his own sheep by name, and leads them out. When he has brought them all out, he goes ahead of them and the sheep follow, because they know his voice. They will not follow a stranger; they will run away from him, because they do not recognize the voice of strangers.'

This was a parable that Jesus told them, but they did not understand what he meant by it. So Jesus spoke again: 'In very truth I tell you, I am the door of the sheepfold. The sheep paid no heed to any who came before me, for they were all thieves and robbers. I am the door; anyone who comes into the fold through me will be safe. He will go in and out and find pasture.'

O Lord, save your people,
and give your blessing
unto your inheritance,
which you have purchased
with the precious blood of your Christ.

Shepherd them under your right hand,
and cover them under your wings,
and grant unto them to fight the good fight,
and to finish the course,
and to keep the faith,
immutably,
unblameably,
and irreprovably,
through our Lord Jesus Christ,
your beloved Son,
with whom to you,
and to the Holy Spirit,
be glory, honour and worship for ever.

Apostolic Constitutions, 4th century

Day 7

Under God's Protection

P RAISED BE THE God and Father of our Lord Jesus Christ! In his great mercy by the resurrection of Jesus Christ from the dead, he gave us new birth into a living hope, the hope of an inheritance, reserved in heaven for you, which nothing can destroy or spoil or wither. Because you put your faith in God, you are under the protection of his power until the salvation now in readiness is revealed at the end of time.

This is cause for great joy, even though for a little while you may have had to suffer trials of many kinds. Even gold passes through the assayer's fire, and much more precious than perishable gold is faith which stands the test. These trials come so that your faith may prove itself worthy of all praise, glory, and honour when Jesus Christ is revealed.

What is before us, we know not, whether we shall live or die; but this we know, that all things are ordered and sure. Everything is ordered with unerring wisdom and unbounded love by thee, our God, who art love. Grant us in all things to see thy hand; through Jesus Christ our Lord.

Charles Simeon, 1759–1836

God's Providence

Day 1

God's Care for the Earth

You care for the earth and make it fruitful;
you enrich it greatly,
filling its great channels with rain.
In this way you prepare the earth
and provide grain for its people.
You water its furrows, level its ridges,
soften it with showers, and bless its growth.
You crown the year with your good gifts;
places where you have passed drip with plenty;
the open pastures are lush
and the hills wreathed in happiness;
the meadows are clothed with sheep
and the valleys decked with grain,
so that with shouts of joy they break into song.

O God our Father, we would thank you for all the bright things of life. Help is to see them, and to count them, and to remember them, that our lives may flow in ceaseless praise; for the sake of Jesus Christ our Lord.

J. H. Jowett, 1846–1923

Day 2

The Laws of Nature

Did you proclaim the rules that govern the heavens
or determine the laws of nature on the earth?
Can you command the clouds
to envelop you in a deluge of rain?
If you bid lightning speed on its way,
will it say to you, 'I am ready'?
Who put wisdom in depths of darkness
and veiled understanding in secrecy?

Can you hunt prey for the lioness
and satisfy the appetite of young lions,
as they crouch in the lair
or lie in wait in the covert?
Who provides the raven with its quarry
when its fledgelings cry aloud,
croaking for lack of food?

Do you know when the mountain goats give birth?
Do you attend the wild doe when she is calving?
Can you count the months that they carry their young
or know the time of their delivery,
when they crouch down to open their wombs
and deliver their offspring,
when the fawns growing and thriving in the open country
leave and do not return?

Does your skill teach the hawk to use its pinions
and spread its wings towards the south?
Do you instruct the eagle to soar aloft
and build its nest high up?
It dwells among the rocks and there it has its nest,
secure on a rocky crag;

O Heavenly Father, who has filled the world with beauty; open, we beseech thee, our eyes to behold thy gracious hand in all thy works; that rejoicing in thy whole creation, we may learn to serve thee with gladness; for the sake of him by whom all things were made, thy Son, Jesus Christ our Lord.

Book of Common Prayer, USA, 1928

Day 3

Elijah and the Drought

THE WORD OF the Lord came to Elijah: 'Leave this place, turn eastwards, and go into hiding in the wadi of Kerith east of the Jordan. You are to drink from the stream, and I have commanded the ravens to feed you there.' Elijah did as the Lord had told him: he went and stayed in the wadi of Kerith east of the Jordan, and the ravens brought him bread and meat morning and evening, and he drank from the stream.

After a while the stream dried up, for there had been no rain in the land. Then the word of the Lord came to him: 'Go now to Zarephath, a village of Sidon, and stay there; I have commanded a widow there to feed you.' He went off to Zarephath, and when he reached the entrance to the village, he saw a widow gathering sticks. He called to her, 'Please bring me a little water in a pitcher to drink.'

As she went to fetch it, he called after her, 'Bring me, please, a piece of bread as well.' But she answered, 'As the Lord your God lives, I have no food baked, only a handful of flour in a jar and a little oil in a flask. I am just gathering two or three sticks to go and cook it for my son and myself before we die.' 'Have no fear,' said Elijah, 'go and do as you have said. But first make me a small cake from what you have and bring it out to me, and after that make something for your son and yourself. For this is the word of the Lord the God of Israel: "The jar of flour will not give out, nor the flask of oil fail, until the Lord sends rain on the land".' She went and did as Elijah had said, and there was food for him and for her and her family for a long time.

> *Thou God of truth and love,*
> *We seek thy perfect way,*
> *Ready thy choice to approve,*
> *Thy providence to obey:*
> *Enter into thy wise design,*
> *And sweetly lose our will in thine.*
>
> Charles Wesley, 1707–88

Day 4

A Greater Happiness

Answer me when I call,
God, the upholder of my right!
When I was hard pressed you set me free;
be gracious to me and hear my prayer.

Men of rank, how long will you dishonour my glorious one,
setting your heart on empty idols and resorting to false gods?
Know that the Lord has singled out for himself his loyal servant;
the Lord hears when I call to him.

Let awe restrain you from sin;
while you rest, meditate in silence:
offer your due of sacrifice,
and put your trust in the Lord.

There are many who say, 'If only we might see good times!
Let the light of your face shine on us, Lord.'
But you have put into my heart a greater happiness
than others had from grain and wine in plenty.

Now in peace I shall lie down and sleep;
for it is you alone, Lord, who let me live in safety.

*I thank you, Father, that in you I find my greatest happiness, as I meditate
in silence and live each day in the safety of your love.*

Philip Law

Day 5

God my Saviour

Hear, Lord, when I call aloud;
show me favour and answer me.

'Come,' my heart has said,
'seek his presence.'
I seek your presence, Lord;
do not hide your face from me,
nor in your anger turn away your servant,
whose help you have been;
God my saviour, do not reject me or forsake me.
Though my father and my mother forsake me,
the Lord will take me into his care.

Well I know that I shall see the goodness of the Lord
in the land of the living.
Wait for the Lord; be strong and brave,
and put your hope in the Lord.

Almighty God, who in thy wisdom hast so ordered our earthly life that we needs must walk by faith and not by sight; grant us such faith in thee that, amidst all things that pass our understanding, we may believe in thy fatherly care, and ever be strengthened by the assurance that underneath are the everlasting arms; through Jesus Christ our Lord.

Source unknown

Day 6

Shipwrecked!

W HEN IT WAS decided that we should sail for Italy, Paul and some other prisoners were handed over to a centurion named Julius, of the Augustan Cohort. The centurion found an Alexandrian vessel bound for Italy and put us on board. Before very long a violent wind swept down from the landward side. It caught the ship and, as it was impossible to keep head to wind, we had to give way and run before it. Next day, as we were making very heavy weather, they began to lighten the ship; and on the third day they jettisoned the ship's gear with their own hands. For days on end there was no sign of either sun or stars, the storm was raging unabated, and our last hopes of coming through alive began to fade.

When they had gone for a long time without food, Paul stood up and said, 'I urge you not to lose heart; not a single life will be lost, only the ship. Last night there stood by me an angel of the God whose I am and whom I worship. "Do not be afraid, Paul," he said, "it is ordained that you shall appear before Caesar; and, be assured, God has granted you the lives of all who are sailing with you." So take heart, men! I trust God: it will turn out as I have been told; we are to be cast ashore on an island.'

When day broke, they sighted a bay with a sandy beach, on which they decided, if possible, to run ashore. But they found themselves caught between cross-currents and ran the ship aground, so that the bow stuck fast and remained immovable, while the stern was being pounded to pieces by the breakers. The soldiers thought they had better kill the prisoners for fear that any should swim away and escape; but the centurion was determined to bring Paul safely through, and prevented them from carrying out their plan. He gave orders that those who could swim should jump overboard first and get to land; the rest were to follow, some on planks, some on parts of the ship. And thus it was that all came safely to land.

O my God, by whose loving providence sorrows, difficulties, trials, dangers, become means of grace, lessons of patience, channels of hope, grant us good will to use and not abuse these our privileges; and of thy great goodness keep us alive through this dying life, that out of death thou mayest raise us up to immortality. For his sake who is the Life, Jesus Christ our Lord.

Christina Rossetti, 1830–94

Day 7

God Will Provide a Way

L ET ME REMIND you, my friends, that our ancestors were all under the cloud, and all of them passed through the Red Sea; so they all received baptism into the fellowship of Moses in cloud and sea. They all ate the same supernatural food, and all drank the same supernatural drink; for they drank from the supernatural rock that accompanied their travels and that rock was Christ. Yet most of them were not accepted by God, for the wilderness was strewn with their corpses.

These events happened as warnings to us not to set our desires on evil things as they did. Do not be idolaters, like some of them; as scripture says, 'The people sat down to feast and rose up to revel.' Let us not commit fornication; some of them did, and twenty-three thousand died in one day. Let us not put the Lord to the test as some of them did; they were destroyed by the snakes. Do not grumble as some of them did; they were destroyed by the Destroyer.

All these things that happened to them were symbolic, and were recorded as a warning for us, upon whom the end of the ages has come. If you think you are standing firm, take care, or you may fall. So far you have faced no trial beyond human endurance; God keeps faith and will not let you be tested beyond your powers, but when the test comes he will at the same time provide a way out and so enable you to endure.

> *Look from the dwelling-place you have prepared for us,*
> *hear us your servants,*
> *and deliver us*
> *from every temptation of the devil and of humankind;*
> *do not stop helping us,*
> *and do not punish us with that which we cannot bear;*
> *for we are unable to overcome what is opposed to us;*
> *but you are able, Lord,*
> *to save us from everything that is against us.*
>
> *Save us, O God,*
> *from the difficulties of the world,*
> *according to your goodness.*

Liturgy of St James

God's Guidance

Day 1

The Lord Is my Shepherd

The Lord is my shepherd; I lack for nothing.
He makes me lie down in green pastures,
he leads me to water where I may rest;
he revives my spirit;
for his name's sake he guides me in the right paths.
Even were I to walk through a valley of deepest darkness
I should fear no harm, for you are with me;
your shepherd's staff and crook afford me comfort.

You spread a table for me in the presence of my enemies;
you have richly anointed my head with oil,
and my cup brims over.
Goodness and love unfailing will follow me
all the days of my life,
and I shall dwell in the house of the Lord
throughout the years to come.

O good Shepherd, seek me out, and bring me home to your fold again. Deal favourably with me according to your grace, till I may dwell in your house all the days of my life, and praise you for ever and ever with those who are there.

Jerome, c.342–420

Day 2

Lead Me and Teach Me

Make your paths known to me, Lord;
teach me your ways.
Lead me by your faithfulness and teach me,
for you are God my saviour;
in you I put my hope all day long.

Remember, Lord, your tender care and love unfailing,
for they are from of old.
Do not remember the sins and offences of my youth,
but remember me in your unfailing love,
in accordance with your goodness, Lord.

The Lord is good and upright;
therefore he teaches sinners the way they should go.
He guides the humble in right conduct,
and teaches them his way.

Thy way, not mine, O Lord,
However dark it be;
Lead me by thine own hand,
Choose out the path for me.

Smooth let it be or rough,
It will be still the best;
Winding or straight, it leads
Right onward to thy rest.

Take thou my cup, and it
With joy or sorrow fill,
As best to thee may seem;
Choose thou my good and ill.

Not mine, not mine the choice
In things or great or small;
Be thou my guide, my strength,
My wisdom and my all.

Horatius Bonar, 1808–89

Day 3

Shun Evil and Do Good

It is the Lord who directs a person's steps;
he holds him firm and approves of his conduct.
Though he may fall, he will not go headlong,
for the Lord grasps him by the hand.

If you shun evil and do good,
you will live at peace for ever;
for the Lord is a lover of justice
and will not forsake his loyal servants.

The lawless are banished for ever
and the children of the wicked cut off,
while the righteous will possess the land
and live there for ever.

A righteous person speaks words of wisdom
and justice is always on his lips.
The law of his God is in his heart;
his steps do not falter.

We beseech thee to give us tender consciences, that we may flee from all evil. We desire, as much as is possible in this state of trial, to be kept in paths of safety; we ask not for wealth, reputation, honour, or prosperity; but we pray for a calm and peaceful spirit; for every opportunity of leading a holy life; and for such circumstances in this world as may be most free from temptation. We pray for thy preserving grace, for holiness of life, and for eternal salvation at the last.

Henry Thornton, 1760–1815

Day 4

Hold a Steady Course

Happy are they whose way of life is blameless,
who conform to the law of the Lord.
Happy are they who obey his instruction,
who set their heart on finding him;
who have done no wrong,
but have lived according to his will.

You, Lord, have laid down your precepts
that are to be kept faithfully.
If only I might hold a steady course,
keeping your statutes!
Then, if I fixed my eyes on all your commandments,
I should never be put to shame.

I shall praise you in sincerity of heart
as I learn your just decrees.
I shall observe your statutes;
do not leave me forsaken!

I have rejoiced in the path of your instruction
as one rejoices over wealth of every kind.
I shall meditate on your precepts
and keep your paths before my eyes.

*May your Spirit, O Christ, lead me in the right way, keeping me safe from
all forces of evil and destruction. And, free from all malice, may I search
diligently in your Holy Word to discover with the eyes of my mind your
commandments. Finally, give me the strength of will to put those commandments into practice through all the days of my life.*

Bede, 672–735

Day 5

I Have Chosen your Precepts

Peace is the reward of those who love your law;
no pitfalls beset their path.
I hope for your deliverance, Lord,
and I fulfil your commandments;
gladly I heed your instruction
and love it dearly.
I heed your precepts and your instruction,
for all my life lies open before you.

Let my cry of joy reach you, Lord;
give me insight as you have promised.
Let my prayers for favour reach you;
be true to your promise and save me.
Let your praise pour from my lips,
for you teach me your statutes.
Let the music of your promises be on my tongue,
for your commandments are justice itself.

May your hand be prompt to help me,
for I have chosen your precepts;
I long for your deliverance, Lord,
and your law is my delight.
Let me live to praise you;
let your decrees be my help.
I have strayed like a lost sheep;
come, search for your servant,
for I have not forgotten your commandments.

Countless voices seek to guide,
many paths there are to choose,
if we turn to either side
firm ground soon our feet will lose.
Take us by the hand we pray,
lead us on the narrow way.

Lord, through dusty ways ahead,
save the stumbling here below,
be on every path we tread,
show lost sheep which way to go.
Guide us through the sheepfold's door,
till we come to joy once more.

Ernest Yang Yin-liu, 1934

Day 6

The Paths of Wisdom

Get wisdom, get understanding;
do not forget or turn a deaf ear to what I say.

Do not forsake her, and she will watch over you;
love her, and she will safeguard you;
cherish her, and she will lift you high;
if only you embrace her, she will bring you to honour.
She will set a becoming garland on your head;
she will bestow on you a glorious crown.

Listen, my son, take my words to heart,
and the years of your life will be many.
I shall guide you in the paths of wisdom;
I shall lead you in honest ways.
When you walk nothing will impede you,
and when you run nothing will bring you down.
Cling to instruction and never let it go;
guard it well, for it is your life.

Do not take to the course of the wicked
or follow the way of evildoers;
do not set foot on it, but avoid it,
turn from it, and go on your way.

*O font of wisdom, send her from your throne of might, to be with me, to
work with me, to act in me, to speak in me, to order all my thoughts and
words and deeds and plans according to your will and to the glory of your
name.*

Aelred of Rievaulx, c.1109–67

Day 7

The Way Ahead

My son, attend to my words,
pay heed to my sayings;
do not let them slip from your sight,
keep them fixed in your mind;
for they are life to those who find them,
and health to their whole being.

Guard your heart more than anything you treasure,
for it is the source of all life.
Keep your mouth from crooked speech
and banish deceitful talk from your lips.
Let your eyes look straight before you,
fix your gaze on what lies ahead.

Mark out the path that your feet must take,
and your ways will be secure.

*O God, the King eternal, drive far from us all wrong desires, incline our
hearts to keep your law, and guide our feet into the way of peace; that
having done your will with cheerfulness during the day, we may, when
night comes, rejoice to give you thanks; through Jesus Christ our Lord*

William Reed Huntingdon, 1838–1909

WEEK 10

God's Promises

Day 1

God's Covenant with Abraham

THE LORD said to Abram, 'Leave your own country, your kin, and your father's house, and go to a country that I will show you. I shall make you into a great nation; I shall bless you and make your name so great that it will be used in blessings: those who bless you, I shall bless; those who curse you, I shall curse. All the peoples on earth will wish to be blessed as you are blessed.'

Abram, who was seventy-five years old, set out as the Lord had bidden him.

After this the word of the Lord came to Abram in a vision. He said, 'Do not be afraid, Abram; I am your shield. Your reward will be very great.' He brought Abram outside and said, 'Look up at the sky, and count the stars, if you can. So many will your descendants be.'

Abram put his faith in the Lord, who reckoned it to him as righteousness.

> *Lord, be thy word my rule,*
> *In it may I rejoice;*
> *Thy glory be my aim,*
> *Thy holy will my choice.*
>
> *Thy promises my hope;*
> *Thy providence my guard*
> *Thine arm my strong support;*
> *Thyself my great reward.*
>
> Christopher Wordsworth, 1807–85

Day 2

The Faith of Abraham

IT WAS NOT through law that Abraham and his descendants were given the promise that the world should be their inheritance, but through righteousness that came from faith. If the heirs are those who hold by the law, then faith becomes pointless and the promise goes for nothing; law can bring only retribution, and where there is no law there can be no breach of law. The promise was made on the ground of faith in order that it might be a matter of sheer grace, and that it might be valid for all Abraham's descendants, not only for those who hold by the law, but also for those who have Abraham's faith. For he is the father of us all, as scripture says: I have appointed you to be father of many nations.

In the presence of God, the God who makes the dead live and calls into being things that are not, Abraham had faith. When hope seemed hopeless, his faith was such that he became father of many nations, in fulfilment of the promise, So shall your descendants be. His faith did not weaken when he considered his own body, which was as good as dead, for he was about a hundred years old, and the deadness of Sarah's womb; no distrust made him doubt God's promise, but, strong in faith, he gave glory to God, convinced that what he had promised he was able to do. And that is why Abraham's faith was counted to him as righteousness.

The words counted to him were meant to apply not only to Abraham but to us; our faith too is to be counted, the faith in the God who raised Jesus our Lord from the dead.

God of Abraham, who makes the dead live and calls into being things that are not, strengthen our faith so that, even when hope seems hopeless, we may trust in your promises and give you glory.

Philip Law

Day 3

A Better Plan

FAITH GIVES SUBSTANCE to our hopes and convinces us of realities we do not see. It was for their faith that the people of old won God's approval.

By faith Abraham obeyed the call to leave his home for a land which he was to receive as a possession; he went away without knowing where he was to go. By faith he settled as an alien in the land which had been promised him, living in tents with Isaac and Jacob, who were heirs with him to the same promise. For he was looking forward to a city with firm foundations, whose architect and builder is God.

By faith even Sarah herself was enabled to conceive, though she was past the age, because she judged that God who had promised would keep faith. Therefore from one man, a man as good as dead, there sprang descendants as numerous as the stars in the heavens or the countless grains of sand on the seashore.

By faith Abraham, when put to the test, offered up Isaac: he had received the promises, and yet he was ready to offer his only son, of whom he had been told, 'Through the line of Isaac your descendants shall be traced.' For he reckoned that God had power even to raise from the dead and it was from the dead, in a sense, that he received him back.

These won God's approval because of their faith; and yet they did not receive what was promised, because, with us in mind, God had made a better plan, that only with us should they reach perfection.

O Lord God,
who called your servants
to ventures of which we cannot see the ending,
by paths as yet untrodden,
through perils unknown:

give us faith
to go out with a good courage,
not knowing where we are going,
but only that your hand is leading us,
and your love supporting us;
to the glory of your name.

Eric Milner-White, 1884–1963 and
G. W. Briggs, 1875–1959

Day 4

Jacob's Ladder

J ACOB SET OUT from Beersheba and journeyed towards Harran. He came to
a certain shrine and, because the sun had gone down, he stopped for the
night. He took one of the stones there and, using it as a pillow under his head,
he lay down to sleep. In a dream he saw a ladder, which rested on the ground
with its top reaching to heaven, and angels of God were going up and down
on it.

The Lord was standing beside him saying, 'I am the Lord, the God of your
father Abraham and the God of Isaac. This land on which you are lying I shall
give to you and your descendants. They will be countless as the specks of dust
on the ground, and you will spread far and wide, to west and east, to north and
south. All the families of the earth will wish to be blessed as you and your
descendants are blessed. I shall be with you to protect you wherever you go,
and I shall bring you back to this land. I shall not leave you until I have done
what I have promised you.'

When Jacob woke from his sleep he said, 'Truly the Lord is in this place, and
I did not know it.' He was awestruck and said, 'How awesome is this place! This
is none other than the house of God; it is the gateway to heaven.' Early in the
morning, when Jacob awoke, he took the stone on which his head had rested,
and set it up as a sacred pillar, pouring oil over it. He named that place Beth-el.

*O Gracious Master, thou seekest us and we seek thee; find us and be found
of us. If not the illumination of Jacob, yet give us his good will and holy fear
when he awaked out of sleep and said: 'Surely the Lord is in this place; and
I knew it not. How dreadful is this place!' Everywhere thou art present:
teach us everywhere to discern thee, rejoicing unto thee with reverence.*

Christina Rossetti, 1830–94

Day 5

The House of God

REMEMBER THEN YOUR former condition, Gentiles as you are by birth. You were at that time separate from Christ, excluded from the community of Israel, strangers to God's covenants and the promise that goes with them. Yours was a world without hope and without God. Once you were far off, but now in union with Christ Jesus you have been brought near through the shedding of Christ's blood. For he is himself our peace. Gentiles and Jews, he has made the two one, and in his own body of flesh and blood has broken down the barrier of enmity which separated them; for he annulled the law with its rules and regulations, so as to create out of the two a single new humanity in himself, thereby making peace. This was his purpose, to reconcile the two in a single body to God through the cross, by which he killed the enmity. So he came and proclaimed the good news: peace to you who were far off, and peace to those who were near; for through him we both alike have access to the Father in the one Spirit.

Thus you are no longer aliens in a foreign land, but fellow-citizens with God's people, members of God's household. You are built on the foundation of the apostles and prophets, with Christ Jesus himself as the corner-stone. In him the whole building is bonded together and grows into a holy temple in the Lord. In him you also are being built with all the others into a spiritual dwelling for God.

> *Almighty God, ever-loving Father,*
> *your care extends beyond the boundaries of race and nation*
> *to the hearts of all who live.*
> *May the walls, which prejudice raises between us,*
> *crumble beneath the shadow of your outstretched arm.*
> *We ask this through Christ our Lord.*
>
> Liturgy of the Hours

Day 6

Promises beyond Price

G OD'S DIVINE POWER has bestowed on us everything that makes for life
and true religion, through our knowledge of him who called us by his
own glory and goodness. In this way he has given us his promises, great beyond
all price, so that through them you may escape the corruption with which lust
has infected the world, and may come to share in the very being of God.

With all this in view, you should make every effort to add virtue to your
faith, knowledge to virtue, self-control to knowledge, fortitude to self-control,
piety to fortitude, brotherly affection to piety, and love to brotherly affection.

If you possess and develop these gifts, you will grow actively and effectively
in the knowledge of our Lord Jesus Christ. Whoever lacks them is wilfully
blind; he has forgotten that his past sins were washed away. All the more then,
my friends, do your utmost to establish that God has called and chosen you. If
you do this, you will never stumble, and there will be rich provision for your
entry into the eternal kingdom of our Lord and Saviour Jesus Christ.

O Lord, who art the hope of all the ends of the earth, let me never be desti-
tute of a well-grounded hope, nor yet possessed with a vain presumption:
suffer me not to think thou wilt either be reconciled to my sins, or reject my
repentance; but give me, I beseech thee, such a hope as may be answerable
to the only ground of hope, thy promises.

The Whole Duty of Man, c.1658

Day 7

God's Day will Come

I N THE LAST days there will come scoffers who live self-indulgent lives; they will mock you and say: 'What has happened to his promised coming? Our fathers have been laid to rest, but still everything goes on exactly as it always has done since the world began.' In maintaining this they forget that there were heavens and earth long ago, created by God's word out of water and with water; and that the first world was destroyed by water, the water of the flood. By God's word the present heavens and earth are being reserved for burning; they are being kept until the day of judgement when the godless will be destroyed.

Here is something, dear friends, which you must not forget: in the Lord's sight one day is like a thousand years and a thousand years like one day. It is not that the Lord is slow in keeping his promise, as some suppose, but that he is patient with you. It is not his will that any should be lost, but that all should come to repentance.

But the day of the Lord will come like a thief. On that day the heavens will disappear with a great rushing sound, the elements will be dissolved in flames, and the earth with all that is in it will be brought to judgement. Since the whole universe is to dissolve in this way, think what sort of people you ought to be, what devout and dedicated lives you should live! Look forward to the coming of the day of God, and work to hasten it on; that day will set the heavens ablaze until they fall apart, and will melt the elements in flames. Relying on his promise we look forward to new heavens and a new earth, in which justice will be established.

Look in compassion, O Heavenly Father, upon this troubled and divided world. Though we cannot trace thy footsteps or understand thy working, give us grace to trust thee now with an understanding and faith, and when thine own time is come, reveal, O Lord, thy new heaven and new earth, wherein dwelleth righteousness, and where the Prince of Peace ruleth, thy Son, our Saviour Jesus Christ.

Charles John Vaughan, 1816–97

God's Kingdom

Day 1

Heaven's King

Why are the nations in turmoil?
Why do the peoples hatch their futile plots?
Kings of the earth stand ready,
and princes conspire together
against the Lord and his anointed king.
'Let us break their fetters,' they cry,
'let us throw off their chains!'

He who sits enthroned in the heavens laughs,
the Lord derides them;
then angrily he rebukes them,
threatening them in his wrath.
'I myself have enthroned my king', he says,
'on Zion, my holy mountain.'

I shall announce the decree of the Lord:
'You are my son,' he said to me;
'this day I become your father.
Ask of me what you will:
I shall give you nations as your domain,
the earth to its farthest ends as your possession.
You will break them with a rod of iron,
shatter them like an earthen pot.'

Be mindful, then, you kings;
take warning, you earthly rulers:
worship the Lord with reverence;
tremble, and pay glad homage to the king,
for fear the Lord may become angry
and you may be struck down in mid-course;
for his anger flares up in a moment.
Happy are all who find refuge in him!

*Mighty God, may the nations acknowledge you as king. May they turn
from their futile ways, and revere the earth as your domain.*
Philip Law

Day 2

An Everlasting Kingdom

I shall extol you, my God and King,
and bless your name for ever and ever.
Every day I shall bless you
and praise your name for ever and ever.
Great is the Lord and most worthy of praise;
his greatness is beyond all searching out.
One generation will commend your works to the next
and set forth your mighty deeds.

People will speak of the glorious splendour of your majesty;
I shall meditate on your wonderful deeds.
People will declare your mighty and terrible acts,
and I shall tell of your greatness.
They will recite the story of your abounding goodness
and sing with joy of your righteousness.

All your creatures praise you, Lord,
and your loyal servants bless you.
They talk of the glory of your kingdom
and tell of your might,
to make known to mankind your mighty deeds,
the glorious majesty of your kingdom.

Your kingdom is an everlasting kingdom,
and your dominion endures throughout all generations.

Let all the world in every corner sing
My God and King.
The heavens are not too high,
His praise may thither fly:
The earth is not too low,
His praises there may grow.
Let all the world in every corner sing
    My God and King.
                        George Herbert, 1593–1633

Day 3

The New Jerusalem

See, I am creating new heavens and a new earth!
The past will no more be remembered
nor will it ever come to mind.
Rejoice and be for ever filled with delight at what I create;
for I am creating Jerusalem as a delight
and her people as a joy;
I shall take delight in Jerusalem
and rejoice in my people;
the sound of weeping, the cry of distress
will be heard in her no more.
No child there will ever again die in infancy,
no old man fail to live out his span of life.
He who dies at a hundred is just a youth,
and if he does not attain a hundred he is thought accursed!

My people will build houses and live in them,
plant vineyards and eat their fruit;
they will not build for others to live in
or plant for others to eat.
They will be as long-lived as a tree,
and my chosen ones will enjoy the fruit of their labour.
They will not toil to no purpose
or raise children for misfortune,
because they and their issue after them
are a race blessed by the Lord.
Even before they call to me, I shall answer,
and while they are still speaking I shall respond.
The wolf and the lamb will feed together
and the lion will eat straw like the ox,
and as for the serpent, its food will be dust.
Neither hurt nor harm will be done in all my holy mountain,
says the Lord.

> *Come, thou long-expected Jesus,*
> *Born to set thy people free;*
> *From our fears and sins release us,*
> *Let us find our rest in thee.*
>
> *Israel's strength and consolation,*
> *Hope of all the world thou art;*
> *Dear desire of every nation,*
> *Joy of every longing heart.*
>
> Charles Wesley, 1707–88

Day 4

The Promised King

T HE DAYS ARE coming,' says the Lord, 'when I shall bestow on Israel and Judah all the blessings I have promised them.

'In those days, at that time, I shall make a righteous Branch spring from David's line; he will maintain law and justice in the land.

'In those days Judah will be kept safe and Jerusalem will live undisturbed. This will be the name given to him: The Lord our Righteousness.'

For these are the words of the Lord: 'David will never lack a successor on the throne of Israel, nor will there ever be lacking a levitical priest to present whole-offerings, to burn grain-offerings, and to make other offerings every day.'

These are the words of the Lord: 'It would be as unthinkable to annul the covenant that I made for the day and the night, so that they should fall out of their proper order, as to annul my covenant with my servant David, so that he would have none of his line to sit on his throne; likewise it would be unthinkable to annul my covenant with the levitical priests who minister to me.

'Like the innumerable host of heaven or the countless sands of the sea, I shall increase the descendants of my servant David and the Levites who minister to me.'

> O Lord; O King, resplendent on the citadel of Heaven,
> all hail continually;
> and of your clemency upon your people still have mercy.
>
> O Christ, enthroned as King above,
> whom the nine orders of angels in their beauty praise without ceasing,
> upon us, your servants, ever have mercy.
>
> Dunstan, c.908–88

Day 5

The Ancient in Years

I N THE FIRST year that Belshazzar was king of Babylon, a dream and visions came to Daniel as he lay on his bed. Then he wrote down the dream, and here his account begins.

> As I was looking,
> thrones were set in place
> and the Ancient in Years took his seat;
> his robe was white as snow,
> his hair like lamb's wool.
> His throne was flames of fire
> and its wheels were blazing fire;
> a river of fire flowed from his presence.
> Thousands upon thousands served him
> and myriads upon myriads were in attendance.
> The court sat, and the books were opened.

I was still watching in visions of the night and I saw one like a human being coming with the clouds of heaven; he approached the Ancient in Years and was presented to him. Sovereignty and glory and kingly power were given to him, so that all peoples and nations of every language should serve him; his sovereignty was to be an everlasting sovereignty which was not to pass away, and his kingly power was never to be destroyed.

O God and Father of all, whom the whole heavens adore: let the whole earth also worship you, all kingdoms obey you, all tongues confess and bless you, and the sons of men love you and serve you in peace, through Jesus Christ our Lord.

Eric Milner-White, 1884–1963

Day 6

God Will Be All in All

IF THE DEAD are not raised, it follows that Christ was not raised; and if Christ was not raised, your faith has nothing to it and you are still in your old state of sin. It follows also that those who have died within Christ's fellowship are utterly lost. If it is for this life only that Christ has given us hope, we of all people are most to be pitied.

But the truth is, Christ was raised to life – the firstfruits of the harvest of the dead. For since it was a man who brought death into the world, a man also brought resurrection of the dead. As in Adam all die, so in Christ all will be brought to life; but each in proper order: Christ the firstfruits, and afterwards, at his coming, those who belong to Christ.

Then comes the end, when he delivers up the kingdom to God the Father, after deposing every sovereignty, authority, and power. For he is destined to reign until God has put all enemies under his feet; and the last enemy to be deposed is death. Scripture says, 'He has put all things in subjection under his feet.' But in saying all things, it clearly means to exclude God who made all things subject to him; and when all things are subject to him, then the Son himself will also be made subject to God who made all things subject to him, and thus God will be all in all.

O Lord, who hast set before us the great hope that thy kingdom shall come on earth, and hast taught us to pray for its coming: Give us grace to discern the signs of its dawning, and to work for the perfect day when thy will shall be done on earth as it is in heaven; through Jesus Christ our Lord.

Percy Dearmer, 1867–1936

Day 7

The Final Victory

FLESH AND BLOOD can never possess the kingdom of God, the perishable cannot possess the imperishable. Listen! I will unfold a mystery: we shall not all die, but we shall all be changed in a flash, in the twinkling of an eye, at the last trumpet-call. For the trumpet will sound, and the dead will rise imperishable, and we shall be changed. This perishable body must be clothed with the imperishable, and what is mortal with immortality. And when this perishable body has been clothed with the imperishable and our mortality has been clothed with immortality, then the saying of scripture will come true: 'Death is swallowed up; victory is won!' 'O Death, where is your victory? O Death, where is your sting?' The sting of death is sin, and sin gains its power from the law. But thanks be to God! He gives us victory through our Lord Jesus Christ.

O Lord, you have freed us from the fear of death. You have made the end of our life here into the beginning of true life for us. You give rest to our bodies for a time in sleep, and then you waken them again with the sound of the last trumpet. Our earthly body, formed by your hands, you consign in trust to the earth, and then once more you reclaim it, transfiguring with immortality and grace whatever in us is mortal or deformed.

Macrina, 4th century

WEEK 12

God's Glory

Day 1

God's Glorious Name

Lord our sovereign,
how glorious is your name throughout the world!
Your majesty is praised as high as the heavens,
from the mouths of babes and infants at the breast.
You have established a bulwark against your adversaries
to restrain the enemy and the avenger.

When I look up at your heavens, the work of your fingers,
at the moon and the stars you have set in place,
what is a frail mortal, that you should be mindful of him,
a human being, that you should take notice of him?

Yet you have made him little less than a god,
crowning his head with glory and honour.
You make him master over all that you have made,
putting everything in subjection under his feet:
all sheep and oxen, all the wild beasts,
the birds in the air, the fish in the sea,
and everything that moves along ocean paths.

Lord our sovereign,
how glorious is your name throughout the world!

All glory and thanks, all honour and power, all love and obedience, be to the blessed and undivided Trinity, one God Eternal. The heavens declare thy glory, the earth confesses thy providence, the sea manifests thy power, and every spirit, and every understanding creature celebrates thy greatness for ever and ever. All glory and majesty, all praises and dominion be unto thee, O God, Father, Son and Holy Ghost, for ever and ever.

Jeremy Taylor, 1613–67

Day 2

Who Is the King of Glory?

To the Lord belong the earth and everything in it,
the world and all its inhabitants.
For it was he who founded it on the seas
and planted it firm on the waters beneath.

Who may go up the mountain of the Lord?
Who may stand in his holy place?
One who has clean hands and a pure heart,
who has not set his mind on what is false
or sworn deceitfully.
Such a one shall receive blessing from the Lord,
and be vindicated by God his saviour.
Such is the fortune of those who seek him,
who seek the presence of the God of Jacob.

Lift up your heads, you gates,
lift them up, you everlasting doors,
that the king of glory may come in.
Who is he, this king of glory?
The Lord of Hosts, he is the king of glory.

King of Glory, King of Peace
I will love thee;
And that love may never cease
I will move thee.
Thou hast granted my request,
Thou has heard me;
Thou didst note my working breast,
Thou hast spared me.

Seven whole days, not one in seven,
I will praise thee;
In my heart, though not in heaven,
I can raise thee.
Small it is in this poor sort
To enrol thee:
E'en Eternity's too short
To extol thee.

George Herbert, 1593–1633

Day 3

Cry Glory!

Ascribe to the Lord, you angelic powers,
ascribe to the Lord glory and might.
Ascribe to the Lord the glory due to his name;
in holy attire worship the Lord.

The voice of the Lord echoes over the waters;
the God of glory thunders;
the Lord thunders over the mighty waters,
the voice of the Lord in power,
the voice of the Lord in majesty.

The voice of the Lord makes flames of fire burst forth;
the voice of the Lord makes the wilderness writhe in travail,
the Lord makes the wilderness of Kadesh writhe.
The voice of the Lord makes the hinds calve;
he strips the forest bare,
and in his temple all cry, 'Glory!'

Glory to thee,
and praise, and blessing, and thanksgiving,
with the voices and convert of voices
of angels and of men,
of all thy saints in heaven,
and of all thy creature in heaven or earth,
and of me, beneath their feet,
unworthy and wretched sinner,
thy abject creature,
now, in this day and hour,
and every day till my last breath,
and till the end of the world.
And for ages upon ages.

Lancelot Andrewes, 1555–1626

Day 4

Song of the Redeemed

Let the wilderness and the parched land be glad,
let the desert rejoice and burst into flower.
Let it flower with fields of asphodel,
let it rejoice and shout for joy.
The glory of Lebanon is given to it,
the splendour too of Carmel and Sharon;
these will see the glory of the Lord,
the splendour of our God.
Then the eyes of the blind will be opened,
and the ears of the deaf unstopped.
Then the lame will leap like deer,
and the dumb shout aloud;
for water will spring up in the wilderness
and torrents flow in the desert.
The mirage will become a pool,
the thirsty land bubbling springs;
instead of reeds and rushes, grass will grow
in country where wolves have their lairs.
And a causeway will appear there;
it will be called the Way of Holiness.
But by that way those the Lord has redeemed will return.
The Lord's people, set free, will come back
and enter Zion with shouts of triumph,
crowned with everlasting joy.
Gladness and joy will come upon them,
while suffering and weariness flee away.

From glory to glory advancing, we praise thee, O Lord
thy name with the Father and Spirit be ever adored.
From strength to strength we go forward on Zion's highway,
to appear before God in the city of infinite day.

Thanksgiving and glory and worship, and blessing and love,
one heart and one song have the saints upon earth and above.
Ever more, O Lord, to thy servants thy presence be nigh;
ever fit us by service on earth for thy service on high.

Liturgy of St James

Day 5

Clear the Way!

A voice cries:
'Clear a road through the wilderness for the Lord,
prepare a highway across the desert for our God.
Let every valley be raised,
every mountain and hill be brought low,
uneven ground be made smooth,
and steep places become level.
Then will the glory of the Lord be revealed
and all mankind together will see it.
The Lord himself has spoken.'

A voice says, 'Proclaim!'
and I asked, 'What shall I proclaim?'
'All mortals are grass,
they last no longer than a wild flower of the field.
The grass withers, the flower fades,
when the blast of the Lord blows on them.
Surely the people are grass!
The grass may wither, the flower fade,
but the word of our God will endure for ever.'

Glory be to thee, O Lord, glory to thee;
glory to thee,
and glory to thine all-holy Name,
for all thy divine perfections in them;
for thine incomprehensible and
unimaginable goodness
and thy pity toward sinners
and unworthy men.

Lancelot Andrewes, 1555–1626

Day 6

A Glorious Vision

AFTER THIS I had a vision: a door stood open in heaven. There in heaven stood a throne. On it sat One whose appearance was like jasper or cornelian, and round it was a rainbow, bright as an emerald. In a circle about this throne were twenty-four other thrones, and on them were seated twenty-four elders, robed in white and wearing gold crowns. From the throne came flashes of lightning and peals of thunder. Burning before the throne were seven flaming torches, the seven spirits of God, and in front of it stretched what looked like a sea of glass or a sheet of ice.

In the centre, round the throne itself, were four living creatures, covered with eyes in front and behind. The first creature was like a lion, the second like an ox, the third had a human face, and the fourth was like an eagle in flight. Each of the four living creatures had six wings, and eyes all round and inside them. Day and night unceasingly they sing:

> Holy, holy, holy is God the sovereign Lord of all, who was, and is, and is to come!

Whenever the living creatures give glory and honour and thanks to the One who sits on the throne, who lives for ever and ever, the twenty-four elders prostrate themselves before the One who sits on the throne and they worship him who lives for ever and ever. As they lay their crowns before the throne they cry:

> You are worthy, O Lord our God, to receive glory and honour and power, because you created all things; by your will they were created and have their being!

Holy, holy, holy, Lord God almighty,
who is and who was and who is to come.
Let us praise and exalt him above all for ever.
Worthy are you, O Lord our God, to receive praise, glory, honour and blessing.
Let us praise and exalt him above all for ever.
Worthy is the lamb that was slain to receive power and divinity, wisdom and
strength, honour glory and blessing.
Let us praise and exalt him above all for ever.
Let us bless the Father, the Son, and the Holy Spirit.
Let us praise and exalt him above all for ever.

Francis of Assisi, 1182–1226

Day 7

The City of God

❦

O NE OF THE seven angels who held the seven bowls full of the seven last plagues came and spoke to me. 'Come,' he said, 'and I will show you the bride, the wife of the Lamb.' So in the spirit he carried me away to a great and lofty mountain, and showed me Jerusalem, the Holy City, coming down out of heaven from God. It shone with the glory of God; it had the radiance of some priceless jewel, like a jasper, clear as crystal. It had a great and lofty wall with twelve gates, at which were stationed twelve angels.

The wall was built of jasper, while the city itself was of pure gold, bright as clear glass. The foundations of the city wall were adorned with precious stones of every kind. The twelve gates were twelve pearls, each gate fashioned from a single pearl. The great street of the city was of pure gold, like translucent glass.

I saw no temple in the city, for its temple was the sovereign Lord God and the Lamb. The city did not need the sun or the moon to shine on it, for the glory of God gave it light, and its lamp was the Lamb. By its light shall the nations walk, and to it the kings of the earth shall bring their splendour.

O Good Jesu, word of the Father, the brightness of the Father's glory, whom angels desire to behold; teach us to do your will; that guided by your good Spirit, we may come to that blessed city where there is everlasting day.

Gregory, 7th century

WEEK 13

God's Holiness

Day 1

Holy Ground

W HILE TENDING THE sheep of his father-in-law Jethro, priest of Midian, Moses led the flock along the west side of the wilderness and came to Horeb, the mountain of God. There an angel of the Lord appeared to him as a fire blazing out from a bush. Although the bush was on fire, it was not being burnt up, and Moses said to himself, 'I must go across and see this remarkable sight. Why ever does the bush not burn away?' When the Lord saw that Moses had turned aside to look, he called to him out of the bush, 'Moses, Moses!' He answered, 'Here I am!' God said, 'Do not come near! Take off your sandals, for the place where you are standing is holy ground.' Then he said, 'I am the God of your father, the God of Abraham, Isaac, and Jacob.' Moses hid his face, for he was afraid to look at God.

The Lord said, 'I have witnessed the misery of my people in Egypt and have heard them crying out because of their oppressors. I know what they are suffering and have come down to rescue them from the power of the Egyptians. Come, I shall send you to Pharaoh, and you are to bring my people Israel out of Egypt.' 'But who am I', Moses said to God, 'that I should approach Pharaoh and that I should bring the Israelites out of Egypt?' God answered, 'I am with you. This will be your proof that it is I who have sent you: when you have brought the people out of Egypt, you will all worship God here at this mountain.'

Moses said to God, 'If I come to the Israelites and tell them that the God of their forefathers has sent me to them, and they ask me his name, what am I to say to them?'

God answered, 'I am that I am. Tell them that I am has sent you to them.' He continued, 'You are to tell the Israelites that it is the Lord, the God of their forefathers, the God of Abraham, Isaac, and Jacob, who has sent you to them. This is my name for ever; this is my title in every generation.'

Holy and Eternal Father, God of Abraham, Isaac and Jacob, we praise and thank you for all that you are and all that you yet will be: hope for the helpless, help for the needy, justice for the poor, liberator of the captives, the holy and righteous judge who condemns and will defeat all tyranny and oppression.
Philip Law

Day 2

God's Holy Way

I call to mind the deeds of the Lord;
I recall your wonderful acts of old;
I reflect on all your works
and consider what you have done.
Your way, God, is holy;
what god is as great as our God?
You are a God who works miracles;
you have shown the nations your power.
With your strong arm you rescued your people,
the descendants of Jacob and Joseph.
The waters saw you, God,
they saw you and writhed in anguish;
the ocean was troubled to its depths.
The clouds poured down water, the skies thundered,
your arrows flashed hither and thither.
The sound of your thunder was in the whirlwind,
lightning-flashes lit up the world,
the earth shook and quaked.
Your path was through the sea,
your way through mighty waters,
and none could mark your footsteps.

Holy God,
holy and mighty,
holy immortal one,
have mercy upon us.

Source unknown,
Eastern Orthodox

Day 3

Holy Is the Lord

The Lord has become King; let peoples tremble.
He is enthroned on the cherubim; let the earth shake.
The Lord is great in Zion;
he is exalted above all the peoples.
Let them extol your great and terrible name.
Holy is he.

The King in his might loves justice.
You have established equity;
you have dealt justly and righteously in Jacob.
Exalt the Lord our God
and bow down at his footstool.
Holy is he.

Moses and Aaron were among his priests,
and Samuel was among those who invoked his name;
they called to the Lord, and he answered them.
He spoke to them in a pillar of cloud;
they kept his decrees and the statute he gave them.

O Lord our God, you answered them;
you were a God who forgave them,
yet you called them to account for their misdeeds.
Exalt the Lord our God,
and bow down towards his holy mountain;
for holy is the Lord our God.

Great and terrible God, we bow down before your throne of grace, conscious of your holiness and thankful that you are also a God who forgives.

Philip Law

Day 4

The Lord of Hosts

I SAW THE LORD seated on a throne, high and exalted, and the skirt of his robe filled the temple. Seraphim were in attendance on him. Each had six wings: with one pair of wings they covered their faces and with another their bodies, and with the third pair they flew. They were calling to one another,

Holy, holy, holy is the Lord of Hosts:
the whole earth is full of his glory.

As each called, the threshold shook to its foundations at the sound, while the house began to fill with clouds of smoke. Then I said,

Woe is me! I am doomed,
for my own eyes have seen the King, the Lord of Hosts,
I, a man of unclean lips,
I, who dwell among a people of unclean lips.

One of the seraphim flew to me, carrying in his hand a glowing coal which he had taken from the altar with a pair of tongs. He touched my mouth with it and said,

This has touched your lips;
now your iniquity is removed
and your sin is wiped out.

> *You are God and we praise you,*
> *you are the Lord and we acclaim you;*
> *you are the eternal Father,*
> *all creation worships you.*
> *To you all angels, all the powers of heaven,*
> *cherubim and seraphim sing in endless praise,*
> *holy, holy, holy, Lord God of power and might,*
> *heaven and earth are full of your glory.*
>
> From the *Te Deum*

Day 5

The Holy One

Who has measured the waters of the sea in the hollow of his hand,
or with its span gauged the heavens?
Who has held all the soil of the earth in a bushel,
or weighed the mountains on a balance,
the hills on a pair of scales?
Who has directed the Spirit of the Lord?
What counsellor stood at his side to instruct him?
With whom did he confer to gain discernment?
Who taught him this path of justice,
or taught him knowledge,
or showed him the way of wisdom?

Do you not know, have you not heard,
were you not told long ago,
have you not perceived ever since the world was founded,
that God sits enthroned on the vaulted roof of the world,
and its inhabitants appear as grasshoppers?
He stretches out the skies like a curtain,
spreads them out like a tent to live in;

To whom, then, will you liken me,
whom set up as my equal?
asks the Holy One.
Do you not know, have you not heard?
The Lord, the eternal God,
creator of earth's farthest bounds,
does not weary or grow faint;
his understanding cannot be fathomed.

There is no God besides you,
there is none holy besides you,
you are the Lord,
the God of knowledge,
the God of the saints,
holy above all holy beings.
Apostolic Constitutions, 4th century

Day 6

My Ways are not Your Ways

Seek the Lord while he is present,
call to him while he is close at hand.

Let the wicked abandon their ways
and the evil their thoughts:
let them return to the Lord, who will take pity on them,
and to our God, for he will freely forgive.

For my thoughts are not your thoughts,
nor are your ways my ways.
This is the word of the Lord.

But as the heavens are high above the earth,
so are my ways high above your ways
and my thoughts above your thoughts.

*Thou art great, O Lord, thou art great, and greatly to be praised, and of thy
greatness there is no end. The heavens are far raised from the earth, but thy
majesty is much further exalted above all our thoughts and conceptions.*

Robert Leighton, 1611–84

Day 7

A Devouring Fire

IT IS NOT to the tangible, blazing fire of Sinai that you have come, with its darkness, gloom, and whirlwind, its trumpet-blast and oracular voice, which the people heard and begged to hear no more; for they could not bear the command, 'If even an animal touches the mountain, it must be stoned to death.' So appalling was the sight that Moses said, 'I shudder with fear.'

No, you have come to Mount Zion, the city of the living God, the heavenly Jerusalem, to myriads of angels, to the full concourse and assembly of the first-born who are enrolled in heaven, and to God the judge of all, and to the spirits of good men made perfect, and to Jesus the mediator of a new covenant, whose sprinkled blood has better things to say than the blood of Abel. See that you do not refuse to hear the voice that speaks. Those who refused to hear the oracle speaking on earth found no escape; still less shall we escape if we reject him who speaks from heaven. Then indeed his voice shook the earth, but now he has promised, 'Once again I will shake not only the earth, but the heavens also.' The words once again point to the removal of all created things, of all that is shaken, so that what cannot be shaken may remain. The kingdom we are given is unshakeable; let us therefore give thanks to God for it, and so worship God as he would be worshipped, with reverence and awe; for our God is a devouring fire.

O God, mercifully grant that the fire of your love may burn up in us all the things which displease you, and make us fit to live in your heavenly King-dom; for the sake of Jesus Christ our Saviour.

The Breviary

God's Justice

Day 1

The Just Ruler

God, endow the king with your own justice,
his royal person with your righteousness,
that he may govern your people rightly
and deal justly with your oppressed ones.

May hills and mountains provide your people
with prosperity in righteousness.
May he give judgement for the oppressed among the people
and help to the needy;
may he crush the oppressor.

May he fear you as long as the sun endures,
and as the moon throughout the ages.
May he be like rain falling on early crops,
like showers watering the earth.

In his days may righteousness flourish,
prosperity abound until the moon is no more.
For he will rescue the needy who appeal for help,
the distressed who have no protector.

He will have pity on the poor and the needy,
and deliver the needy from death;
he will redeem them from oppression and violence
and their blood will be precious in his eyes.

*O Christ, thou hast bidden us pray for the coming of thy Father's kingdom,
in which his righteousness will be done on earth. As we have mastered
nature that we may gain wealth, help us now to master the social relations
of mankind that we may gain justice and a world of brothers.*

Walter Rauschenbusch, 1861–1918

Day 2

Justice and Equity

Great is the Lord and most worthy of praise;
he is more to be feared than all gods.
For the gods of the nations are idols every one;
but the Lord made the heavens.

Declare among the nations, 'The Lord is King;
the world is established immovably;
he will judge the peoples with equity.'

Let the heavens rejoice and the earth be glad,
let the sea resound and everything in it,
let the fields exult and all that is in them;
let all the trees of the forest shout for joy
before the Lord when he comes,
when he comes to judge the earth.
He will judge the world with justice
and peoples by his faithfulness.

O sun of righteousness, in all unclouded glory, supreme dispenser of justice,
in that great day when you strictly judge all nations,
we earnestly beseech you, upon this your people,
who here stand before your presence,
in your pity, Lord, have mercy on us.

Dunstan, c.908–88

Day 3

Justice for the Oppressed

Praise the Lord.
My soul, praise the Lord.
As long as I live I shall praise the Lord;
I shall sing psalms to my God all my life long.

Put no trust in princes
or in any mortal, for they have no power to save.
When they breathe their last breath,
they return to the dust,
and on that day their plans come to nothing.

Happy is he whose helper is the God of Jacob,
whose hope is in the Lord his God,
maker of heaven and earth,
the sea, and all that is in them;
who maintains faithfulness for ever
and deals out justice to the oppressed.
The Lord feeds the hungry
and sets the prisoner free.

The Lord restores sight to the blind
and raises those who are bowed down;
the Lord loves the righteous
and protects the stranger in the land;
the Lord gives support to the fatherless and the widow,
but thwarts the course of the wicked.

The Lord will reign for ever, Zion,
your God for all generations.
Praise the Lord.

God of love, you see all the suffering, injustice, and misery which reign in this world; have pity, we pray, on what you have created; in your mercy look upon the poor, the oppressed, the destitute, and all who are heavy-laden; fill our hearts with deep compassion for those who suffer, and hasten the coming of your kingdom of justice and truth; for the sake of Jesus Christ our Lord.

Eugene Bersier, 1831–89

Day 4

The Wages of Sin

THIS WORD OF the Lord came to me: 'What do you all mean by repeating this proverb in the land of Israel:

"Parents eat sour grapes,
and their children's teeth are set on edge?"

'As I live, says the Lord God, this proverb will never again be used by you in Israel. Every living soul belongs to me; parent and child alike are mine. It is the person who sins that will die.

'If someone who is wicked renounces all his sinful ways and keeps all my laws, doing what is just and right, he will live; he will not die. None of the offences he has committed will be remembered against him; because of his righteous conduct he will live. Have I any desire for the death of a wicked person? says the Lord God. Is not my desire rather that he should mend his ways and live?

'If someone who is righteous turns from his righteous ways and commits every kind of abomination that the wicked practise, is he to do this and live? No, none of his former righteousness will be remembered in his favour; because he has been faithless and has sinned, he must die.'

> *God eternal, all that is hidden is known to you,*
> *all that will come to pass you see before it happens;*
> *it is not your will that sinners should die:*
> *you want them to repent and be saved.*
> *Look, then, on this poor thing,*
> *pitiful, sinful, your servant.*
>
> Papyri, 3rd or 4th century

Day 5

Let Justice Flow on

These are the words of the Lord to the people of Israel:
'If you would live, make your way to me,
who makes destruction flash forth against the mighty
so that destruction comes upon the stronghold.

'You that turn justice to poison
and thrust righteousness to the ground,
you that hate a man who brings the wrongdoer to court
and abominate him who speaks nothing less than truth:
You levy taxes on the poor
and extort a tribute of grain from them,
you bully the innocent, extort ransoms,
and in court push the destitute out of the way.

'Seek good, and not evil,
that you may live,
that the Lord, the God of Hosts, may be with you,
as you claim he is.
Hate evil, and love good;
establish justice in the courts;

'I spurn with loathing your pilgrim-feasts;
I take no pleasure in your sacred ceremonies.
Spare me the sound of your songs;
I shall not listen to the strumming of your lutes.
Instead let justice flow on like a river
and righteousness like a never-failing torrent.'

Strengthen us, O God, to relieve the oppressed, to hear the groans of poor prisoners, to reform the abuses of all professions; that many be made not poor to make a few rich; for Jesus Christ's sake.

Oliver Cromwell, 1599–1658

Day 6

Inescapable Judgement

W E ALL KNOW that God's judgement is just; and do you imagine you that pass judgement on the guilty while committing the same crimes yourself do you imagine that you, any more than they, will escape the judgement of God? Or do you despise his wealth of kindness and tolerance and patience, failing to see that God's kindness is meant to lead you to repentance? In the obstinate impenitence of your heart you are laying up for yourself a store of retribution against the day of retribution, when God's just judgement will be revealed, and he will pay everyone for what he has done. To those who pursue glory, honour, and immortality by steady persistence in well-doing, he will give eternal life; but the retribution of his wrath awaits those who are governed by selfish ambition, who refuse obedience to truth and take evil for their guide.

O Lord, when we consider what we are and remember our mistakes, then, conscious of our sins and misdeeds, our thoughts turn to your terrible day of judgement; our assurance of a favourable verdict lies in our one and only refuge who loves all mankind; and so it is right that we pray you now to grant us the great gift of your merciful forbearance.

Through the grace, mercy and all-embracing love of your only-begotten Son, to whom with you and your holy and life-giving Spirit be all blessing, now and for ever, to the ages of ages.

Source Unknown, Eastern Orthodox

Day 7

The Last Judgement

I SAW THRONES, and on them sat those to whom judgement was committed. I saw the souls of those who, for the sake of God's word and their witness to Jesus, had been beheaded, those who had not worshipped the beast and its image or received its mark on forehead or hand. They came to life again and reigned with Christ for a thousand years, though the rest of the dead did not come to life until the thousand years were ended.

This is the first resurrection. Blessed and holy are those who share in this first resurrection! Over them the second death has no power; but they shall be priests of God and of Christ, and shall reign with him for the thousand years.

When the thousand years are ended, Satan will be let loose from his prison, and he will come out to seduce the nations in the four quarters of the earth. He will muster them for war, the hosts of Gog and Magog, countless as the sands of the sea. They marched over the breadth of the land and laid siege to the camp of God's people and the city that he loves. But fire came down on them from heaven and consumed them. Their seducer, the Devil, was flung into the lake of fire and sulphur, where the beast and the false prophet had been flung to be tormented day and night for ever.

I saw a great, white throne, and the One who sits upon it. From his presence earth and heaven fled away, and there was no room for them any more. I saw the dead, great and small, standing before the throne; and books were opened. Then another book, the book of life, was opened. The dead were judged by what they had done, as recorded in these books. The sea gave up the dead that were in it, and Death and Hades gave up the dead in their keeping. Everyone was judged on the record of his deeds. Then Death and Hades were flung into the lake of fire. This lake of fire is the second death; into it were flung any whose names were not to be found in the book of life.

O thou that beholdest all things, we have sinned against thee in thought, word, and deed; blot out our transgressions, be merciful to us sinners, and grant that our names may be found written in the Book of Life, for the sake of Christ Jesus our Saviour.

Nerses, 4th century

WEEK 15

God's Grace

Day 1

Divine Forgiveness

Happy is he whose offence is forgiven,
whose sin is blotted out!
Happy is he to whom the Lord imputes no fault,
in whose spirit there is no deceit.

While I refused to speak, my body wasted away
with day-long moaning.
For day and night
your hand was heavy upon me;
the sap in me dried up as in summer drought.

When I acknowledged my sin to you,
when I no longer concealed my guilt,
but said, 'I shall confess my offence to the Lord,'
then you for your part remitted the penalty of my sin.

So let every faithful heart pray to you
in the hour of anxiety;
when great floods threaten
they shall not touch him.

O most merciful Father, who dost put away the sins of those who truly repent, we come before thy throne in the name of Jesus Christ, that for his sake alone thou wilt have compassion on us, and let not our sins be a cloud between thee and us.

John Colet, 1467–1519

Day 2

Divine Blessing

May God be gracious to us and bless us,
may he cause his face to shine on us,
that your purpose may be known on earth,
your saving power among all nations.

Let the peoples praise you, God;
let all peoples praise you.
Let nations rejoice and shout in triumph;
for you judge the peoples with equity
and guide the nations of the earth.
Let the peoples praise you, God;
let all peoples praise you.

The earth has yielded its harvest.
May God, our God, bless us.
God grant us his blessing,
that all the ends of the earth may fear him.

May the Lord bless us
and take care of us;
may the Lord be kind and gracious to us;
may the Lord look on us with favour
and give us peace.
                              Numbers 6.24–26, adapted

Day 3

Divine Compassion

I love the Lord, for he has heard me
and listened to my prayer;
he has given me a hearing
and all my days I shall cry to him.

The cords of death bound me,
Sheol held me in its grip.
Anguish and torment held me fast;
then I invoked the Lord by name,
'Lord, deliver me, I pray.'

Gracious is the Lord and righteous;
our God is full of compassion.
The Lord preserves the simple-hearted;
when I was brought low, he saved me.

We thank you, O Father, for your readiness to hear and to forgive; for your great love to us, in spite of our unworthiness; for the many blessings we enjoy above our deserving, hoping, or asking. You have been so good to us in our ingratitude, thoughtlessness, and forgetfulness of you. For your pity, long-suffering, gentleness and tenderness, we bow our heads in humble thankfulness of heart. We worship you who are infinite love, infinite compassion, infinite power. Accept our praise and gratitude; through Jesus Christ our Lord and Saviour.

C. J. N. Child

Day 4

Divine Comfort

These are the words of the high and exalted One,
who is enthroned for ever, whose name is holy:
I dwell in a high and holy place
and with him who is broken and humble in spirit,
to revive the spirit of the humble,
to revive the courage of the broken.

I shall not be always accusing,
I shall not continually nurse my wrath,
else the spirit of the creatures whom I made
would be faint because of me.

For a brief time I was angry at the guilt of Israel.
I smote him in my anger and withdrew my favour,
but he was wayward and went his own way.

I have seen his conduct,
yet I shall heal him and give him relief;
I shall bring him comfort in full measure,
and on the lips of those who mourn him
I shall create words of praise.

Comfort, we ask you, most Gracious God,
all who are cast down and faint of heart
amidst the sorrows and difficulties of the world:
and grant that, by the quickening power of the Holy Spirit,
they may be lifted up to you with hope and courage,
and enabled to go upon their way
rejoicing in your love;
through Jesus Christ our Lord

Richard Meux Benson, 1824–1915

Day 5

Divine Pity

THE WORD OF the Lord came to Jonah: 'Go to the great city of Nineveh; go and denounce it in the words I give you.' Jonah obeyed and went at once to Nineveh. Then he proclaimed: 'In forty days Nineveh will be overthrown!'

The people of Nineveh took to heart this warning from God; they declared a public fast, and high and low alike put on sackcloth. When God saw what they did and how they gave up their wicked ways, he relented and did not inflict on them the punishment he had threatened.

This greatly displeased Jonah. In anger he prayed to the Lord: 'It is just as I feared, Lord. I knew that you are a gracious and compassionate God, long-suffering, ever constant, always ready to relent and not inflict punishment. Now take away my life, Lord: I should be better dead than alive.'

Jonah went out and sat down to the east of Nineveh, where he made himself a shelter and sat in its shade, waiting to see what would happen in the city. The Lord God ordained that a climbing gourd should grow up above Jonah's head to throw its shade over him and relieve his discomfort, and he was very glad of it. But at dawn the next day God ordained that a worm should attack the gourd, and it withered; and when the sun came up God ordained that a scorching wind should blow from the east. The sun beat down on Jonah's head till he grew faint, and he prayed for death; 'I should be better dead than alive,' he said.

At this God asked, 'Are you right to be angry over the gourd?' 'Yes,' Jonah replied, 'mortally angry!' But the Lord said, 'You are sorry about the gourd, though you did not have the trouble of growing it, a plant which came up one night and died the next. And should not I be sorry about the great city of Nineveh, with its hundred and twenty thousand people who cannot tell their right hand from their left, as well as cattle without number?'

O thou gracious and gentle and condescending God, the God of peace, Father of mercy, God of all comfort; see I lament before thee the evil of my heart; I acknowledge that I am too much disposed to anger, jealousy and revenge, to ambition and pride, which often give rise to discord and bitter feelings between me and others. Too often have I thus offended and grieved both thee, O long-suffering Father, and my fellow men.

Johann Arndt, 1558–1621

Day 6

Divine Peace

N OW THAT WE have been justified through faith, we are at peace with God through our Lord Jesus Christ, who has given us access to that grace in which we now live; and we exult in the hope of the divine glory that is to be ours. More than this: we even exult in our present sufferings, because we know that suffering is a source of endurance, endurance of approval, and approval of hope. Such hope is no fantasy; through the Holy Spirit he has given us, God's love has flooded our hearts.

It was while we were still helpless that, at the appointed time, Christ died for the wicked. Even for a just man one of us would hardly die, though perhaps for a good man one might actually brave death; but Christ died for us while we were yet sinners, and that is God's proof of his love towards us. And so, since we have now been justified by Christ's sacrificial death, we shall all the more certainly be saved through him from final retribution. For if, when we were God's enemies, we were reconciled to him through the death of his Son, how much more, now that we have been reconciled, shall we be saved by his life! But that is not all: we also exult in God through our Lord Jesus, through whom we have now been granted reconciliation.

Let us give thanks to God the Father, through his Son, in the Holy Spirit, who for his great mercy and his love for us has had pity on us, and when we were dead in sin, gave us new life in Christ, that together we might be a new creation. Acknowledging our divinity, because we have become sharers in the divine nature through the birth of the Messiah, we submit ourselves to Christ, who will judge us in truth because he ransomed us in mercy, who with the Father and the Holy Spirit reigns for ever and ever.

Leo the Great, d.461

Day 7

Divine Grace

Y OU ONCE WERE dead because of your sins and wickedness; you followed the ways of this present world order, obeying the commander of the spiritual powers of the air, the spirit now at work among God's rebel subjects. We too were once of their number: we were ruled by our physical desires, and did what instinct and evil imagination suggested. In our natural condition we lay under the condemnation of God like the rest of mankind. But God is rich in mercy, and because of his great love for us, he brought us to life with Christ when we were dead because of our sins; it is by grace you are saved.

And he raised us up in union with Christ Jesus and enthroned us with him in the heavenly realms, so that he might display in the ages to come how immense are the resources of his grace, and how great his kindness to us in Christ Jesus. For it is by grace you are saved through faith; it is not your own doing. It is God's gift, not a reward for work done. There is nothing for anyone to boast of; we are God's handiwork, created in Christ Jesus for the life of good deeds which God designed for us.

Blessed be the glory of the Lord, for the essential perfections of his Godhead, and his incomprehensible greatness, his dominion and omnipotence, his eternity and providence, his holiness and justice, his wisdom and truth, his goodness and mercy, but above all, for the unspeakable riches of his exceeding abundant grace and love in Christ Jesus.

John Henry Hobart, 1774–1830

WEEK 16

God's Wisdom

Day 1

Deeper Than Anyone Can Fathom

Consider God's handiwork; who can straighten what he has made crooked?

When things go well, be glad; but when they go ill, consider this: God has set the one alongside the other in such a way that no one can find out what is to happen afterwards.

In my futile existence I have seen it all, from the righteous perishing in their righteousness to the wicked growing old in wickedness.

Do not be over-righteous and do not be over-wise. Why should you destroy yourself?

Do not be over-wicked and do not be a fool. Why die before your time?

It is good to hold on to the one thing and not lose hold of the other; for someone who fears God will succeed both ways.

Wisdom makes the possessor of wisdom stronger than ten rulers in a city.

There is no one on earth so righteous that he always does right and never does wrong.

All this I have put to the test of wisdom. I said, 'I am resolved to be wise,' but wisdom was beyond my reach – whatever has happened lies out of reach, deep down, deeper than anyone can fathom.

> *Holy and infinite! Limitless, boundless*
> *All thy perfections and power and praise!*
> *Ocean of mystery! Awful and soundless*
> *All thine unsearchable judgements and ways!*
>
> Frances Ridley Havergal, 1836–79

Day 2

A Hymn to Wisdom

There are mines for silver
and places where gold is refined.
Iron is won from the earth
and copper smelted from the ore.
Man sets his hand to the granite rock
and lays bare the roots of the mountains;
he cuts galleries in the rocks,
and gems of every kind meet his eye;
he dams up the sources of the streams
and brings the hidden riches of the earth to light.

But where can wisdom be found,
and where is the source of understanding?
No one knows the way to it,
nor is it to be found in the land of the living.
'It is not in us,' declare the ocean depths;
the sea declares, 'It is not with me.'
Red gold cannot buy it,
nor can its price be weighed out in silver.
Where, then, does wisdom come from?
Where is the source of understanding?

God alone understands the way to it,
he alone knows its source;
for he can see to the ends of the earth
and observe every place under heaven.
And he said to mankind:
'The fear of the Lord is wisdom,
and to turn from evil, that is understanding!'

O gracious and holy Father,
give us wisdom to perceive thee,
intelligence to understand thee,
diligence to seek thee,
patience to wait for thee,
eyes to behold thee,
a heart to meditate upon thee,
and a life to proclaim thee.

Benedict, 480–c.550

Day 3

Spiritual Treasure

My son, if you take my words to heart
and treasure my commandments deep within you,
giving your attention to wisdom
and your mind to understanding,
if you cry out for discernment
and invoke understanding,
if you seek for her as for silver
and dig for her as for buried treasure,
then you will understand the fear of the Lord
and attain to knowledge of God.

It is the Lord who bestows wisdom
and teaches knowledge and understanding.
Out of his store he endows the upright with ability.
For those whose conduct is blameless he is a shield,
guarding the course of justice
and keeping watch over the way of his loyal servants.
You will then understand what is right and just
and keep only to the good man's path,
for wisdom will sink into your mind,
and knowledge will be your heart's delight.

Give us, O Lord, we humbly beseech thee, a wise, a sober, a patient understanding, a courageous heart; a soul full of devotion to do thee service, strength against all temptations, through Jesus Christ our Lord.

William Laud, 1573–1645

Day 4

A Tree of Life

Happy is he who has found wisdom,
he who has acquired understanding,
for wisdom is more profitable than silver,
and the gain she brings is better than gold!
She is more precious than red coral,
and none of your jewels can compare with her.
In her right hand is long life,
in her left are riches and honour.
Her ways are pleasant ways
and her paths all lead to prosperity.

She is a tree of life to those who grasp her,
and those who hold fast to her are safe.
By wisdom the Lord laid the earth's foundations
and by understanding he set the heavens in place;
by his knowledge the springs of the deep burst forth
and the clouds dropped dew.

Grant me, O Lord, heavenly wisdom, that I may learn to seek thee above all things, and to understand all other things as they are, according to the order of thy wisdom.

Thomas à Kempis, 1380–1471

Day 5

The Law of the Lord

The law of the Lord is perfect and revives the soul.
The Lord's instruction never fails;
it makes the simple wise.

The precepts of the Lord are right
and give joy to the heart.
The commandment of the Lord is pure
and gives light to the eyes.

The fear of the Lord is unsullied; it abides for ever.
The Lord's judgements are true and righteous every one,
more to be desired than gold, pure gold in plenty,
sweeter than honey dripping from the comb.

It is through them that your servant is warned;
in obeying them is great reward.

Who is aware of his unwitting sins?
Cleanse me of any secret fault.
Hold back your servant also from wilful sins,
lest they get the better of me.
Then I shall be blameless,
innocent of grave offence.

May the words of my mouth and the thoughts of my mind
be acceptable to you,
Lord, my rock and my redeemer!

Lord, you are to be blessed and praised; all good things come from you: you are in our words and in our thoughts, and in all that we do.

Teresa of Avila, 1515–82

Day 6

The Mind of the Lord

How deep are the wealth
and the wisdom and the knowledge of God!
How inscrutable his judgements,
how unsearchable his ways!

Who knows the mind of the Lord?
Who has been his counsellor?
Who has made a gift to him first,
and earned a gift in return?
From him and through him and for him all things exist
to him be glory for ever!

You are the Wisdom, uncreated and eternal,
the supreme first cause, above all being,
sovereign Godhead, sovereign goodness,
watching unseen the God-inspired wisdom of Christian people.
Raise us, we pray, that we may totally respond
to the supreme, unknown, ultimate, and splendid height
of your words, mysterious and inspired.

The Cloud of Unknowing, 14th century

Day 7

Christ our Wisdom

S CRIPTURE SAYS, 'I will destroy the wisdom of the wise, and bring to nothing the cleverness of the clever.' Where is your wise man now, your man of
learning, your subtle debater of this present age? God has made the wisdom of
this world look foolish! As God in his wisdom ordained, the world failed to
find him by its wisdom, and he chose by the folly of the gospel to save those
who have faith. Jews demand signs, Greeks look for wisdom, but we proclaim
Christ nailed to the cross; and though this is an offence to Jews and folly to
Gentiles, yet to those who are called, Jews and Greeks alike, he is the power of
God and the wisdom of God.

The folly of God is wiser than human wisdom, and the weakness of God
stronger than human strength. My friends, think what sort of people you are,
whom God has called. Few of you are wise by any human standard, few powerful or of noble birth. Yet, to shame the wise, God has chosen what the world
counts folly, and to shame what is strong, God has chosen what the world
counts weakness. He has chosen things without rank or standing in the world,
mere nothings, to overthrow the existing order. So no place is left for any
human pride in the presence of God. By God's act you are in Christ Jesus; God
has made him our wisdom, and in him we have our righteousness, our holiness, our liberation. Therefore, in the words of scripture, 'If anyone must boast,
let him boast of the Lord.'

> *O Lord Jesus Christ, wisdom and word of God, dwell in our hearts, we
> beseech thee, by thy most Holy Spirit that out of the abundance of our
> hearts our mouths may speak thy praise.*
>
> Christina Rossetti, 1830–94

WEEK 17

God's Faithfulness

Day 1

From the Depths

You are my hope, Lord God,
my trust since my childhood.
On you I have leaned from birth;
you brought me from my mother's womb;
to you I offer praise at all times.
You have made me suffer many grievous hardships,
yet you revive me once more
and lift me again from earth's watery depths.

Restore me to honour, and comfort me again;
then I shall praise you on the harp
for your faithfulness, my God;
on the lyre I shall sing to you,
the Holy One of Israel.
Songs of joy will be on my lips;
I shall sing to you because you have redeemed me.

From the depths, O Lord, you lifted me. Though I suffer many hardships, you revive me. For you are my hope, Lord God, and in your faithfulness I will find my joy.

Philip Law

Day 2

Fountain of Life and Light

Lord, your unfailing love reaches to the heavens,
your faithfulness to the skies.
Your righteousness is like the lofty mountains,
your justice like the great deep;
Lord who saves man and beast,
how precious is your unfailing love!
Gods and frail mortals seek refuge in the shadow of your wings.
They are filled with the rich plenty of your house,
and you give them to drink from the stream of your delights;
for with you is the fountain of life,
and by your light we are enlightened.

*Come, O thou eternal light, salvation, comfort, be our light in darkness,
our salvation in life, our comfort in death; and lead us in the straight way
to everlasting life, that we may praise thee, for ever.*

Bernhard Albrecht, 1569–1636

Day 3

Cleansed from Sin

God, be gracious to me in your faithful love;
in the fullness of your mercy blot out my misdeeds.
Wash away all my iniquity
and cleanse me from my sin.
For well I know my misdeeds,
and my sins confront me all the time.

Against you only have I sinned
and have done what displeases;
you are right when you accuse me
and justified in passing sentence.

From my birth I have been evil,
sinful from the time my mother conceived me.
You desire faithfulness in the inmost being,
so teach me wisdom in my heart.

Sprinkle me with hyssop, so that I may be cleansed;
wash me, and I shall be whiter than snow.
Let me hear the sound of joy and gladness;
you have crushed me, but make me rejoice again.

God,
to whom all hearts are open,
to whom all wills speak
and from whom no secret is hidden,
I beg you,
so to cleanse the intent of my heart
with the unutterable gift of your grace,
that I may perfectly love you
and worthily praise you.
The Cloud of Unknowing, 14th century

Day 4

God Is my Refuge

God, be gracious to me; be gracious,
for I have made you my refuge.
I shall seek refuge in the shadow of your wings
until the storms are past.

I shall call to God Most High,
to the God who will fulfil his purpose for me.

My heart is steadfast, God,
my heart is steadfast.
I shall sing and raise a psalm.

I shall praise you among the peoples, Lord,
among the nations I shall raise a psalm to you,
for your unfailing love is as high as the heavens;
your faithfulness reaches to the skies.

God, be exalted above the heavens;
let your glory be over all the earth.

Give us, O Lord, a steadfast heart, which no unworthy affection may drag downwards; give us an unconquered heart, which no tribulation can wear out; give us an upright heart, which no unworthy purpose may tempt aside.

Thomas Aquinas, 1225–74

Day 5

God Is my Rock

It is good to give thanks to the Lord,
to sing psalms to your name, Most High,
to declare your love in the morning
and your faithfulness every night
to the music of a ten-stringed harp,
to the sounding chords of the lyre.

Your acts, Lord, fill me with exultation;
I shout in triumph at your mighty deeds.
The righteous flourish like a palm tree,
they grow tall as a cedar on Lebanon;
planted in the house of the Lord,
and flourishing in the courts of our God,
they still bear fruit in old age;
they are luxuriant, wide-spreading trees.
They declare that the Lord is just:
my rock, in him there is no unrighteousness.

O Almighty God, we humbly ask you to make us like trees planted by the waterside, that we may bear fruits of good living in due season. Forgive us past offences, sanctify us now, and direct all that we should be in the future, for Christ's sake.

Source unknown, Nigerian

Day 6

God Is Ever Faithful

The Lord is gracious and compassionate,
long-suffering and ever faithful.
The Lord is good to all;
his compassion rests upon all his creatures.

In all his promises the Lord keeps faith,
he is unchanging in all his works;
the Lord supports all who stumble
and raises all who are bowed down.

All raise their eyes to you in hope,
and you give them their food when it is due.
You open your hand
and satisfy every living creature with your favour.

The Lord is righteous in all his ways,
faithful in all he does;
the Lord is near to all who call to him,
to all who call to him in sincerity.
He fulfils the desire of those who fear him;
he hears their cry for help and saves them.

Our God, you open your hand, and fill all things living with plenteousness;
to you we commit all those are dear to us; watch over them, we pray, and
provide all things needful for their souls and bodies, now and for evermore;
through Jesus Christ our Lord.

Nerses, 4th century

Day 7

God does not Forget

Shout for joy, you heavens; earth, rejoice;
break into songs of triumph, you mountains,
for the Lord has comforted his people
and has had pity on them in their distress.

But Zion says,
'The Lord has forsaken me;
my Lord has forgotten me.'

Can a woman forget the infant at her breast,
or a mother the child of her womb?
But should even these forget,
I shall never forget you.

Hark, my soul! It is the Lord;
'Tis thy Saviour, hear his word;
Jesus speaks, and speaks to thee:
'Say, poor sinner, lov'st thou me?'

'Can a woman's tender care
Cease towards the child she bare?
Yes, she may forgetful be,
Yet will I remember thee.

Mine is an unchanging love,
Higher than the heights above;
Deeper than the depths beneath,
Free and faithful, strong as death.'

Lord, it is my chief complaint
That my love is weak and faint;
Yet I love thee and adore,
Oh, for grace to love thee more!

William Cowper, 1731–1800

God's Goodness

Day 1

Rest in God

O NE DAY NAOMI, Ruth's mother-in-law, said to her, 'My daughter, I want to see you settled happily. Now there is our kinsman Boaz, whose girls you have been with. Tonight he will be winnowing barley at the threshing-floor. Bathe and anoint yourself with perfumed oil, then get dressed and go down to the threshing-floor; but do not make yourself known to the man until he has finished eating and drinking. When he lies down make sure you know the place where he is. Then go in, turn back the covering at his feet and lie down. He will tell you what to do.' 'I will do everything you say,' replied Ruth.

She went down to the threshing-floor and did exactly as her mother-in-law had told her. About midnight the man woke with a start; he turned over, and there, lying at his feet, was a woman! 'Who are you?', he said. 'Sir, it is I, Ruth,' she replied. 'Spread the skirt of your cloak over me, for you are my next-of-kin.' Boaz said, 'The Lord bless you, my daughter!'

She lay at his feet till next morning, but rose before it was light enough for one man to recognize another; Boaz said to her, 'Take the cloak you are wearing, and hold it out.' When she did so, he poured in six measures of barley and lifted it for her to carry, and she went off to the town.

When she came to her mother-in-law, Naomi asked, 'How did things go with you, my daughter?' Ruth related all that the man had done for her, and she added, 'He gave me these six measures of barley; he would not let me come home to my mother-in-law empty-handed.' Naomi said, 'Wait, my daughter, until you see what will come of it; he will not rest till he has settled the matter this very day.'

So Boaz took Ruth and she became his wife. When they had come together the Lord caused her to conceive, and she gave birth to a son. Naomi took the child and laid him in her own lap, and she became his foster-mother.

O sweetest love of God, too little known, whoever has found you will be at rest. Let everything change, O my God, that I may rest in you. How sweet to me is your presence, you who are the sovereign good! I will draw near to you in silence, and will uncover your feet, that it may please you to unite me with yourself, making my soul your bride. I will rejoice in nothing until I am in your arms; O Lord, I beseech you, leave me not for a moment.

John of the Cross, 1542–91

Day 2

A Rock of Refuge

In you, Lord, I have found refuge;
let me never be put to shame.
By your saving power deliver me,
bend down and hear me,
come quickly to my rescue.
Be to me a rock of refuge,
a stronghold to keep me safe.

You are my rock and my stronghold;
lead and guide me for the honour of your name.
Set me free from the net that has been hidden to catch me;
for you are my refuge.
Into your hand I commit my spirit.
You have delivered me, Lord, you God of truth.

How great is your goodness,
stored up for those who fear you,
made manifest before mortal eyes
for all who turn to you for shelter.

You will hide them under the cover of your presence
from those who conspire together;
you keep them in your shelter,
safe from contentious tongues.

Blessed be the Lord,
whose unfailing love for me was wonderful
when I was in sore straits.

My God,
I pray that I may so know you and love you
that I may rejoice in you.
And if I may not do so fully in this life,
let me go steadily on
to the day when I come to fullness of life.
Meanwhile let my mind meditate on your eternal goodness,
let my tongue speak of it,
let my heart live it,
let my mouth speak it,
let my soul hunger for it,
and my whole being desire it,
until I enter into your joy.

Anselm, 1033–1109

Day 3

Taste and See

I shall bless the Lord at all times;
his praise will be ever on my lips.
In the Lord I shall glory;
the humble will hear and be glad.

The angel of the Lord is on guard
round those who fear him, and he rescues them.
Taste and see that the Lord is good.
Happy are they who find refuge in him!

The eyes of the Lord are on the righteous;
his ears are open to their cry.
The Lord sets his face against wrongdoers
to cut off all memory of them from the earth.

When the righteous cry for help, the Lord hears
and sets them free from all their troubles.
The Lord is close to those whose courage is broken;
he saves those whose spirit is crushed.

*O Lord, the helper of the helpless, the hoper of those who are past hope, the
saviour of the tempest-tossed, the harbour of the voyagers, the physician of
the sick; you know each soul and our prayer, each home and its need;
become to each one of us what we most dearly require, receiving us all into
your kingdom, making us children of light; and pour on us your peace and
love, O Lord our God.*

Liturgy of St Basil the Great

Day 4

God's Tender Care

God, my desire is to do your will;
your law is in my heart.

In the great assembly I have proclaimed what is right;
I do not hold back my words,
as you know, Lord.
I have not kept your goodness hidden in my heart;
I have proclaimed your faithfulness and saving power,
and have not concealed your unfailing love and truth
from the great assembly.

You, Lord, will not withhold
your tender care from me;
may your love and truth for ever guard me.
For misfortunes beyond counting
press on me from all sides;
my iniquities have overtaken me,
and I cannot see;
they are more in number than the hairs of my head;
my courage fails.

Show me favour, Lord, and save me;
Lord, come quickly to my help.

*O Saviour of the world, the Son, Lord Jesus: stir up thy strength and help
us, we humbly beseech thee.*
*By thy cross and precious blood thou hast redeemed us; save us and help us,
we humbly beseech thee.*
*Let the pitifulness of thy great mercy loose us from our sins, we humbly
beseech thee.*
*Make it appear that thou art our Saviour and mighty deliverer: O save,
that we may praise thee, we humbly beseech thee.*

Source unknown, 12th century

Day 5

Trust in God's Goodness

Lord, you keep those of firm purpose
untroubled because of their trust in you.

Trust in the Lord for ever,
for he is an eternal rock.
He has brought low
all who dwell high in a towering city;
he levels it to the ground
and lays it in the dust,
so that the oppressed and the poor
may tread it underfoot.

The path of the righteous is smooth,
and you, Lord, make level the way for the upright.
We have had regard to the path prescribed in your laws,
your name and your renown are our heart's desire.
With all my heart I long for you in the night,
at dawn I seek for you;
for, when your laws prevail on earth,
the inhabitants of the world learn what justice is.

You, Lord, give perfect peace
to those who keep their purpose firm
and put their trust in you.
We follow your will and put our trust in you;
you are all that we desire.

Isaiah 26.3, 8, adapted

Day 6

The Good News

The Spirit of the Lord God is upon me
because the Lord has anointed me;
he has sent me to announce good news to the humble,
to bind up the broken-hearted,
to proclaim liberty to captives,
release to those in prison;
to proclaim a year of the Lord's favour
and a day of the vengeance of our God;
to comfort all who mourn,
to give them garlands instead of ashes,
oil of gladness instead of mourners' tears,
a garment of splendour for the heavy heart.
They will be called trees of righteousness,
planted by the Lord for his adornment.

Buildings long in ruins will be rebuilt
and sites long desolate restored;
they will repair the ruined cities
which for generations have lain desolate.

Sovereign Lord,
fill us with your Spirit,
that we may bring good news to the poor
and heal the broken-hearted;
that we may announce release to the captives
of injustice and oppression,
freedom to those in the prison of despair;
that we may proclaim that the time has come
when you will save your people
and defeat their enemies;
that we may comfort all who mourn.

Isaiah 61.1, 2, adapted

Day 7

God Knows your Needs

A SK, AND YOU will receive; seek, and you will find; knock, and the door will be opened to you. For everyone who asks receives, those who seek find, and to those who knock, the door will be opened.

'Would any of you offer his son a stone when he asks for bread, or a snake when he asks for a fish? If you, bad as you are, know how to give good things to your children, how much more will your heavenly Father give good things to those who ask him!

'Are not two sparrows sold for a penny? Yet without your Father's knowledge not one of them can fall to the ground. As for you, even the hairs of your head have all been counted. So do not be afraid; you are worth more than any number of sparrows.'

> *Almighty God, the fountain of all wisdom,*
> *you know our needs before we ask*
> *and our ignorance in asking;*
> *have compassion on our weakness,*
> *and give us those things*
> *which for our unworthiness we dare not*
> *and for our blindness we cannot ask,*
> *for the sake of your Son, Jesus Christ our Lord.*

Ministry to the Sick: Authorized Alternative Services

God's Kindness

Day 1

The Dance of Praise

Lord my God, I cried to you and you healed me.
You have brought me up, Lord, from Sheol,
and saved my life as I was sinking into the abyss.

Sing a psalm to the Lord, all you his loyal servants;
give thanks to his holy name.
In his anger is distress, in his favour there is life.
Tears may linger at nightfall,
but rejoicing comes in the morning.

To you, Lord, I called
and pleaded with you for mercy:
'What profit is there in my death,
in my going down to the pit?
Can the dust praise you?
Can it proclaim your truth?
Hear, Lord, and be gracious to me;
Lord, be my helper.'

You have turned my laments into dancing;
you have stripped off my sackcloth and clothed me with joy,
that I may sing psalms to you without ceasing.
Lord my God, I shall praise you for ever.

Great is, O King, our happiness
in thy kingdom, thou, our King.
We dance before thee, our King
by the strength of thy kingdom.

May our feet be made strong;
let us dance before thee, eternal.
Give you praise, all angels,
to him above who is worthy cause of praise

Zulu Nazarite Church

Day 2

Trust in the Lord

Patiently I waited for the Lord;
he bent down to me and listened to my cry.
He raised me out of the miry pit,
out of the mud and clay;
he set my feet on rock
and gave me a firm footing.

On my lips he put a new song,
a song of praise to our God.
Many will look with awe
and put their trust in the Lord.
Happy is he who puts his trust in the Lord
and does not look to the arrogant and treacherous.

Lord my God, great things you have done;
your wonders and your purposes are for our good;
none can compare with you.
I would proclaim them and speak of them,
but they are more than I can tell.

Faithful God, our trust is in you. Deliver us from the bondage of evil, and grant that we may hereafter be your devoted servants, serving you in the freedom of holy love; for Jesus Christ's sake.

Eugène Bersier, 1831–89

Day 3

A Heart at Peace

My heart, be at peace once more,
for the Lord has granted you full deliverance.
You have rescued me from death,
my eyes from weeping,
my feet from stumbling.

I shall walk in the presence of the Lord
in the land of the living.
I was sure I should be swept away;
my distress was bitter.
In my alarm I cried,
'How faithless are all my fellow-creatures!'

How can I repay the Lord
for all his benefits to me?
I shall lift up the cup of salvation
and call on the Lord by name.
I shall pay my vows to the Lord
in the presence of all his people.

O God, you are the unsearchable abyss of peace,
the ineffable sea of love,
and the fountain of all blessings.
Water us with plenteous streams
from the riches of your grace,
and from the most sweet springs of your kindness.
Make us children of quietness and heirs of peace.

Clement of Alexandria, c.150-c.215

Day 4

The Lord Deals Kindly

Lord, the earth is filled with your unfailing love;
teach me your statutes.
You have dealt kindly with your servant,
fulfilling your word, Lord.

Give me insight, give me knowledge,
for I put my trust in your commandments.
Before I was chastened I went astray,
but now I pay heed to your promise.

You are good, and you do what is good;
teach me your statutes.
I know, Lord, that your decrees are just
and even in chastening you keep faith with me.

Let your love comfort me,
as you have promised me, your servant.

O God, who declarest thy almighty power most chiefly in showing mercy
and pity, mercifully grant unto us a measure of thy grace, that we, running
the way of thy commandments, may obtain thy gracious promises, and be
made partakers of thy heavenly treasure; through Jesus Christ our Lord.

Gelasian Sacramentary, 5th century

Day 5

God Comforts his People

Comfort my people; bring comfort to them,
says your God;
speak kindly to Jerusalem
and proclaim to her
that her term of bondage is served,
her penalty is paid;
for she has received at the Lord's hand
double measure for all her sins.

Climb to a mountaintop,
you that bring good news to Zion;
raise your voice and shout aloud,
you that carry good news to Jerusalem,
raise it fearlessly;
say to the cities of Judah, 'Your God is here!'

Here is the Lord God; he is coming in might,
coming to rule with powerful arm.
His reward is with him,
his recompense before him.

Like a shepherd he will tend his flock
and with his arm keep them together;
he will carry the lambs in his bosom
and lead the ewes to water.

We have wandered and strayed from thy way, carried away by our perverse desires and wild impulses. Our heart does not revere thy living word, and our tongue refuses to praise thy benefits.

But thou art our sublime Father in heaven and we your children are of lowly clay. Thou art our creator and we the work of thy hands. Thou art the shepherd and we the flock that thou hast redeemed in thy mercy.

Giulio Cesare Paschale, 16th century

Day 6

God's Constancy

I shall wait patiently
because I take this to heart:

The Lord's love is surely not exhausted,
nor has his compassion failed;
they are new every morning,
so great is his constancy.
'The Lord', I say, 'is all that I have;
therefore I shall wait for him patiently.'

The Lord is good to those who look to him,
to anyone who seeks him;
it is good to wait in patience
for deliverance by the Lord.
It is good for a man
to bear the yoke from youth.

Let him sit alone in silence
if it is heavy on him;
let him lie face downwards on the ground,
and there may yet be hope;
let him offer his cheek to the smiter
and endure full measure of abuse.

For rejection by the Lord
does not last for ever.
He may punish, yet he will have compassion
in the fullness of his unfailing love.

Kindness flows from you, Lord, pure and continual.
You had cast us off, as was only just, but mercifully you forgave us;
you hated us and you were reconciled to us, you cursed us and you blessed us;
you banished us from paradise, and you called us back again.

Basil the Great, 330–79

Day 7

God's Mercy

T HERE WAS A time when we too were lost in folly and disobedience and were slaves to passions and pleasures of every kind. Our days were passed in malice and envy; hateful ourselves, we loathed one another. But when the kindness and generosity of God our Saviour dawned upon the world, then, not for any good deeds of our own, but because he was merciful, he saved us through the water of rebirth and the renewing power of the Holy Spirit, which he lavished upon us through Jesus Christ our Saviour, so that, justified by his grace, we might in hope become heirs to eternal life.

Goodness I have none to plead,
Sinfulness in all I see,
I can only bring my need;
God be merciful to me.

Broken heart and downcast eyes
Dare not lift themselves to thee;
Yet thou canst interpret sighs:
God be merciful to me.

John Samuel Bewley Monsell, 1811–75

WEEK 20

God's Love

Day 1

God's Unfailing Love

Lord, your unfailing love reaches to the heavens,
your faithfulness to the skies.
Your righteousness is like the lofty mountains,
your justice like the great deep;
Lord who saves man and beast,
how precious is your unfailing love!
Gods and frail mortals seek refuge in the shadow of your wings.
They are filled with the rich plenty of your house,
and you give them to drink from the stream of your delights;
for with you is the fountain of life,
and by your light we are enlightened.
Continue your love unfailing to those who know you,
and your saving power towards the honest of heart.

O Lord, help me to learn that love is your meaning.
Help me to see, both here and elsewhere,
that before you made us, you loved us;
and that you love has never slackened,
nor ever shall.
In this love all your works have been done,
and in this love you have made everything serve us;
and in this love our life is everlasting.

Julian of Norwich, 1342–c.1416, adapted

Day 2

Love from Heaven

God, be gracious to me; be gracious,
for I have made you my refuge.
I shall seek refuge in the shadow of your wings
until the storms are past.

I shall call to God Most High,
to the God who will fulfil his purpose for me.
He will send from heaven and save me,
and my persecutors he will put to scorn.
May God send his love, unfailing and sure.

I shall praise you among the peoples, Lord,
among the nations I shall raise a psalm to you,
for your unfailing love is as high as the heavens;
your faithfulness reaches to the skies.

God, be exalted above the heavens;
let your glory be over all the earth.

Late have I loved you,
O Beauty so ancient and so new.
You called, and broke through my defences,
and now I long for you.
You breathed your fragrance on me,
and I drew in my breath
and now I pant for you.
I tasted you, and now I hunger and thirst for you.
You touched me,
and I burn for your peace.

Augustine of Hippo, 354-430

Day 3

Longing for God

God, you are my God; I seek you eagerly
with a heart that thirsts for you
and a body wasted with longing for you,
like a dry land, parched and devoid of water.
With such longing I see you in the sanctuary
and behold your power and glory.

Your unfailing love is better than life;
therefore I shall sing your praises.
Thus all my life I bless you;
in your name I lift my hands in prayer.
I am satisfied as with a rich feast
and there is a shout of praise on my lips.

I call you to mind on my bed
and meditate on you in the night watches,
for you have been my help
and I am safe in the shadow of your wings.

O Lord our God,
under the shadow of your wings we will rest.
Defend and support us,
bear us up when we are little,
and we know that even down to our grey hairs
you will carry us.

Augustine of Hippo, 354–430

Day 4

Let Me Know of your Love

Lord, hear my prayer;
listen to my plea;
in your faithfulness and righteousness answer me.

Do not bring your servant to trial,
for no person living is innocent before you.
I thirst for you like thirsty land,
I lift my outspread hands to you.

Lord, answer me soon;
my spirit faints.
Do not hide your face from me
or I shall be like those who go down to the abyss.

In the morning let me know of your love,
for I put my trust in you.
Show me the way that I must take,
for my heart is set on you.

O thou infinite goodness and love, be pleased to pardon all the defects of my love to thee, and all the excesses of my love to earthly things; and turn my inclinations and affections from all vain objects to thy blessed self, who art the worthiest of all love; and to conquer all my prejudice, and for ever win my heart. O show thyself to me as a pardoning God; full of compassion, ready to forgive, and willing to save me. Yea, make me to know so much of the love wherewith thou has loved me, that I may make better returns of love the gracious giver of all my good. Touch my heart with such a powerful sense of thy loveliness and loving-kindness, that I may experience stronger desires and inclinations after thee, and greater complacence and delight in thee; and may I leave all other things, in comparison of my best and dearest Lord, as if I loved them not.

Hannah More, 1745–1833

Day 5

God's Love for his People

When Israel was a youth, I loved him;
out of Egypt I called my son;
but the more I called, the farther they went from me;
they must needs sacrifice to the baalim
and burn offerings to images.

It was I who taught Ephraim to walk,
I who took them in my arms;
but they did not know that
I secured them with reins
and led them with bonds of love,
that I lifted them like a little child to my cheek,
that I bent down to feed them.

I am not going to let loose my fury,
I shall not turn and destroy Ephraim,
for I am God, not a mortal;
I am the Holy One in your midst.
I shall not come with threats.

Lord of Compassion,
you loved me; you called to me
as a mother calls to her child.
But the more you called to me,
the more I turned away.
Yet you were the one who taught me to walk;
you took me up in your arms.
You drew me to you; you picked me up,
and held me to your cheek.
You bent down to me and fed me.
Lord of Compassion,
do not give me up; do not abandon me.
do not punish me in your anger!

Philip Law

Day 6

God's Love Revealed in Christ

WITH ALL THIS in mind, what are we to say? If God is on our side, who is against us? He did not spare his own Son, but gave him up for us all; how can he fail to lavish every other gift upon us? Who will bring a charge against those whom God has chosen? Not God, who acquits! Who will pronounce judgement? Not Christ, who died, or rather rose again; not Christ, who is at God's right hand and pleads our cause! Then what can separate us from the love of Christ? Can affliction or hardship? Can persecution, hunger, nakedness, danger, or sword? 'We are being done to death for your sake all day long, as scripture says, 'we have been treated like sheep for slaughter and yet, throughout it all, overwhelming victory is ours through him who loved us.' For I am convinced that there is nothing in death or life, in the realm of spirits or superhuman powers, in the world as it is or the world as it shall be, in the forces of the universe, in heights or depths nothing in all creation that can separate us from the love of God in Christ Jesus our Lord.

Dear Saviour, I will love thee with all my powers, and strive and pray that I may love thee more and more, as fervently as ever any of the saints have done, I will give my self unto thee, and despise all other things in comparison of thee; and when I have once tasted of this all-saving sacrifice which was given for me, I am persuaded that neither life nor death, pleasure nor pain, things present or things to come, shall ever be able to separate me from the love of God which is in Christ Jesus our Lord.

Thomas Comber, 1645–99

Day 7

God Is Love

G OD IS LOVE. This is how he showed his love among us: he sent his only Son into the world that we might have life through him. This is what love really is: not that we have loved God, but that he loved us and sent his Son as a sacrifice to atone for our sins. If God thus loved us, my dear friends, we also must love one another. God has never been seen by anyone, but if we love one another, he himself dwells in us; his love is brought to perfection within us.

This is how we know that we dwell in him and he dwells in us: he has imparted his Spirit to us. Moreover, we have seen for ourselves, and we are witnesses, that the Father has sent the Son to be the Saviour of the world. If anyone acknowledges that Jesus is God's Son, God dwells in him and he in God. Thus we have come to know and believe in the love which God has for us.

God of Love,
we thank you for giving us life
and for showing us the meaning of love.
You showed your love among us
by sending your only Son into the world
as a sacrifice for our sins.

God of Love,
if you loved us so much,
we also must love one another.
You have never been seen by anyone,
but if we love one another
you yourself dwell in us
and your love is brought to perfection in us.

God of Love,
we know that you dwell in us
because you have imparted to us your Spirit,
and because you have sent your Son
to be the Saviour of the world.

Philip Law

PART TWO

God with Us

The Promised Messiah

Day 1

The Child of Promise

The people that walked in darkness
have seen a great light;
on those who lived in a land as dark as death
a light has dawned.

For a child has been born to us, a son is given to us;
he will bear the symbol of dominion on his shoulder,
and his title will be:
Wonderful Counsellor, Mighty Hero,
Eternal Father, Prince of Peace.

Wide will be the dominion
and boundless the peace
bestowed on David's throne and on his kingdom,
to establish and support it
with justice and righteousness
from now on, for evermore.
The zeal of the Lord of Hosts will do this.

Wonderful Counsellor,
give us the wisdom of your counsels,

Mighty Hero,
show us the glory of your mightiness.

Eternal Father,
hold us in the arms of your unfailing love.

Prince of Peace,
unite us in the service of your kingdom.

From now on, for evermore.

Philip Law

Day 2

God's Chosen Servant

Here is my servant, whom I uphold,
my chosen one, in whom I take delight!
I have put my Spirit on him;
he will establish justice among the nations.

He will not shout or raise his voice,
or make himself heard in the street.

He will not break a crushed reed
or snuff out a smouldering wick;
unfailingly he will establish justice.

He will never falter or be crushed
until he sets justice on earth,
while coasts and islands await his teaching.

These are the words of the Lord who is God,
who created the heavens and stretched them out,
who fashioned the earth
and everything that grows in it,
giving breath to its people
and life to those who walk on it:

'I the Lord have called you with righteous purpose
and taken you by the hand;
I have formed you, and destined you
to be a light for peoples,
a lamp for nations,
to open eyes that are blind,
to bring captives out of prison,
out of the dungeon where they lie in darkness.'

*O God, who looked on us when we had fallen down into death, and
resolved to redeem us by the advent of your only begotten Son; grant, we
beg you, that those who confess his glorious incarnation may also be
admitted to the fellowship of their Redeemer, through the same Jesus Christ
our Lord.*

Ambrose, c.340–97

Day 3

The Suffering Prophet

My servant will achieve success,
he will be raised to honour, high and exalted.

Time was when many were appalled at you, my people;
so now many nations recoil at the sight of him,
and kings curl their lips in disgust.
His form, disfigured, lost all human likeness;
his appearance so changed he no longer looked like a man.
They see what they had never been told
and their minds are full of things unheard before.

Who could have believed what we have heard?
To whom has the power of the Lord been revealed?

He grew up before the Lord like a young plant
whose roots are in parched ground;
he had no beauty, no majesty to catch our eyes,
no grace to attract us to him.

He was despised, shunned by all,
pain-racked and afflicted by disease;
we despised him, we held him of no account,
an object from which people turn away their eyes.

Yet it was our afflictions he was bearing,
our pain he endured,
while we thought of him as smitten by God,
struck down by disease and misery.

But he was pierced for our transgressions,
crushed for our iniquities;
the chastisement he bore restored us to health
and by his wounds we are healed.

Thou who art the life of men, behold me dead in trespasses and sins. I come to thee, O Lord, as thou dost call me: I come to thee that I may have life. Thou art the physician of my soul, who has borne stripes thyself, that all my sickness might be healed.

Have pity on me, therefore gracious Lord, O Lord, be merciful unto me; heal my soul, for I have sinned against thee.

Sabine Baring-Gould, 1834–1924

Day 4

The Lamb of God

We had all strayed like sheep,
each of us going his own way,
but the Lord laid on him
the guilt of us all.

He was maltreated, yet he was submissive
and did not open his mouth;
like a sheep led to the slaughter,
like a ewe that is dumb before the shearers,
he did not open his mouth.

He was arrested and sentenced and taken away,
and who gave a thought to his fate –
how he was cut off from the world of the living,
stricken to death for my people's transgression?

He was assigned a grave with the wicked,
a burial-place among felons,
though he had done no violence,
had spoken no word of treachery.

Yet the Lord took thought for his oppressed servant
and healed him who had given himself as a sacrifice for sin.
He will enjoy long life and see his children's children,
and in his hand the Lord's purpose will prosper.

By his humiliation my servant will justify many;
after his suffering he will see light and be satisfied;
it is their guilt he bears.

Therefore I shall allot him a portion with the great,
and he will share the spoil with the mighty,
because he exposed himself to death
and was reckoned among transgressors,
for he bore the sin of many
and interceded for transgressors.

O Lamb of God, who takest away the sin of the world, look upon us and have mercy upon us, thou who art thyself both victim and priest, thyself both reward and redeemer, keep safe from evil those whom thou hast redeemed, O Saviour of the World.

Irenaeus, c.140–c.202

Day 5

The Lord's Shepherd

F OR THE Lord God says: 'Now I myself shall take thought for my sheep and search for them.

'As a shepherd goes in search of his sheep when his flock is scattered from him in every direction, so I shall go in search of my sheep and rescue them, no matter where they were scattered in a day of cloud and darkness.

'I shall lead them out from the nations, gather them in from different lands, and bring them home to their own country. I shall shepherd them on the mountains of Israel and by its streams, wherever there is a settlement.

'I shall feed them on good grazing-ground, and their pasture will be Israel's high mountains. There they will rest in good pasture, and find rich grazing on the mountains of Israel.

'I myself shall tend my flock, and find them a place to rest, says the Lord God.

'I shall search for the lost, recover the straggler, bandage the injured, strengthen the sick, leave the healthy and strong to play, and give my flock their proper food.

'I shall set over them one shepherd to take care of them, my servant David; he will care for them and be their shepherd.

'I, the Lord, shall be their God, and my servant David will be prince among them. I, the Lord, have spoken.'

> *Praise him, Praise him! Jesus, our blessed redeemer;*
> *Sing, O earth, his wonderful love proclaim!*
> *Hail him, hail him! Highest archangels in glory,*
> *Strength and honour give to his holy name.*
> *Like a shepherd, Jesus will guard his children,*
> *In his arms he carries them all day long;*
> *O ye saints that dwell in the mountains of Zion,*
> *Praise him, praise him! Ever in joyful song.*
>
> Frances Jane Van Alstyne, 1820–1915

Day 6

The Great High Priest

This is the Lord's oracle to my lord:
'Sit at my right hand,
and I shall make your enemies your footstool.'

The Lord extends the sway of your powerful sceptre, saying,
'From Zion reign over your enemies.'

You gain the homage of your people
on the day of your power.
Arrayed in holy garments, a child of the dawn,
you have the dew of your youth.

The Lord has sworn an oath and will not change his mind:
'You are a priest for ever,
a Melchizedek in my service.'

God, we thank thee for thy great mercies: praise be to thee for the incarnation of Jesus: praise be to thee for the obedience of Jesus: praise be to thee for the blood of Jesus; for he is ours, and he is thine, and we are his. He is our sacrifice, and thy satisfaction; our glorious head, and thine only-begotten Son; our intercessor, and thy beloved; our merciful High Priest, and thine anointed King.

Henry Alford, 1810–71

Day 7

The Righteous King

A branch will grow from the stock of Jesse,
and a shoot will spring from his roots.
On him the spirit of the Lord will rest:
a spirit of wisdom and understanding,
a spirit of counsel and power,
a spirit of knowledge and fear of the Lord;
and in the fear of the Lord will be his delight.
He will not judge by outward appearances
or decide a case on hearsay;
but with justice he will judge the poor
and defend the humble in the land with equity;
like a rod his verdict will strike the ruthless,
and with his word he will slay the wicked.

He will wear the belt of justice,
and truth will be his girdle.

There will be neither hurt nor harm in all my holy mountain;
for the land will be filled with the knowledge of the Lord,
as the waters cover the sea.

Blessed be he who in his love stooped to redeem mankind! Blessed be the King who made himself poor to enrich the needy! Blessed be he who came to fulfil the types and emblems of the prophets! Blessed be he who made creation to rejoice with the wealth and treasure of his Father!

Ephraem the Syrian, c.306–73

WEEK 22

The Christ Is Born

Day 1

Mary and Joseph

THE ANGEL GABRIEL was sent by God to Nazareth, a town in Galilee, with a message for a girl betrothed to a man named Joseph, a descendant of David; the girl's name was Mary. The angel went in and said to her, 'Greetings, most favoured one! The Lord is with you.' But she was deeply troubled by what he said and wondered what this greeting could mean. Then the angel said to her, 'Do not be afraid, Mary, for God has been gracious to you; you will conceive and give birth to a son, and you are to give him the name Jesus. He will be great, and will be called Son of the Most High. The Lord God will give him the throne of his ancestor David, and he will be king over Israel for ever; his reign shall never end.' 'How can this be?' said Mary. 'I am still a virgin.' The angel answered, 'The Holy Spirit will come upon you, and the power of the Most High will overshadow you; for that reason the holy child to be born will be called Son of God.' 'I am the Lord's servant,' said Mary; 'may it be as you have said.' Then the angel left her.

Being a man of principle, and at the same time wanting to save her from exposure, Joseph made up his mind to have the marriage contract quietly set aside. He had resolved on this, when an angel of the Lord appeared to him in a dream and said, 'Joseph, son of David, do not be afraid to take Mary home with you to be your wife. It is through the Holy Spirit that she has conceived. She will bear a son; and you shall give him the name Jesus, for he will save his people from their sins.' All this happened in order to fulfil what the Lord declared through the prophet: 'A virgin will conceive and bear a son, and he shall be called Emmanuel,' a name which means 'God is with us'.

Christ our God Incarnate, whose Virgin Mother was blessed in bearing thee, but still more blessed in keeping thy word; grant us, who honour the exaltation of her lowliness, to follow the example of her devotion to thy will, who livest, and reignest with the Father and the Holy Spirit, one God, now and for ever.

William Bright, 1824–1901

Day 2

Magnificat

MARY SET OUT and hurried away to a town in the uplands of Judah. She went into Zechariah's house and greeted Elizabeth. Then Elizabeth was filled with the Holy Spirit and exclaimed in a loud voice, 'God's blessing is on you above all women, and his blessing is on the fruit of your womb. Happy is she who has had faith that the Lord's promise to her would be fulfilled!'

And Mary said:

My soul tells out the greatness of the Lord,
my spirit has rejoiced in God my Saviour;
for he has looked with favour on his servant,
lowly as she is.
From this day forward
all generations will count me blessed,
for the Mighty God has done great things for me.
His name is holy,
his mercy sure from generation to generation
toward those who fear him.
He has shown the might of his arm,
he has routed the proud and all their schemes;
he has brought down monarchs from their thrones,
and raised on high the lowly.
He has filled the hungry with good things,
and sent the rich away empty.
He has come to the help of Israel his servant,
as he promised to our forefathers;
he has not forgotten to show mercy
to Abraham and his children's children for ever.

> *O Jesus living in Mary,*
> *come and live in thy servants,*
> *in the spirit of thy sanctity,*
> *in the fullness of thy strength,*
> *in the reality of thy virtues,*
> *in the perfection of thy ways,*
> *in the communion of thy mysteries,*
> *be Lord over every opposing power,*
> *in thine own Spirit, to the glory of the Father.*
>
> Jean-Jaques Olier, 1608–57

Day 3

The Birth of Jesus

I N THOSE DAYS a decree was issued by the emperor Augustus for a census to be taken throughout the Roman world. This was the first registration of its kind; it took place when Quirinius was governor of Syria. Everyone made his way to his own town to be registered. Joseph went up to Judaea from the town of Nazareth in Galilee, to register in the city of David called Bethlehem, because he was of the house of David by descent; and with him went Mary, his betrothed, who was expecting her child. While they were there the time came for her to have her baby, and she gave birth to a son, her firstborn. She wrapped him in swaddling clothes, and laid him in a manger, because there was no room for them at the inn.

Let your goodness, Lord, appear to us, that we, made in your image, con-
form ourselves to it. In our one strength we cannot imitate your majesty,
power and wonder; nor is it fitting for us to try. But your mercy reaches
from the heavens, through the clouds, to the earth below. You have come to
us as a small child, but you have brought us the greatest of all gifts, the gift
of eternal love. Caress us with your tiny hands, embrace us with your tiny
arms, and pierce our hearts with your soft, sweet cries.

Bernard of Clairvaux, 1090–1153

Day 4

Angels and Shepherds

N OW IN THIS same district there were shepherds out in the fields, keeping watch through the night over their flock. Suddenly an angel of the Lord appeared to them, and the glory of the Lord shone round them. They were terrified, but the angel said, 'Do not be afraid; I bring you good news, news of great joy for the whole nation. Today there has been born to you in the city of David a deliverer – the Messiah, the Lord. This will be the sign for you: you will find a baby wrapped in swaddling clothes, and lying in a manger.' All at once there was with the angel a great company of the heavenly host, singing praise to God:

> Glory to God in highest heaven,
> and on earth peace to all in whom he delights.

After the angels had left them and returned to heaven the shepherds said to one another, 'Come, let us go straight to Bethlehem and see this thing that has happened, which the Lord has made known to us.' They hurried off and found Mary and Joseph, and the baby lying in the manger. When they saw the child, they related what they had been told about him; and all who heard were astonished at what the shepherds said. But Mary treasured up all these things and pondered over them. The shepherds returned glorifying and praising God for what they had heard and seen; it had all happened as they had been told.

> *Send, O God, into the darkness of this troubled world, the light of your Son: let the star of your hope touch the minds of all people with the bright beams of mercy and truth; and so direct our steps that we may always walk in the way revealed to us, as the shepherds of Bethlehem walked with joy to the manger where he dwelt, who now and ever reigns in our hearts, Jesus Christ our Lord.*
>
> John Wallace Suter, 1859–1942

Day 5

King of the Jews

AFTER JESUS' BIRTH astrologers from the east arrived in Jerusalem, asking, 'Where is the new-born king of the Jews? We observed the rising of his star, and we have come to pay him homage.' King Herod was greatly perturbed when he heard this, and so was the whole of Jerusalem. He called together the chief priests and scribes of the Jews, and asked them where the Messiah was to be born. 'At Bethlehem in Judaea,' they replied, 'for this is what the prophet wrote: "Bethlehem in the land of Judah, you are by no means least among the rulers of Judah; for out of you shall come a ruler to be the shepherd of my people Israel."'

Then Herod summoned the astrologers to meet him secretly, and ascertained from them the exact time when the star had appeared. He sent them to Bethlehem, and said, 'Go and make a careful search for the child, and when you have found him, bring me word, so that I may go myself and pay him homage.'

After hearing what the king had to say they set out; there before them was the star they had seen rising, and it went ahead of them until it stopped above the place where the child lay. They were overjoyed at the sight of it and, entering the house, they saw the child with Mary his mother and bowed low in homage to him; they opened their treasure chests and presented gifts to him: gold, frankincense, and myrrh. Then they returned to their own country by another route, for they had been warned in a dream not to go back to Herod.

O God, who guided by a star the Wise Men to the worship of your Son: lead to yourself, we pray, the wise and the great in every land, that unto you every knee may now, and every thought be brought into allegiance; through Jesus Christ our Lord.

The Book of Common Worship, South India, adapted

Day 6

Refuge in Egypt

A N ANGEL OF the Lord appeared to Joseph in a dream, and said, 'Get up, take the child and his mother and escape with them to Egypt, and stay there until I tell you; for Herod is going to search for the child to kill him.' So Joseph got up, took mother and child by night, and sought refuge with them in Egypt, where he stayed till Herod's death. This was to fulfil what the Lord had declared through the prophet: 'Out of Egypt I have called my son.'

When Herod realized that the astrologers had tricked him he flew into a rage, and gave orders for the massacre of all the boys aged two years or under, in Bethlehem and throughout the whole district, in accordance with the time he had ascertained from the astrologers. So the words spoken through Jeremiah the prophet were fulfilled: 'A voice was heard in Rama, sobbing in bitter grief; it was Rachel weeping for her children, and refusing to be comforted, because they were no more.'

We remember today, O God, the slaughter of the holy innocents of Bethlehem by King Herod. Receive, we pray, into the arms of your mercy all innocent victims; and by your great might frustrate all evil designs, and establish your rule of justice, love and peace; through Jesus Christ our Lord.

The Book of Common Prayer, USA, adapted

Day 7

The Presentation in the Temple

E IGHT DAYS LATER the time came to circumcise him, and he was given the name Jesus, the name given by the angel before he was conceived.

Then, after the purification had been completed in accordance with the law of Moses, they brought him up to Jerusalem to present him to the Lord. There was at that time in Jerusalem a man called Simeon. This man was upright and devout, one who watched and waited for the restoration of Israel, and the Holy Spirit was upon him. It had been revealed to him by the Holy Spirit that he would not see death until he had seen the Lord's Messiah. Guided by the Spirit he came into the temple; and when the parents brought in the child Jesus to do for him what the law required, he took him in his arms, praised God, and said:

> Now, Lord, you are releasing your servant in peace,
> according to your promise.
> For I have seen with my own eyes
> the deliverance you have made ready in full view of all nations:
> a light that will bring revelation to the Gentiles
> and glory to your people Israel.

The child's father and mother were full of wonder at what was being said about him. Simeon blessed them and said to Mary his mother, 'This child is destined to be a sign that will be rejected; and you too will be pierced to the heart. Many in Israel will stand or fall because of him; and so the secret thoughts of many will be laid bare.'

> *Come, and with divine songs let us also go to meet Christ, and let us receive him whose salvation Simeon saw. This is he whom David announced: this is he whose words the prophets uttered, who for our sakes has taken flesh and speaks to us in his new law. Let us worship him.*
>
> Ancient Orthodox Liturgy

WEEK 23

Son of God

Day 1

The Boy Jesus in the Temple

N OW IT WAS the practice of his parents to go to Jerusalem every year for the Passover festival; and when he was twelve, they made the pilgrimage as usual. When the festive season was over and they set off for home, the boy Jesus stayed behind in Jerusalem. His parents did not know of this; but supposing that he was with the party they travelled for a whole day, and only then did they begin looking for him among their friends and relations. When they could not find him they returned to Jerusalem to look for him; and after three days they found him sitting in the temple surrounded by the teachers, listening to them and putting questions; and all who heard him were amazed at his intelligence and the answers he gave. His parents were astonished to see him there, and his mother said to him, 'My son, why have you treated us like this? Your father and I have been anxiously searching for you.' 'Why did you search for me?' he said. 'Did you not know that I was bound to be in my Father's house?' But they did not understand what he meant. Then he went back with them to Nazareth, and continued to be under their authority; his mother treasured up all these things in her heart. As Jesus grew he advanced in wisdom and in favour with God and men.

O Lord Jesus Christ, who as a child didst learn and grow in wisdom: grant me so to learn thy holy Word, that I may walk in thy ways and daily grow more like unto thee; who are my Saviour and Lord.

Book of Common Prayer, Ireland

Day 2

John the Baptist

IN THE FIFTEENTH year of the emperor Tiberius, when Pontius Pilate was governor of Judaea, when Herod was tetrarch of Galilee, his brother Philip prince of Ituraea and Trachonitis, and Lysanias prince of Abilene, during the high-priesthood of Annas and Caiaphas, the word of God came to John son of Zechariah in the wilderness. And he went all over the Jordan valley proclaiming a baptism in token of repentance for the forgiveness of sins, as it is written in the book of the prophecies of Isaiah:

A voice cries in the wilderness,
'Prepare the way for the Lord;
clear a straight path for him.'

Crowds of people came out to be baptized by him, and he said to them: 'Vipers' brood! Who warned you to escape from the wrath that is to come? Prove your repentance by the fruit you bear; and do not begin saying to yourselves, "We have Abraham for our father." I tell you that God can make children for Abraham out of these stones. Already the axe is laid to the roots of the trees; and every tree that fails to produce good fruit is cut down and thrown on the fire.'

The people asked him, 'Then what are we to do?' He replied, 'Whoever has two shirts must share with him who has none, and whoever has food must do the same.' Among those who came to be baptized were tax-collectors, and they said to him, 'Teacher, what are we to do?' He told them, 'Exact no more than the assessment.' Some soldiers also asked him, 'And what of us?' To them he said, 'No bullying; no blackmail; make do with your pay!'

The people were all agog, wondering about John, whether perhaps he was the Messiah, but he spoke out and said to them all: 'I baptize you with water; but there is one coming who is mightier than I am. I am not worthy to unfasten the straps of his sandals. He will baptize you with the Holy Spirit and with fire. His winnowing-shovel is ready in his hand, to clear his threshing-floor and gather the wheat into his granary; but the chaff he will burn on a fire that can never be put out.'

In this and many other ways he made his appeal to the people and announced the good news.

Almighty and merciful God, the fountain of all goodness, who knows the thoughts of our hearts, we confess that we have sinned against you, and done what you see as evil. Wash us, we implore you, from the stains of our past sins, and give us grace and power to put away all hurtful things so that, being delivered from the bondage of sin, we may produce the good fruits of repentance.

Alcuin of York, 735–804

Day 3

The Baptism of Jesus

THEN JESUS arrived at the Jordan from Galilee, and came to John to be baptized by him. John tried to dissuade him. 'Do you come to me?' he said. 'It is I who need to be baptized by you.' Jesus replied, 'Let it be so for the present; it is right for us to do all that God requires.' Then John allowed him to come. No sooner had Jesus been baptized and come up out of the water than the heavens were opened and he saw the Spirit of God descending like a dove to alight on him. And there came a voice from heaven saying, 'This is my beloved Son, in whom I take delight.'

> *Blessing and honour and thanksgiving and praise, more than we can utter, more than we can conceive, be unto thee, O holy and glorious Trinity, Father, Son and Holy Spirit, by all angels, by all men, all creatures, for ever and ever.*
>
> Thomas Ken, 1637–1711

Day 4

Jesus Is Tempted in the Desert

FULL OF THE Holy Spirit, Jesus returned from the Jordan, and for forty days he wandered in the wilderness, led by the Spirit and tempted by the devil. During that time he ate nothing, and at the end of it he was famished. The devil said to him, 'If you are the Son of God, tell this stone to become bread.' Jesus answered, 'Scripture says, "Man is not to live on bread alone."'

Next the devil led him to a height and showed him in a flash all the kingdoms of the world. 'All this dominion will I give to you,' he said, 'and the glory that goes with it; for it has been put in my hands and I can give it to anyone I choose. You have only to do homage to me and it will all be yours.' Jesus answered him, 'Scripture says, "You shall do homage to the Lord your God and worship him alone."'

The devil took him to Jerusalem and set him on the parapet of the temple. 'If you are the Son of God,' he said, 'throw yourself down from here; for scripture says, "He will put his angels in charge of you," and again, "They will support you in their arms for fear you should strike your foot against a stone."' Jesus answered him, 'It has been said, "You are not to put the Lord your God to the test."'

So, having come to the end of all these temptations, the devil departed, biding his time.

> *God of the desert,*
> *as we follow Jesus into the unknown,*
> *may we recognize the tempter when he comes;*
> *let it be your bread we eat,*
> *your world we serve*
> *and you alone we worship.*
>
> A New Zealand Prayer Book

Day 5

The First Disciples

T HE NEXT DAY John saw Jesus coming towards him. 'There is the Lamb of God,' he said, 'who takes away the sin of the world. He it is of whom I said, "After me there comes a man who ranks ahead of me"; before I was born, he already was. I did not know who he was; but the reason why I came, baptizing in water, was that he might be revealed to Israel.'

John testified again: 'I saw the Spirit come down from heaven like a dove and come to rest on him. I did not know him; but he who sent me to baptize in water had told me, "The man on whom you see the Spirit come down and rest is the one who is to baptize in Holy Spirit." I have seen it and have borne witness: this is God's Chosen One.'

The next day again, John was standing with two of his disciples when Jesus passed by. John looked towards him and said, 'There is the Lamb of God!' When the two disciples heard what he said, they followed Jesus.

Praise the name of the Lord.
We praise you,
we sing to you,
we bless you,
for your great glory,
O Lord our King,
Father of Christ – the spotless Lamb,
who takes away the sin of the world.

Praise becomes you,
worship becomes you,
glory becomes you,
God and Father,
through your Son,
in the Holy Spirit,
for ever and ever.
Amen.

Apostolic Constitutions, 4th century

Day 6

The Marriage at Cana

TWO DAYS LATER there was a wedding at Cana-in-Galilee. The mother of Jesus was there, and Jesus and his disciples were also among the guests. The wine gave out, so Jesus' mother said to him, 'They have no wine left.' He answered, 'That is no concern of mine. My hour has not yet come.' His mother said to the servants, 'Do whatever he tells you.' There were six stone water-jars standing near, of the kind used for Jewish rites of purification; each held from twenty to thirty gallons. Jesus said to the servants, 'Fill the jars with water,' and they filled them to the brim. 'Now draw some off,' he ordered, 'and take it to the master of the feast'; and they did so. The master tasted the water now turned into wine, not knowing its source, though the servants who had drawn the water knew. He hailed the bridegroom and said, 'Everyone else serves the best wine first, and the poorer only when the guests have drunk freely; but you have kept the best wine till now.'

So Jesus performed at Cana-in-Galilee the first of the signs which revealed his glory and led his disciples to believe in him.

You are the guest who filled the jars with good wine.
Fill my mouth with your praise.
Ephraem the Syrian, c.306–73

Day 7

Jesus and Nicodemus

O NE OF THE Pharisees, called Nicodemus, a member of the Jewish Council, came to Jesus by night. 'Rabbi,' he said, 'we know that you are a
teacher sent by God; no one could perform these signs of yours unless God
were with him.' Jesus answered, 'In very truth I tell you, no one can see the
kingdom of God unless he has been born again.' 'But how can someone be
born when he is old?' asked Nicodemus. 'Can he enter his mother's womb a
second time and be born?' Jesus answered, 'In very truth I tell you, no one can
enter the kingdom of God without being born from water and spirit. Flesh can
give birth only to flesh; it is spirit that gives birth to spirit. You ought not to be
astonished when I say, "You must all be born again." The wind blows where it
wills; you hear the sound of it, but you do not know where it comes from or
where it is going. So it is with everyone who is born from the Spirit.'

'How is this possible?' asked Nicodemus. 'You a teacher of Israel and igno-
rant of such things!' said Jesus. 'In very truth I tell you, we speak of what we
know, and testify to what we have seen, and yet you all reject our testimony. If
you do not believe me when I talk to you about earthly things, how are you to
believe if I should talk about the things of heaven?

'No one has gone up into heaven except the one who came down from
heaven, the Son of Man who is in heaven. Just as Moses lifted up the serpent in
the wilderness, so the Son of Man must be lifted up, in order that everyone
who has faith may in him have eternal life.

'God so loved the world that he gave his only Son, that everyone who has
faith in him may not perish but have eternal life. It was not to judge the world
that God sent his Son into the world, but that through him the world might be
saved.'

*To thee, O Christ, O Word of the Father, we offer up our lowly praises and
unfeigned hearty thanks: who for love of our fallen race didst most wonder-
fully and humbly choose to be made man, and to take our nature as never
more to lay it by; so that we might be born again by thy Spirit and restored
in the image of God; to whom, one blessed Trinity, be ascribed all honour,
might, majesty, and dominion, now and for ever.*

Lancelot Andrewes, 1555–1626

WEEK 24

Gift of God

Day 1

Jesus and the Samaritan Woman

NEWS NOW REACHED the Pharisees that Jesus was winning and baptizing more disciples than John; although, in fact, it was his disciples who were baptizing, not Jesus himself. When Jesus heard this, he left Judaea and set out once more for Galilee. He had to pass through Samaria, and on his way came to a Samaritan town called Sychar, near the plot of ground which Jacob gave to his son Joseph; Jacob's well was there. It was about noon, and Jesus, tired after his journey, was sitting by the well.

His disciples had gone into the town to buy food. Meanwhile a Samaritan woman came to draw water, and Jesus said to her, 'Give me a drink.' The woman said, 'What! You, a Jew, ask for a drink from a Samaritan woman?' (Jews do not share drinking vessels with Samaritans.) Jesus replied, 'If only you knew what God gives, and who it is that is asking you for a drink, you would have asked him and he would have given you living water.' 'Sir,' the woman said, 'you have no bucket and the well is deep, so where can you get "living water"? Are you greater than Jacob our ancestor who gave us the well and drank from it himself, he and his sons and his cattle too?' Jesus answered, 'Everyone who drinks this water will be thirsty again; but whoever drinks the water I shall give will never again be thirsty. The water that I shall give will be a spring of water within him, welling up and bringing eternal life.' 'Sir,' said the woman, 'give me this water, and then I shall not be thirsty, nor have to come all this way to draw water.'

> *Almighty God, from whom every good prayer cometh, and who pourest out on all who desire it the Spirit of grace and supplications; deliver us, when we draw nigh to thee, from coldness of heart and wanderings of mind; that with steadfast thoughts and kindled affections we may worship thee in spirit and truth; through Jesus Christ our Lord.*
>
> William Bright, 1824–1901

Day 2

Good News to the Poor

THEN JESUS, armed with the power of the Spirit, returned to Galilee; and reports about him spread through the whole countryside. He taught in their synagogues and everyone sang his praises. He came to Nazareth, where he had been brought up, and went to the synagogue on the sabbath day as he regularly did. He stood up to read the lesson and was handed the scroll of the prophet Isaiah. He opened the scroll and found the passage which says,

> The Spirit of the Lord is upon me
> because he has anointed me;
> he has sent me to announce good news to the poor,
> to proclaim release for prisoners
> and recovery of sight for the blind;
> to let the broken victims go free,
> to proclaim the year of the Lord's favour.

He rolled up the scroll, gave it back to the attendant, and sat down; and all eyes in the synagogue were fixed on him.

He began to address them: 'Today', he said, 'in your hearing this text has come true.' There was general approval; they were astonished that words of such grace should fall from his lips.

> *Jesus, preaching good tidings to the poor,*
> *proclaiming release to the captives,*
> *setting at liberty them that are bound,*
> *I adore thee.*
>
> *Jesus, friend of the poor,*
> *feeder of the hungry,*
> *healer of the sick,*
> *I adore thee.*
>
> *Jesus, denouncing the oppressor,*
> *instructing the simple,*
> *going about doing good,*
> *I adore thee.*
>
> *Jesus, teacher of patience,*
> *pattern of gentleness,*
> *prophet of the kingdom of heaven,*
> *I adore thee.*

A Book of Prayers for Students

Day 3

The First Healings

COMING DOWN TO Capernaum, a town in Galilee, he taught the people on the sabbath, and they were amazed at his teaching, for what he said had the note of authority. Now there was a man in the synagogue possessed by a demon, an unclean spirit. He shrieked at the top of his voice, 'What do you want with us, Jesus of Nazareth? Have you come to destroy us? I know who you are – the Holy One of God.' Jesus rebuked him: 'Be silent', he said, 'and come out of him.' Then the demon, after throwing the man down in front of the people, left him without doing him any injury. Amazement fell on them all and they said to one another: 'What is there in this man's words? He gives orders to the unclean spirits with authority and power, and they go.' So the news spread, and he was the talk of the whole district.

On leaving the synagogue he went to Simon's house. Simon's mother-in-law was in the grip of a high fever; and they asked him to help her. He stood over her and rebuked the fever. It left her, and she got up at once and attended to their needs.

At sunset all who had friends ill with diseases of one kind or another brought them to him; and he laid his hands on them one by one and healed them. Demons also came out of many of them, shouting, 'You are the Son of God.' But he rebuked them and forbade them to speak, because they knew he was the Messiah.

> *Remember, O Lord,*
> *the sick and afflicted,*
> *and those troubled by unclean spirits,*
> *for it is from you that their speedy healing comes,*
> *O God,*
> *and their salvation.*
>
> Liturgy of St James

Day 4

The Miraculous Catch of Fish

O NE DAY AS he stood by the lake of Gennesaret, with people crowding in on him to listen to the word of God, he noticed two boats lying at the water's edge; the fishermen had come ashore and were washing their nets. He got into one of the boats, which belonged to Simon, and asked him to put out a little way from the shore; then he went on teaching the crowds as he sat in the boat. When he had finished speaking, he said to Simon, 'Put out into deep water and let down your nets for a catch.' Simon answered, 'Master, we were hard at work all night and caught nothing; but if you say so, I will let down the nets.' They did so and made such a huge catch of fish that their nets began to split. So they signalled to their partners in the other boat to come and help them. They came, and loaded both boats to the point of sinking. When Simon saw what had happened he fell at Jesus's knees and said, 'Go, Lord, leave me, sinner that I am!' For he and all his companions were amazed at the catch they had made; so too were his partners James and John, Zebedee's sons. 'Do not be afraid,' said Jesus to Simon; 'from now on you will be catching people.' As soon as they had brought the boats to land, they left everything and followed him.

Blessed are you, O Christ our God; you revealed your wisdom to simple fisherfolk, sending down upon them your Holy Spirit, and through them you caught the whole world in your net. Glory to you, lover of humankind.

Liturgy of St John Chrysostom, 4th century

Day 5

The Sower

O N ANOTHER OCCASION he began to teach by the lakeside. The crowd that gathered round him was so large that he had to get into a boat on the lake and sit there, with the whole crowd on the beach right down to the water's edge. And he taught them many things by parables.

As he taught he said: 'Listen! A sower went out to sow. And it happened that as he sowed, some of the seed fell along the footpath; and the birds came and ate it up. Some fell on rocky ground, where it had little soil, and it sprouted quickly because it had no depth of earth; but when the sun rose it was scorched, and as it had no root it withered away. Some fell among thistles; and the thistles grew up and choked the corn, and it produced no crop. And some of the seed fell into good soil, where it came up and grew, and produced a crop; and the yield was thirtyfold, sixtyfold, even a hundredfold.' He added, 'If you have ears to hear, then hear.'

He went on: 'Do you not understand this parable? How then are you to understand any parable? The sower sows the word. With some the seed falls along the footpath; no sooner have they heard it than Satan comes and carries off the word which has been sown in them. With others the seed falls on rocky ground; as soon as they hear the word, they accept it with joy, but it strikes no root in them; they have no staying-power, and when there is trouble or perse-cution on account of the word, they quickly lose faith. With others again the seed falls among thistles; they hear the word, but worldly cares and the false glamour of wealth and evil desires of all kinds come in and choke the word, and it proves barren. But there are some with whom the seed is sown on good soil; they accept the word when they hear it, and they bear fruit thirtyfold, sixtyfold, or a hundredfold.'

> *Christ, the gardener of souls, who sowest the good seed, givest the increase, softening and watering with the showers of thy grace, warming and illumi-nating with the sun of thy favour; look on the little seed of eternal life thy hands have planted in my heart, quicken and cherish it, and bid it grown, first the blade, then the ear, afterwards the full corn in the ear, bringing forth daily fresh virtues, adorned daily with more heavenly graces, striving ever for the perfection which is in thee. Let the knowledge of thee increase in me here, that it may be full hereafter. Let the love of thee grow daily more and more here, that it may be perfect hereafter. Let my mind meditate, my tongue speak, my heart desire and love thee, till I enter into the joy of my Lord, there to remain for ever and ever.*
>
> Sabine Baring-Gould, 1834–1924

Day 6

The Calming of the Storm

T HAT DAY, in the evening, he said to them, 'Let us cross over to the other side of the lake.' So they left the crowd and took him with them in the boat in which he had been sitting; and some other boats went with him. A fierce squall blew up and the waves broke over the boat until it was all but swamped. Now he was in the stern asleep on a cushion; they roused him and said, 'Teacher, we are sinking! Do you not care?' He awoke and rebuked the wind, and said to the sea, 'Silence! Be still!' The wind dropped and there was a dead calm. He said to them, 'Why are you such cowards? Have you no faith even now?' They were awestruck and said to one another, 'Who can this be? Even the wind and the sea obey him.'

> *Serene Son of God, whose will subdued the troubled waters and laid to rest the fears of men, let thy majesty master us, thy power of calm control us; that for our fears we may have faith, and for our disquietude perfect trust in thee; who dost live and govern all things, world without end.*
>
> John Wallace Suter, 1859–1942

Day 7

A Double Healing

WHILE HE WAS by the lakeside, there came a synagogue president named Jairus; and when he saw him, he threw himself down at his feet and pleaded with him. 'My little daughter is at death's door,' he said. 'I beg you to come and lay your hands on her so that her life may be saved.' So Jesus went with him, accompanied by a great crowd which pressed round him.

Among them was a woman who had suffered from haemorrhages for twelve years; and in spite of long treatment by many doctors, on which she had spent all she had, she had become worse rather than better. She had heard about Jesus, and came up behind him in the crowd and touched his cloak; for she said, 'If I touch even his clothes, I shall be healed.' And there and then the flow of blood dried up and she knew in herself that she was cured of her affliction. Aware at once that power had gone out of him, Jesus turned round in the crowd and asked, 'Who touched my clothes?' His disciples said to him, 'You see the crowd pressing round you and yet you ask, "Who touched me?"' But he kept looking around to see who had done it. Then the woman, trembling with fear because she knew what had happened to her, came and fell at his feet and told him the whole truth. He said to her, 'Daughter, your faith has healed you. Go in peace, free from your affliction.'

While he was still speaking, a message came from the president's house, 'Your daughter has died; why trouble the teacher any more?' But Jesus, over-hearing the message as it was delivered, said to the president of the synagogue, 'Do not be afraid; simply have faith.' Then he allowed no one to accompany him except Peter and James and James' brother John. They came to the president's house, where he found a great commotion, with loud crying and wailing. So he went in and said to them, 'Why this crying and commotion? The child is not dead: she is asleep'; and they laughed at him. After turning everyone out, he took the child's father and mother and his own companions into the room where the child was. Taking hold of her hand, he said to her, '*Talitha cum*,' which means, 'Get up, my child.' Immediately the girl got up and walked about – she was twelve years old.

> *Lord Jesus, open our ears,*
> *heal our wounds and purify our lives,*
> *as you did those who came to you;*
> *then we shall hear and perceive what is true*
> *amidst the sounds of the world,*
> *and find wholeness in ourselves.*
>
> Origen, 185–254, adapted

The Sermon on the Mount: I

Day 1

Beatitudes

Blessed are the poor in spirit;
the kingdom of Heaven is theirs.
Blessed are the sorrowful;
they shall find consolation.
Blessed are the gentle;
they shall have the earth for their possession.
Blessed are those who hunger and thirst to see right prevail;
they shall be satisfied.
Blessed are those who show mercy;
mercy shall be shown to them.
Blessed are those whose hearts are pure;
they shall see God.
Blessed are the peacemakers;
they shall be called God's children.
Blessed are those who are persecuted in the cause of right;
the kingdom of Heaven is theirs.
'Blessed are you, when you suffer insults and persecution and calumnies of
every kind for my sake. Exult and be glad, for you have a rich reward in
heaven; in the same way they persecuted the prophets before you.

Give ear, O Lord, unto our prayer,
and attend to the voice of our supplication.
Make us poor in spirit: that ours may be the kingdom of heaven.
Make us to mourn for sin: that we may be comforted by thy grace.
Make us meek: that we may inherit the earth.
Make us to hunger and thirst after righteousness:
that we may be filled therewith.
Make us merciful: that we may obtain mercy.
Make us pure in heart: that we may see thee.
Make us peacemakers: that we may be called thy children.
Make us willing to be persecuted for righteousness' sake:
that our reward may be great in heaven.

Book of Common Order, 1562

Day 2

Salt and Light

YOU ARE SALT to the world. And if salt becomes tasteless, how is its saltness to be restored? It is good for nothing but to be thrown away and trodden underfoot.

You are light for all the world. A town that stands on a hill cannot be hidden. When a lamp is lit, it is not put under the meal-tub, but on the lamp-stand, where it gives light to everyone in the house. Like the lamp, you must shed light among your fellows, so that, when they see the good you do, they may give praise to your Father in heaven.

> *Lord, grant me, I pray,*
> *in the name of Jesus Christ, the Son,*
> *that love which knows no fall,*
> *so that my lamp*
> *may feel his kindling touch*
> *and know no quenching;*
> *burning for me*
> *and giving light to others.*
>
> Columbanus, c. 543–615

Day 3

Dealing with Anger

Y OU HAVE HEARD that our forefathers were told, "Do not commit murder; anyone who commits murder must be brought to justice." But what I tell you is this: Anyone who nurses anger against his brother must be brought to justice. Whoever calls his brother "good for nothing" deserves the sentence of the court; whoever calls him "fool" deserves hell-fire. So if you are presenting your gift at the altar and suddenly remember that your brother has a grievance against you, leave your gift where it is before the altar. First go and make your peace with your brother; then come back and offer your gift. If someone sues you, come to terms with him promptly while you are both on your way to court; otherwise he may hand you over to the judge, and the judge to the officer, and you will be thrown into jail. Truly I tell you: once you are there you will not be let out until you have paid the last penny.'

O God, who of thy great love to man didst reconcile earth to heaven through thine only-begotten Son: grant that we who by the darkness of our sins are turned aside from brotherly love, may be filled with his Spirit shed abroad within us, and embrace our friends in thee and our enemies for thy sake; through Jesus Christ our Lord.

Mozarabic Liturgy, 7th century

Day 4

Beyond Retaliation

Y OU HAVE HEARD that they were told, "An eye for an eye, a tooth for a tooth." But what I tell you is this: Do not resist those who wrong you. If anyone slaps you on the right cheek, turn and offer him the other also. If anyone wants to sue you and takes your shirt, let him have your cloak as well. If someone in authority presses you into service for one mile, go with him two. Give to anyone who asks; and do not turn your back on anyone who wants to borrow.'

> *O Lord Jesus Christ, give us a measure of thy spirit that we may be enabled to obey thy teaching to pacify anger, to take part in pity, and not to be vindictive, ever entrusting our spirit to immortal God, who with thee and the Holy Spirit liveth and reigneth world without end.*
>
> Apollonius, 2nd century, adapted

Day 5

Love without Limits

Y OU HAVE HEARD that they were told, "Love your neighbour and hate your enemy." But what I tell you is this: Love your enemies and pray for your persecutors; only so can you be children of your heavenly Father, who causes the sun to rise on good and bad alike, and sends the rain on the innocent and the wicked. If you love only those who love you, what reward can you expect? Even the tax-collectors do as much as that. If you greet only your brothers, what is there extraordinary about that? Even the heathen do as much. There must be no limit to your goodness, as your heavenly Father's goodness knows no bounds.'

> *Pour into our hearts the spirit of unselfishness, so that, when our cup over-flows, we may seek to share our happiness with our brethren. O thou God of love, who makest thy sun to rise on the evil and on the good, and sendest rain on the just and the unjust, grant that we may become more and more thy true children, by receiving into our souls more of thine own spirit of ungrudging and unwearying kindness; which we ask in the name of Jesus Christ.*
>
> John Hunter, 1849–1917

Day 6

The Praise of God

B E CAREFUL NOT to parade your religion before others; if you do, no reward awaits you with your Father in heaven.

'So, when you give alms, do not announce it with a flourish of trumpets, as the hypocrites do in synagogues and in the streets to win the praise of others. Truly I tell you: they have their reward already. But when you give alms, do not let your left hand know what your right is doing; your good deed must be secret, and your Father who sees what is done in secret will reward you.'

> *Teach us to look, in all our ends,*
> *on thee for judge, and not our friends;*
> *that we, with thee, may walk uncowed*
> *by fear or favour of the crowd.*
>
> Rudyard Kipling, 1865–1936

Day 7

True Prayer

AGAIN, WHEN YOU pray, do not be like the hypocrites; they love to say their prayers standing up in synagogues and at street corners for everyone to see them. Truly I tell you: they have their reward already. But when you pray, go into a room by yourself, shut the door, and pray to your Father who is in secret; and your Father who sees what is done in secret will reward you.

'In your prayers do not go babbling on like the heathen, who imagine that the more they say the more likely they are to be heard. Do not imitate them, for your Father knows what your needs are before you ask him.'

Lord, I know not what I ought to ask of you. You only know what I need. You know better than I know myself. O Father, give to your child what he himself knows not how to ask. Teach me to pray. Pray yourself in me.

François Fénelon, 1651–1715

The Sermon on the Mount: II

Day 1

The Lord's Prayer

This is how you should pray:

> Our Father in heaven,
> may your name be hallowed;
> your kingdom come,
> your will be done,
> on earth as in heaven.
> Give us today our daily bread.
> Forgive us the wrong we have done,
> as we have forgiven those who have wronged us.
> And do not put us to the test,
> but save us from the evil one.

We thank you, O Lord and Master, for teaching us how to pray simply and sincerely to you, and for hearing us when we so call upon you. We thank you for saving us from our sins and sorrows, and for directing us all ways this day. Lead us ever onwards to yourself; for the sake of Jesus Christ our Lord and Saviour. Amen.

John of the Russian Church, 19th century

Day 2

Treasure in Heaven

D O NOT STORE up for yourselves treasure on earth, where moth and rust destroy, and thieves break in and steal; but store up treasure in heaven, where neither moth nor rust will destroy, nor thieves break in and steal. For where your treasure is, there will your heart be also.

'No one can serve two masters; for either he will hate the first and love the second, or he will be devoted to the first and despise the second. You cannot serve God and Money.'

Most loving Father, who has taught us to dread nothing save the loss of thee, preserve me from faithless fears and worldly anxieties, from corrupting passions and unhallowed love of earthly treasures; and grant that no clouds of this mortal life may hide me from the light of that love which is immortal and which thou hast manifested unto us in thy Son, Jesus Christ our Lord.

William Bright, 1824–1901

Day 3

Do Not Be Anxious

T HIS IS WHY I tell you not to be anxious about food and drink to keep you
alive and about clothes to cover your body. Surely life is more than food,
the body more than clothes. Look at the birds in the sky; they do not sow and
reap and store in barns, yet your heavenly Father feeds them. Are you not
worth more than the birds? Can anxious thought add a single day to your life?
And why be anxious about clothes? Consider how the lilies grow in the fields;
they do not work, they do not spin; yet I tell you, even Solomon in all his splendour was not attired like one of them. If that is how God clothes the grass in
the fields, which is there today and tomorrow is thrown on the stove, will he
not all the more clothe you? How little faith you have! Do not ask anxiously,
"What are we to eat? What are we to drink? What shall we wear?" These are the
things that occupy the minds of the heathen, but your heavenly Father knows
that you need them all. Set your mind on God's kingdom and his justice before
everything else, and all the rest will come to you as well. So do not be anxious
about tomorrow; tomorrow will look after itself. Each day has troubles enough
of its own.'

> *Cleanse our minds, O Lord, we beseech thee, of all anxious thoughts for*
> *ourselves, that we may learn not to trust in the abundance of what we*
> *have, save as tokens of they goodness and grace, but that we may commit*
> *ourselves in faith to thy keeping, and devote all our energy of soul, mind*
> *and body to the work of thy kingdom and the furthering of the purposes if*
> *thy divine righteousness; through Jesus Christ our Lord.*
>
> Euchologium Anglicanum

Day 4

Do Not Judge

D O NOT JUDGE, and you will not be judged. For as you judge others, so you will yourselves be judged, and whatever measure you deal out to others will be dealt to you. Why do you look at the speck of sawdust in your brother's eye, with never a thought for the plank in your own? How can you say to your brother, "Let me take the speck out of your eye," when all the time there is a plank in your own? You hypocrite! First take the plank out of your own eye, and then you will see clearly to take the speck out of your brother's.'

Lord and Master of our lives, take from us the spirit of laziness, half-heartedness, selfish ambition and idle talk. Give us rather the spirit of integrity, purity of heart, humility, faithfulness and love. Lord and King, help us to see our own errors, and not our neighbours', for your mercy's sake.

Orthodox Liturgy, adapted

Day 5

Concluding Teachings

D O NOT GIVE dogs what is holy; do not throw your pearls to the pigs: they will only trample on them, and turn and tear you to pieces.

'Ask, and you will receive; seek, and you will find; knock, and the door will be opened to you. For everyone who asks receives, those who seek find, and to those who knock, the door will be opened.

'Would any of you offer his son a stone when he asks for bread, or a snake when he asks for a fish? If you, bad as you are, know how to give good things to your children, how much more will your heavenly Father give good things to those who ask him!

'Always treat others as you would like them to treat you: that is the law and the prophets.'

O Lord my God, by honour or dishonour, through evil report or good report, give us grace to seek thee, greater grace to find thee, greater grace to abide with thee, for ever and ever, world without end. By the indwelling of thy most Holy Spirit, and for the only merits and sake of thy Son Jesus Christ.

Christina Rossetti, 1830–94

Day 6

Final Warnings

ENTER BY THE narrow gate. Wide is the gate and broad the road that leads to destruction, and many enter that way; narrow is the gate and constricted the road that leads to life, and those who find them are few.

'Beware of false prophets, who come to you dressed up as sheep while underneath they are savage wolves. You will recognize them by their fruit. Can grapes be picked from briars, or figs from thistles? A good tree always yields sound fruit, and a poor tree bad fruit. A good tree cannot bear bad fruit, or a poor tree sound fruit. A tree that does not yield sound fruit is cut down and thrown on the fire. That is why I say you will recognize them by their fruit.

'Not everyone who says to me, "Lord, Lord" will enter the kingdom of Heaven, but only those who do the will of my heavenly Father. When the day comes, many will say to me, "Lord, Lord, did we not prophesy in your name, drive out demons in your name, and in your name perform many miracles?" Then I will tell them plainly, "I never knew you. Out of my sight; your deeds are evil!"'

O Lord, the Lord whose ways are right, keep us in thy mercy from lip-service and empty forms; from having a name that we live, but being dead.

Help us to worship thee by righteous deeds and lives of holiness; that our prayer also may be set forth in thy sight as the incense, and the lifting up of our hands be as an evening sacrifice.

Christina Rossetti, 1830–94

Day 7

The House on the Rock

S O WHOEVER HEARS these words of mine and acts on them is like a man who had the sense to build his house on rock. The rain came down, the floods rose, the winds blew and beat upon that house; but it did not fall, because its foundations were on rock. And whoever hears these words of mine and does not act on them is like a man who was foolish enough to build his house on sand. The rain came down, the floods rose, the winds blew and battered against that house; and it fell with a great crash.'

When Jesus had finished this discourse the people were amazed at his teaching; unlike their scribes he taught with a note of authority.

Lord Jesus, grant us grace to come to thee in obedience, and by thy constant obedience to abide with thee; that our foundation may be upon the rock of ages, and that underneath us may be the everlasting arms. Hold us fast that we may cleave unto thee; embrace us that we may cling unto thee.

Christina Rossetti, 1830–94

WEEK 27
Teachings about God's Kingdom

Day 1

An Undivided Kingdom

T HEN THEY BROUGHT him a man who was possessed by a demon; he was blind and dumb, and Jesus cured him, restoring both speech and sight. The bystanders were all amazed, and the word went round: 'Can this be the Son of David?' But when the Pharisees heard it they said, 'It is only by Beelzebul prince of devils that this man drives the devils out.'

Knowing what was in their minds, he said to them, 'Every kingdom divided against itself is laid waste; and no town or household that is divided against itself can stand. And if it is Satan who drives out Satan, he is divided against himself; how then can his kingdom stand? If it is by Beelzebul that I drive out devils, by whom do your own people drive them out? If this is your argument, they themselves will refute you. But if it is by the Spirit of God that I drive out the devils, then be sure the kingdom of God has already come upon you.'

Grant us, O Lord Christ, to desire to have thee as our saviour; that thou wilt change and alter all that is within us, as thou didst help the blind to see and the lame to walk; that thy tempers may be formed and begotten in our hearts, thy humility and self-denial, thy love of the Father, the desire of doing his will and seeking only his honour; so that the kingdom of God may be in us now, and our possession for ever, world without end.

William Law, 1686–1761

Day 2

The Wheat and the Darnel

THE KINGDOM OF Heaven is like this. A man sowed his field with good seed; but while everyone was asleep his enemy came, sowed darnel among the wheat, and made off. When the corn sprouted and began to fill out, the darnel could be seen among it. The farmer's men went to their master and said, "Sir, was it not good seed that you sowed in your field? So where has the darnel come from?" "This is an enemy's doing," he replied. "Well then," they said, "shall we go and gather the darnel?" "No," he answered; "in gathering it you might pull up the wheat at the same time. Let them both grow together till harvest; and at harvest time I will tell the reapers, 'Gather the darnel first, and tie it in bundles for burning; then collect the wheat into my barn.'"

Then he sent the people away, and went into the house, where his disciples came to him and said, 'Explain to us the parable of the darnel in the field.' He replied, 'The sower of the good seed is the Son of Man. The field is the world; the good seed stands for the children of the kingdom, the darnel for the children of the evil one, and the enemy who sowed the darnel is the devil. The harvest is the end of time, and the reapers are angels. As the darnel is gathered up and burnt, so at the end of time the Son of Man will send his angels, who will gather out of his kingdom every cause of sin, and all whose deeds are evil; these will be thrown into the blazing furnace, where there will be wailing and grinding of teeth. Then the righteous will shine like the sun in the kingdom of their Father.'

As the grain from which the bread we make is made were once scattered over the fields, and then gathered together and made one, so may your Church be gathered from all over the earth into your kingdom.

Didache, 1st or 2nd century

Day 3

More Parables of the Kingdom

THE KINGDOM OF HEAVEN is like yeast, which a woman took and mixed with three measures of flour till it was all leavened.

'The kingdom of Heaven is like treasure which a man found buried in a field. He buried it again, and in joy went and sold everything he had, and bought the field.

'Again, the kingdom of Heaven is like this. A merchant looking out for fine pearls found one of very special value; so he went and sold everything he had and bought it.

'Again the kingdom of Heaven is like a net cast into the sea, where it caught fish of every kind. When it was full, it was hauled ashore. Then the men sat down and collected the good fish into baskets and threw the worthless away. That is how it will be at the end of time. The angels will go out, and they will separate the wicked from the good, and throw them into the blazing furnace, where there will be wailing and grinding of teeth.

'Have you understood all this?' he asked; and they answered, 'Yes.' So he said to them, 'When, therefore, a teacher of the law has become a learner in the kingdom of Heaven, he is like a householder who can produce from his store things new and old.'

Behold, O Lord, I have thee now who hast all things; I possess thee to whom all things belong, and who canst do all things; detach my heart from all things but thee, O my God, for in all else there is nothing but vanity and vexation of spirit; may my heart be firmly fixed on thee alone, for thou art my treasure, thou art the sovereign truth, perfect happiness, and eternal life.

Sabine Baring-Gould, 1834–1924

Day 4

Self-denial

J ESUS THEN SAID to his disciples, 'Anyone who wishes to be a follower of mine must renounce self; he must take up his cross and follow me. Whoever wants to save his life will lose it, but whoever loses his life for my sake will find it. What will anyone gain by winning the whole world at the cost of his life? Or what can he give to buy his life back? For the Son of Man is to come in the glory of his Father with his angels, and then he will give everyone his due reward. Truly I tell you: there are some of those standing here who will not taste death before they have seen the Son of Man coming in his kingdom.'

Teach us, dear Lord, frequently and attentively to consider this truth: that if I gain the whole world and lose you, in the end I have lost everything; whereas if I lose the world and gain you, in the end I have lost nothing.

John Henry Newman, 1801–90

Day 5

The Greatest in the Kingdom

A T THAT TIME the disciples came to Jesus and asked, 'Who is the greatest in the kingdom of Heaven?' He called a child, set him in front of them, and said, 'Truly I tell you: unless you turn round and become like children, you will never enter the kingdom of Heaven. Whoever humbles himself and becomes like this child will be the greatest in the kingdom of Heaven, and whoever receives one such child in my name receives me. But if anyone causes the downfall of one of these little ones who believe in me, it would be better for him to have a millstone hung round his neck and be drowned in the depths of the sea. Alas for the world that any of them should be made to fall! Such things must happen, but alas for the one through whom they happen!'

O Saviour, meek and lowly of heart, let not our pride refuse thy bidding, to become as little children, in joy and simplicity, in trustfulness one toward another, in lowliness of heart; and by this thine own glory, bring us unto ours; for thy majesty and mercy's sake.

Eric Milner-White, 1884–1963

Day 6

The Great Banquet

HEARING THIS, one of the company said to him, 'Happy are those who will sit at the feast in the kingdom of God!' Jesus answered, 'A man was giving a big dinner party and had sent out many invitations. At dinner-time he sent his servant to tell his guests, "Come please, everything is now ready." One after another they all sent excuses. The first said, "I have bought a piece of land, and I must go and inspect it; please accept my apologies." The second said, "I have bought five yoke of oxen, and I am on my way to try them out; please accept my apologies." The next said, "I cannot come; I have just got married." When the servant came back he reported this to his master. The master of the house was furious and said to him, "Go out quickly into the streets and alleys of the town, and bring in the poor, the crippled, the blind, and the lame." When the servant informed him that his orders had been carried out and there was still room, his master replied, "Go out on the highways and along the hedgerows and compel them to come in; I want my house full. I tell you, not one of those who were invited shall taste my banquet."'

Open our hearts, O God, that we may learn to give love to the loveless, help to the helpless, and hope to those who are living in despair.

Philip Law

Day 7

The Workers in the Vineyard

T HE KINGDOM OF HEAVEN is like this. There was once a land owner who went out early one morning to hire labourers for his vineyard; and after agreeing to pay them the usual day's wage he sent them off to work. Three hours later he went out again and saw some more men standing idle in the market-place. "Go and join the others in the vineyard," he said, "and I will pay you a fair wage"; so off they went. At midday he went out again, and at three in the afternoon, and made the same arrangement as before. An hour before sunset he went out and found another group standing there; so he said to them, "Why are you standing here all day doing nothing?" "Because no one has hired us," they replied; so he told them, "Go and join the others in the vine-yard." When evening fell, the owner of the vineyard said to the overseer, "Call the labourers and give them their pay, beginning with those who came last and ending with the first." Those who had started work an hour before sunset came forward, and were paid the full day's wage. When it was the turn of the men who had come first, they expected something extra, but were paid the same as the others. As they took it, they grumbled at their employer: "These latecomers did only one hour's work, yet you have treated them on a level with us, who have sweated the whole day long in the blazing sun!" The owner turned to one of them and said, "My friend, I am not being unfair to you. You agreed on the usual wage for the day, did you not? Take your pay and go home. I choose to give the last man the same as you. Surely I am free to do what I like with my own money? Why be jealous because I am generous?" So the last will be first, and the first last.'

> *O God, grant unto us that we be not unwise, but understanding thy will. Whatsoever our hand findeth to do, may we do it with our might: that when thou shalt call thy labourers to give them their reward, we may so have run that we may obtain: so have fought the good fight, as to receive the crown of eternal life; through Jesus Christ our Lord.*
>
> Henry Alford, 1810–71

WEEK 28

Teachings about Love and Forgiveness

Day 1

The Two Great Commandments

T HEN ONE OF the scribes, who had been listening to these discussions and had observed how well Jesus answered, came forward and asked him, 'Which is the first of all the commandments?' He answered, 'The first is, "Hear, O Israel: the Lord our God is the one Lord, and you must love the Lord your God with all your heart, with all your soul, with all your mind, and with all your strength." The second is this: "You must love your neighbour as yourself." No other commandment is greater than these.' The scribe said to him, 'Well said, Teacher. You are right in saying that God is one and beside him there is no other. And to love him with all your heart, all your understanding, and all your strength, and to love your neighbour as yourself – that means far more than any whole-offerings and sacrifices.' When Jesus saw how thoughtfully he answered, he said to him, 'You are not far from the kingdom of God.'

> *O most loving Jesu, pattern of charity, who makest all the commandments of the law to consist in love towards God and towards man, grant to us so love thee with all our heart, with all our mind, and all our soul, and our neighbour for thy sake; that the grace of charity and brotherly love may dwell in us, and all envy, harshness, and ill-will may die in us; and fill our hearts with feelings of love, kindness, and compassion, so that by constantly rejoicing in the happiness and good success of others, by sympathizing with them in their sorrows, and putting away all harsh judgments and envious thoughts, we may follow thee, who art thyself the true and perfect love.*
>
> Treasury of Devotion, 1869

Day 2

A Woman Anoints Jesus' Feet

ONE OF THE Pharisees invited Jesus to a meal; he went to the Pharisee's house and took his place at table. A woman who was living an immoral life in the town had learned that Jesus was a guest in the Pharisee's house and had brought oil of myrrh in a small flask. She took her place behind him, by his feet, weeping. His feet were wet with her tears and she wiped them with her hair, kissing them and anointing them with the myrrh. When his host the Pharisee saw this he said to himself, 'If this man were a real prophet, he would know who this woman is who is touching him, and what a bad character she is.' Jesus took him up: 'Simon,' he said, 'I have something to say to you.' 'What is it, Teacher?' he asked. 'Two men were in debt to a moneylender: one owed him five hundred silver pieces, the other fifty. As they did not have the means to pay he cancelled both debts. Now, which will love him more?' Simon replied, 'I should think the one that was let off more.' 'You are right,' said Jesus.

Then turning to the woman, he said to Simon, 'You see this woman? I came to your house: you provided no water for my feet; but this woman has made my feet wet with her tears and wiped them with her hair. You gave me no kiss; but she has been kissing my feet ever since I came in. You did not anoint my head with oil; but she has anointed my feet with myrrh. So, I tell you, her great love proves that her many sins have been forgiven; where little has been forgiven, little love is shown.' Then he said to her, 'Your sins are forgiven.' The other guests began to ask themselves, 'Who is this, that he can forgive sins?' But he said to the woman, 'Your faith has saved you; go in peace.'

Give us, O Lord, a humble spirit, that we never presume upon your mercy, but live always as those who have been much forgiven. Make us tender and compassionate towards those who are overtaken by temptation, considering ourselves, how we have fallen in times past and may fall yet again. Make us watchful and sober-minded, looking ever unto you for grace to stand upright, and to preserve unto the end; through your Son, Jesus Christ our Lord.

Charles John Vaughan, 1816–97

Day 3

Reproof and Reconciliation

I F YOUR BROTHER does wrong, go and take the matter up with him, strictly between yourselves. If he listens to you, you have won your brother over. But if he will not listen, take one or two others with you, so that every case may be settled on the evidence of two or three witnesses. If he refuses to listen to them, report the matter to the congregation; and if he will not listen even to the congregation, then treat him as you would a pagan or a tax-collector.

'Truly I tell you: whatever you forbid on earth shall be forbidden in heaven, and whatever you allow on earth shall be allowed in heaven.

'And again I tell you: if two of you agree on earth about any request you have to make, that request will be granted by my heavenly Father. For where two or three meet together in my name, I am there among them.'

Then Peter came to him and asked, 'Lord, how often am I to forgive my brother if he goes on wronging me? As many as seven times?' Jesus replied, 'I do not say seven times but seventy times seven.'

O Lord Jesus, because, being full of foolishness, we often sin and have to ask pardon, help us to forgive as we would be forgiven, neither mentioning old offences committed against us, nor dwelling upon them in thought, nor being influenced by them in heart but loving our brother freely, as you freely loved us. For you name's sake.

Christina Rossetti, 1830–94

Day 4

The Unmerciful Servant

T HE KINGDOM OF HEAVEN, therefore, should be thought of in this way: There was once a king who decided to settle accounts with the men who served him. At the outset there appeared before him a man who owed ten thousand talents. Since he had no means of paying, his master ordered him to be sold, with his wife, his children, and everything he had, to meet the debt. The man fell at his master's feet. "Be patient with me," he implored, "and I will pay you in full"; and the master was so moved with pity that he let the man go and cancelled the debt. But no sooner had the man gone out than he met a fellow servant who owed him a hundred denarii; he took hold of him, seizing him by the throat, and said, "Pay me what you owe." The man fell at his fellow servant's feet, and begged him, "Be patient with me, and I will pay you"; but he refused, and had him thrown into jail until he should pay the debt. The other servants were deeply distressed when they saw what had happened, and they went to their master and told him the whole story. Then he sent for the man and said, "You scoundrel! I cancelled the whole of your debt when you appealed to me; ought you not to have shown mercy to your fellow servant just as I showed mercy to you?" And so angry was the master that he condemned the man to be tortured until he should pay the debt in full. That is how my heavenly Father will deal with you, unless you each forgive your brother from your hearts.'

Take away, O Lord, from our hearts all suspiciousness, indignation, anger and contention, and whatever is calculated to wound charity and to lessen brotherly love.

Have mercy, O Lord, have mercy on those who seek your mercy; give grace to the needy; make us to live so that we may be found worthy to enjoy the fruition of your grace and that we may attain to eternal life.

Thomas à Kempis, 1380–1471

Day 5

The Good Samaritan

A LAWYER ONCE came forward to test him by asking: 'Teacher, what must I do to inherit eternal life?' Jesus said, 'What is written in the law? What is your reading of it?' He replied, 'Love the Lord your God with all your heart, and with all your soul, with all your strength, and with all your mind; and your neighbour as yourself.' 'That is the right answer,' said Jesus; 'do that and you will have life.'

Wanting to justify his question, he asked, 'But who is my neighbour?' Jesus replied, 'A man was on his way from Jerusalem down to Jericho when he was set upon by robbers, who stripped and beat him, and went off leaving him half dead. It so happened that a priest was going down by the same road, and when he saw him, he went past on the other side. So too a Levite came to the place, and when he saw him went past on the other side. But a Samaritan who was going that way came upon him, and when he saw him he was moved to pity. He went up and bandaged his wounds, bathing them with oil and wine. Then he lifted him on to his own beast, brought him to an inn, and looked after him. Next day he produced two silver pieces and gave them to the innkeeper, and said, "Look after him; and if you spend more, I will repay you on my way back." Which of these three do you think was neighbour to the man who fell into the hands of the robbers?' He answered, 'The one who showed him kindness.' Jesus said to him, 'Go and do as he did.'

> *Show me, O Lord, your mercy, and delight my heart with it. Let me find you whom I so longingly seek. See, here is the man whom the robbers seized, mishandled, and left half dead on the road to Jericho. O kind hearted Samaritan, come to my aid! I am the sheep who wandered into the wilderness – seek after me, and bring me home again to your fold. Do with me what you will, that I may stay by you all the days of my life, and praise you with all those who are with you in heaven for all eternity.*
>
> Jerome, c.342–420

Day 6

The Lost Sheep

ANOTHER TIME, the tax-collectors and sinners were all crowding in to listen to him; and the Pharisees and scribes began murmuring their disapproval: 'This fellow,' they said, 'welcomes sinners and eats with them.' He answered them with this parable: 'If one of you has a hundred sheep and loses one of them, does he not leave the ninety-nine in the wilderness and go after the one that is missing until he finds it? And when he does, he lifts it joyfully on to his shoulders, and goes home to call his friends and neighbours together. "Rejoice with me!" he cries. "I have found my lost sheep." In the same way, I tell you, there will be greater joy in heaven over one sinner who repents than over ninety-nine righteous people who do not need to repent.'

O God our Father, hear me, who am trembling in this darkness, and stretch forth thy hand unto me; hold forth thy light before me; recall me from my wanderings; and, thou being my guide, may I be restored to myself and to thee.

Augustine of Hippo, 354–430

Day 7

The Prodigal Son

A GAIN HE SAID: 'There was once a man who had two sons; and the younger said to his father, "Father, give me my share of the property." So he divided his estate between them. A few days later the younger son turned the whole of his share into cash and left home for a distant country, where he squandered it in dissolute living. He had spent it all, when a severe famine fell upon that country and he began to be in need. So he went and attached himself to one of the local landowners, who sent him on to his farm to mind the pigs. He would have been glad to fill his belly with the pods that the pigs were eating, but no one gave him anything. Then he came to his senses: "How many of my father's hired servants have more food than they can eat," he said, "and here am I, starving to death! I will go at once to my father, and say to him, 'Father, I have sinned against God and against you; I am no longer fit to be called your son; treat me as one of your hired servants.'" So he set out for his father's house. But while he was still a long way off his father saw him, and his heart went out to him; he ran to meet him, flung his arms round him, and kissed him. The son said, "Father, I have sinned against God and against you; I am no longer fit to be called your son." But the father said to his servants, "Quick! Fetch a robe, the best we have, and put it on him; put a ring on his finger and sandals on his feet. Bring the fatted calf and kill it, and let us celebrate with a feast. For this son of mine was dead and has come back to life; he was lost and is found."'

In the evening of this life, I shall appear before you with empty hands for I do not ask you, Lord, to count my works. All our goodness is stained and imperfect. I wish, then, to be clothed with your own goodness, and to receive you yourself eternally, out of your love. I want no other place or crown but you, my beloved.

Lord, even if my conscience were burdened with every sin it is possible to commit, I would still throw myself into your arms, my heart broken with contrition. And I know how tenderly you welcome any prodigal child of yours who comes back to you.

Thérèse of Lisieux, 1873–97

Teachings about Humility

Day 1

Warnings against Pride and Hypocrisy

WHEN HE HAD finished speaking, a Pharisee invited him to a meal, and he came in and sat down. The Pharisee noticed with surprise that he had not begun by washing before the meal. But the Lord said to him, 'You Pharisees clean the outside of cup and plate; but inside you are full of greed and wickedness. You fools! Did not he who made the outside make the inside too? But let what is inside be given in charity, and all is clean.

'Alas for you Pharisees! You pay tithes of mint and rue and every garden herb, but neglect justice and the love of God. It is these you should have practised, without overlooking the others.

'Alas for you Pharisees! You love to have the chief seats in synagogues, and to be greeted respectfully in the street.

'Alas, alas, you are like unmarked graves which people walk over unawares.'

O God, who resists the proud and gives grace to the humble: grant us the virtue of true humility of which your only-begotten Son himself gave us the perfect example; that we may never offend you by our pride and be rejected by our self-assertion; through Jesus Christ our Lord.

Leonine Sacramentary, 6th century

Day 2

The Need for Humility

WHEN HE NOTICED how the guests were trying to secure the places of honour, he spoke to them in a parable: 'When somebody asks you to a wedding feast, do not sit down in the place of honour. It may be that some person more distinguished than yourself has been invited; and the host will come to say to you, "Give this man your seat." Then you will look foolish as you go to take the lowest place. No, when you receive an invitation, go and sit down in the lowest place, so that when your host comes he will say, "Come up higher, my friend." Then all your fellow guests will see the respect in which you are held. For everyone who exalts himself will be humbled; and whoever humbles himself will be exalted.'

Then he said to his host, 'When you are having guests for lunch or supper, do not invite your friends, your brothers or other relations, or your rich neighbours; they will only ask you back again and so you will be repaid. But when you give a party, ask the poor, the crippled, the lame, and the blind. That is the way to find happiness, because they have no means of repaying you. You will be repaid on the day when the righteous rise from the dead.'

O Christ! Who has shown us the beauty of eternal peace and the duty of inseparable love, grant that we may ever think humbly of ourselves, abounding in gentleness and pity towards all, that following the example of your humility and imitating you in all things, we may live in you and never depart from you.

Mozarabic Liturgy, 7th century

Day 3

The Pharisee and the Tax-collector

H ERE IS ANOTHER parable that he told; it was aimed at those who were sure of their own goodness and looked down on everyone else. 'Two men went up to the temple to pray, one a Pharisee and the other a tax-collector. The Pharisee stood up and prayed this prayer: "I thank you, God, that I am not like the rest of mankind – greedy, dishonest, adulterous – or, for that matter, like this tax-collector. I fast twice a week; I pay tithes on all that I get." But the other kept his distance and would not even raise his eyes to heaven, but beat upon his breast, saying, "God, have mercy on me, sinner that I am." It was this man, I tell you, and not the other, who went home acquitted of his sins. For everyone who exalts himself will be humbled; and whoever humbles himself will be exalted.'

> *Humility once exalted the tax-collector,*
> *who bewailed his sin*
> *and cried: 'Be merciful,'*
> *and justified him.*
> *Let him be our example,*
> *for we have all fallen into the abyss of evil.*
> *Let us cry to the Saviour*
> *from the bottom of our heart:*
> *we have sinned, be merciful,*
> *for you alone love us.*
>
> *Lord, you condemned the Pharisee*
> *who, boasting of his works,*
> *justified himself.*
> *You justified the tax-collector*
> *who, humbling himself,*
> *with sorrowful sighing asked for mercy.*
> *For you reject proud thoughts,*
> *but do not despise contrite hearts.*
> *So in humility we prostrate ourselves*
> *before you, who suffered for us.*
> *Grant us forgiveness*
> *and generous mercy.*
>
> From Orthodox Lent, Holy Week and Easter

Day 4

Jesus Blesses the Children

T HEY BROUGHT CHILDREN for him to touch. The disciples rebuked them,
but when Jesus saw it he was indignant, and said to them, 'Let the children
come to me; do not try to stop them; for the kingdom of God belongs to such
as these. Truly I tell you: whoever does not accept the kingdom of God like a
child will never enter it.' And he put his arms round them, laid his hands on
them, and blessed them.

> *To you alone, O Jesus, I must cling,*
> *running to your arms, dear Lord,*
> *there let me hide, safe from all fears,*
> *loving you with the tenderness of a child.*

> Thérèse of Lisieux, 1873–97, adapted

Day 5

Many who are First will be Last

J ESUS LOOKED ROUND at his disciples and said to them, 'How hard it will be for the wealthy to enter the kingdom of God!' They were amazed that he should say this, but Jesus insisted, 'Children, how hard it is to enter the kingdom of God! It is easier for a camel to pass through the eye of a needle than for a rich man to enter the kingdom of God.' They were more astonished than ever, and said to one another, 'Then who can be saved?' Jesus looked at them and said, 'For men it is impossible, but not for God; everything is possible for God.'

'What about us?' said Peter. 'We have left everything to follow you.' Jesus said, 'Truly I tell you: there is no one who has given up home, brothers or sisters, mother, father or children, or land, for my sake and for the gospel, who will not receive in this age a hundred times as much – houses, brothers and sisters, mothers and children, and land and persecutions besides; and in the age to come eternal life. But many who are first will be last, and the last first.'

> *Let me love thee so that the honour, riches, and pleasures of the world may seem unworthy even of hatred – may be not even encumbrances.*
>
> Coventry Patmore, 1823–96

Day 6

Called to Serve

J AMES AND JOHN, the sons of Zebedee, approached him and said, 'Teacher, we should like you to do us a favour.' 'What is it you want me to do for you?' he asked. They answered, 'Allow us to sit with you in your glory, one at your right hand and the other at your left.' Jesus said to them, 'You do not understand what you are asking. Can you drink the cup that I drink, or be baptized with the baptism I am baptized with?' 'We can,' they answered. Jesus said, 'The cup that I drink you shall drink, and the baptism I am baptized with shall be your baptism; but to sit on my right or on my left is not for me to grant; that honour is for those to whom it has already been assigned.'

When the other ten heard this, they were indignant with James and John. Jesus called them to him and said, 'You know that among the Gentiles the recognized rulers lord it over their subjects, and the great make their authority felt. It shall not be so with you; among you, whoever wants to be great must be your servant, and whoever wants to be first must be the slave of all. For the Son of Man did not come to be served but to serve, and to give his life as a ransom for many.'

O God, in whom nothing can live but as it lives in love, grant us the spirit of love which does not want to be rewarded, honoured or esteemed, but only to become the blessing and happiness of everything that wants it; love which is the very joy of life, and thine own goodness and truth within the soul; who thyself art love, and by love our redeemer, from eternity to eternity.

William Law, 1686–1761

Day 7

Jesus and Zacchaeus

E NTERING JERICHO HE made his way through the city. There was a man there named Zacchaeus; he was superintendent of taxes and very rich. He was eager to see what Jesus looked like; but, being a little man, he could not see him for the crowd. So he ran on ahead and climbed a sycamore tree in order to see him, for he was to pass that way. When Jesus came to the place, he looked up and said, 'Zacchaeus, be quick and come down, for I must stay at your house today.' He climbed down as quickly as he could and welcomed him gladly. At this there was a general murmur of disapproval. 'He has gone in to be the guest of a sinner,' they said. But Zacchaeus stood there and said to the Lord, 'Here and now, sir, I give half my possessions to charity; and if I have defrauded anyone, I will repay him four times over.' Jesus said to him, 'Today salvation has come to this house, for this man too is a son of Abraham. The Son of Man has come to seek and to save what is lost.'

I am not worthy, Master and Lord, that you should come beneath the roof of my soul; yet since in your love towards all, you wish to dwell in me, in boldness I come. You command, open the gates, which you alone have made. And you will come in, and enlighten my darkened reasoning. You are blessed for evermore.

John Chrysostom, c.347–407

WEEK 30

Being a Disciple: I

Day 1

The Unforgivable Sin

H E WHO IS NOT with me is against me, and he who does not gather with me scatters.

'So I tell you this: every sin and every slander can be forgiven, except slander spoken against the Spirit; that will not be forgiven. Anyone who speaks a word against the Son of Man will be forgiven; but if anyone speaks against the Holy Spirit, for him there will be no forgiveness, either in this age or in the age to come.

'Get a good tree and its fruit will be good; get a bad tree and its fruit will be bad. You can tell a tree by its fruit. Vipers' brood! How can your words be good when you yourselves are evil? It is from the fullness of the heart that the mouth speaks. Good people from their store of good produce good; and evil people from their store of evil produce evil.

'I tell you this: every thoughtless word you speak you will have to account for on the day of judgement. For out of your own mouth you will be acquitted; out of your own mouth you will be condemned.'

Preserve me, Lord, from the sin which I fear so much: contempt for thy love. May I never sin against the Holy Spirit who is life and union, harmony and peace. May I never be separated from thy Spirit, from the unity of thy peace, by committing the sin which can never be forgiven, neither here nor in the world to come. Keep me, O Lord, among my brothers and kinsfolk that I may proclaim thy peace. Keep me among those who preserve the unity of the Spirit in the bond of peace.

Baldwin, 12th century

Day 2

The Feeding of the Five Thousand

SOME TIME LATER Jesus withdrew to the farther shore of the sea of Galilee (or Tiberias), and a large crowd of people followed him because they had seen the signs he performed in healing the sick. Jesus went up the hillside and sat down with his disciples. It was near the time of Passover, the great Jewish festival. Looking up and seeing a large crowd coming towards him, Jesus said to Philip, 'Where are we to buy bread to feed these people?' He said this to test him; Jesus himself knew what he meant to do. Philip replied, 'We would need two hundred denarii to buy enough bread for each of them to have a little.' One of his disciples, Andrew, the brother of Simon Peter, said to him, 'There is a boy here who has five barley loaves and two fish; but what is that among so many?' Jesus said, 'Make the people sit down.' There was plenty of grass there, so the men sat down, about five thousand of them. Then Jesus took the loaves, gave thanks, and distributed them to the people as they sat there. He did the same with the fish, and they had as much as they wanted. When everyone had had enough, he said to his disciples, 'Gather up the pieces left over, so that nothing is wasted.' They gathered them up, and filled twelve baskets with the pieces of the five barley loaves that were left uneaten.

In the confidence of your goodness and great mercy, O Lord, I draw near to you, as a sick person to the healer, as one hungry and thirsty to the fountain of life, a creature to the creator, a desolate soul to my own tender comforter. Behold, in you is everything that I can or ought to desire. You are my salvation and my redemption, my helper and my strength.

Thomas à Kempis, 1380–1471

Day 3

Jesus Walks on the Water

As soon as they had finished, he made the disciples embark and cross to the other side ahead of him, while he dismissed the crowd; then he went up the hill by himself to pray. It had grown late, and he was there alone. The boat was already some distance from the shore, battling with a head wind and a rough sea. Between three and six in the morning he came towards them, walking across the lake. When the disciples saw him walking on the lake they were so shaken that they cried out in terror: 'It is a ghost!' But at once Jesus spoke to them: 'Take heart! It is I; do not be afraid.'

Peter called to him: 'Lord, if it is you, tell me to come to you over the water.' 'Come,' said Jesus. Peter got down out of the boat, and walked over the water towards Jesus. But when he saw the strength of the gale he was afraid; and beginning to sink, he cried, 'Save me, Lord!' Jesus at once reached out and caught hold of him. 'Why did you hesitate?' he said. 'How little faith you have!' Then they climbed into the boat; and the wind dropped. And the men in the boat fell at his feet, exclaiming, 'You must be the Son of God.'

Saviour Christ, we beseech thee, when the wind is boisterous, and our faith weak and we begin to sink even as we would fain come to thee on the water, stretch forth thy hand, O Lord, as of old to thy fearful disciple, and say to the sea of our difficulties, 'Peace be still': for thy holy Name's sake.

Charles John Vaughan, 1816–97

Day 4

Bread from Heaven

NEXT MORNING the crowd was still on the opposite shore. They had seen only one boat there, and Jesus, they knew, had not embarked with his disciples, who had set off by themselves. Boats from Tiberias, however, had come ashore near the place where the people had eaten the bread over which the Lord gave thanks. When the crowd saw that Jesus had gone as well as his disciples, they went on board these boats and made for Capernaum in search of him. They found him on the other side. 'Rabbi,' they asked, 'when did you come here?' Jesus replied, 'In very truth I tell you, it is not because you saw signs that you came looking for me, but because you ate the bread and your hunger was satisfied. You should work, not for this perishable food, but for the food that lasts, the food of eternal life.'

They asked, 'What sign can you give us, so that we may see it and believe you? What is the work you are doing? Our ancestors had manna to eat in the desert; as scripture says, "He gave them bread from heaven to eat."' Jesus answered, 'In very truth I tell you, it was not Moses who gave you the bread from heaven; it is my Father who gives you the true bread from heaven. The bread that God gives comes down from heaven and brings life to the world.' 'Sir,' they said to him, 'give us this bread now and always.' Jesus said to them, 'I am the bread of life. Whoever comes to me will never be hungry, and whoever believes in me will never be thirsty. But you, as I said, have seen and yet you do not believe. All that the Father gives me will come to me, and anyone who comes to me I will never turn away. I am the living bread that has come down from heaven; if anyone eats this bread, he will live for ever. The bread which I shall give is my own flesh, given for the life of the world.'

This led to a fierce dispute among the Jews. 'How can this man give us his flesh to eat?' they protested. Jesus answered them, 'In very truth I tell you, unless you eat the flesh of the Son of Man and drink his blood you can have no life in you. Whoever eats my flesh and drinks my blood has eternal life, and I will raise him up on the last day. My flesh is real food; my blood is real drink. Whoever eats my flesh and drinks my blood dwells in me and I in him.'

Heavenly Father, we thank you for giving us the living bread to sustain us, even Jesus Christ your only Son. Grant that our souls may be fed and nourished by him, that we may constantly dwell in him and he in us.

Philip Law

Day 5

The Meaning of Defilement

A GROUP OF PHARISEES, with some scribes who had come from Jerusalem, met him and noticed that some of his disciples were eating their food with defiled hands – in other words, without washing them. (For Pharisees and Jews in general never eat without washing their hands, in obedience to ancient tradition; and on coming from the market-place they never eat without first washing. And there are many other points on which they maintain traditional rules, for example in the washing of cups and jugs and copper bowls.) These Pharisees and scribes questioned Jesus: 'Why do your disciples not conform to the ancient tradition, but eat their food with defiled hands?' He answered, 'How right Isaiah was when he prophesied about you hypocrites in these words: "This people pays me lip-service, but their heart is far from me: they worship me in vain, for they teach as doctrines the commandments of men." You neglect the commandment of God, in order to maintain the tradition of men.'

He called the people and said to them, 'Listen to me, all of you, and understand this: nothing that goes into a person from outside can defile him; no, it is the things that come out of a person that defile him.'

When he had left the people and gone indoors, his disciples questioned him about the parable. He said to them, 'Are you as dull as the rest? Do you not see that nothing that goes into a person from outside can defile him, because it does not go into the heart but into the stomach, and so goes out into the drain?' By saying this he declared all foods clean. He went on, 'It is what comes out of a person that defiles him. From inside, from the human heart, come evil thoughts, acts of fornication, theft, murder, adultery, greed, and malice; fraud, indecency, envy, slander, arrogance, and folly; all these evil things come from within, and they are what defile a person.'

> *O God,*
> *be all my love,*
> *all my hope,*
> *all my striving;*
> *let my thoughts and words flow from you,*
> *my daily life be in you,*
> *and every breath I take be from you.*
> John Cassian, 360–435, adapted

Day 6

The Transfiguration

SIX DAYS LATER Jesus took Peter, James, and John with him and led them up a high mountain by themselves. And in their presence he was transfigured; his clothes became dazzling white, with a whiteness no bleacher on earth could equal. They saw Elijah appear and Moses with him, talking with Jesus. Then Peter spoke: 'Rabbi,' he said, 'it is good that we are here! Shall we make three shelters, one for you, one for Moses, and one for Elijah?' For he did not know what to say; they were so terrified. Then a cloud appeared, casting its shadow over them, and out of the cloud came a voice: 'This is my beloved Son; listen to him.' And suddenly, when they looked around, only Jesus was with them; there was no longer anyone else to be seen.

On their way down the mountain, he instructed them not to tell anyone what they had seen until the Son of Man had risen from the dead. They seized upon those words, and discussed among themselves what this 'rising from the dead' could mean. And they put a question to him: 'Why do the scribes say that Elijah must come first?' He replied, 'Elijah does come first to set everything right. How is it, then, that the scriptures say of the Son of Man that he is to endure great suffering and be treated with contempt? However, I tell you, Elijah has already come and they have done to him what they wanted, as the scriptures say of him.'

My Jesus, from all eternity you were pleased to give yourself to us in love. And you planted within us a deep spiritual desire that can only be satisfied by yourself.

My Jesus, how good it is to love you. Let me be like your disciples on Mount Tabor, seeing nothing else but you. Let us be like two bosom friends, neither of whom can ever bear to offend the other.

Jean-Baptiste Marie Vianney, 1786–1859

The Healing of a Boy Possessed by a Spirit

WHEN THEY CAME back to the disciples they saw a large crowd surrounding them and scribes arguing with them. As soon as they saw Jesus the whole crowd were overcome with awe and ran forward to welcome him. He asked them, 'What is this argument about?' A man in the crowd spoke up: 'Teacher, I brought my son for you to cure. He is possessed by a spirit that makes him dumb. Whenever it attacks him, it flings him to the ground, and he foams at the mouth, grinds his teeth, and goes rigid. I asked your disciples to drive it out, but they could not.' Jesus answered: 'What an unbelieving generation! How long shall I be with you? How long must I endure you? Bring him to me.' So they brought the boy to him; and as soon as the spirit saw him it threw the boy into convulsions, and he fell on the ground and rolled about foaming at the mouth. Jesus asked his father, 'How long has he been like this?' 'From childhood,' he replied; 'it has often tried to destroy him by throwing him into the fire or into water. But if it is at all possible for you, take pity on us and help us.' 'If it is possible!' said Jesus. 'Everything is possible to one who believes.' At once the boy's father cried: 'I believe; help my unbelief.' When Jesus saw that the crowd was closing in on them, he spoke sternly to the unclean spirit. 'Deaf and dumb spirit,' he said, 'I command you, come out of him and never go back!' It shrieked aloud and threw the boy into repeated convulsions, and then came out, leaving him looking like a corpse; in fact, many said, 'He is dead.' But Jesus took hold of his hand and raised him to his feet, and he stood up.

Then Jesus went indoors, and his disciples asked him privately, 'Why could we not drive it out?' He said, 'This kind cannot be driven out except by prayer.'

May the wonderful energy of God's healing power flow into me, fill me with new life, and give me peace and calm.

Source unknown

WEEK 31

Being a Disciple: II

Day 1

In the House of Mary and Martha

WHILE THEY WERE on their way Jesus came to a village where a woman named Martha made him welcome. She had a sister, Mary, who seated herself at the Lord's feet and stayed there listening to his words. Now Martha was distracted by her many tasks, so she came to him and said, 'Lord, do you not care that my sister has left me to get on with the work by myself? Tell her to come and give me a hand.' But the Lord answered, 'Martha, Martha, you are fretting and fussing about so many things; only one thing is necessary. Mary has chosen what is best; it shall not be taken away from her.'

I need thee to teach me day by day, according to each day's opportunities and needs. Give me, O my Lord, that purity of conscience which alone can receive, which alone can improve thy inspirations.

My ears are dull, so that I cannot hear thy voice. My eyes are dim, so that I cannot see thy tokens. Thou alone canst quicken my hearing, and purge my sight, and cleanse and renew my heart.

Teach me to sit at thy feet, and to hear thy word.

John Henry Newman, 1801–90

Day 2

The Rich Fool

Someone in the crowd said to him, 'Teacher, tell my brother to divide the family property with me.' He said to the man, 'Who set me over you to judge or arbitrate?' Then to the people he said, 'Beware! Be on your guard against greed of every kind, for even when someone has more than enough, his possessions do not give him life.' And he told them this parable: 'There was a rich man whose land yielded a good harvest. He debated with himself: "What am I to do? I have not the space to store my produce. This is what I will do," said he: "I will pull down my barns and build them bigger. I will collect in them all my grain and other goods, and I will say to myself, 'You have plenty of good things laid by, enough for many years to come: take life easy, eat, drink, and enjoy yourself.'" But God said to him, "You fool, this very night you must surrender your life; and the money you have made, who will get it now?" That is how it is with the man who piles up treasure for himself and remains a pauper in the sight of God.'

> *Grant us, O Lord, the blessing of those whose minds are stayed on you, so that we may be kept in perfect peace: a peace which cannot be broken. Let not our minds rest upon any creature, but only upon the creator; not upon goods, things, houses, lands, inventions or vanities, or foolish fashions, lest, our peace being broken, we become cross and brittle and given over to envy. From all such deliver us, O God, and grant us your peace.*
>
> George Fox, 1624–91

Day 3

Keep Going!

N O ONE WHO does not carry his cross and come with me can be a disciple of mine. Would any of you think of building a tower without first sitting down and calculating the cost, to see whether he could afford to finish it? Otherwise, if he has laid its foundation and then is unable to complete it, everyone who sees it will laugh at him. "There goes the man", they will say, "who started to build and could not finish.'"

O Lord God, when thou givest to thy servants to endeavour any great matter, grant us also to know that it is not the beginning but the continuing of the same until it be thoroughly finished which yieldeth the true glory, through him that for the finishing of thy work laid down his life, thy Son Jesus Christ.

Based on words used by Sir Francis Drake, c.1540–96

Day 4

The Rich Man and Lazarus

THERE WAS ONCE a rich man, who used to dress in purple and the finest linen, and feasted sumptuously every day. At his gate lay a poor man named Lazarus, who was covered with sores. He would have been glad to satisfy his hunger with the scraps from the rich man's table. Dogs used to come and lick his sores. One day the poor man died and was carried away by the angels to be with Abraham. The rich man also died and was buried. In Hades, where he was in torment, he looked up and there, far away, was Abraham with Lazarus close beside him. "Abraham, my father," he called out, "take pity on me! Send Lazarus to dip the tip of his finger in water, to cool my tongue, for I am in agony in this fire." But Abraham said, "My child, remember that the good things fell to you in your lifetime, and the bad to Lazarus. Now he has his consolation here and it is you who are in agony. But that is not all: there is a great gulf fixed between us; no one can cross it from our side to reach you, and none may pass from your side to us." "Then, father," he replied, "will you send him to my father's house, where I have five brothers, to warn them, so that they may not come to this place of torment?" But Abraham said, "They have Moses and the prophets; let them listen to them." "No, father Abraham," he replied, "but if someone from the dead visits them, they will repent." Abraham answered, "If they do not listen to Moses and the prophets they will pay no heed even if someone should rise from the dead."

> *Lord! Teach me to bestow charity willingly, kindly, joyfully, and to believe that by bestowing it I do not lose, but gain, infinitely more than that which I give.*
>
> *Turn my eyes away from hard-hearted people who do not sympathize with the poor, who meet poverty with indifference, who judge, reproach, brand it with shameful names, and weaken my heart against poverty.*

John of Krondstadt, 1829–1908

Day 5

The Unjust Judge

H E TOLD THEM a parable to show that they should keep on praying and never lose heart: 'In a certain city there was a judge who had no fear of God or respect for man, and in the same city there was a widow who kept coming before him to demand justice against her opponent. For a time he refused; but in the end he said to himself, "Although I have no fear of God or respect for man, yet this widow is so great a nuisance that I will give her justice before she wears me out with her persistence."' The Lord said, 'You hear what the unjust judge says. Then will not God give justice to his chosen, to whom he listens patiently while they cry out to him day and night? I tell you, he will give them justice soon enough. But when the Son of Man comes, will he find faith on earth?'

Assist me mercifully, O Lord, in all my supplications and prayers, that I may not draw near to thee with my lips while my heart is far from thee. Give me a hearty desire to pray, and grace to pray faithfully, that I may live under thy most mighty protection here, and praise thee hereafter; through Jesus Christ.

Sabine Baring-Gould, 1834–1924

Day 6

The Rich Young Man

As he was starting out on a journey, a stranger ran up, and, kneeling before him, asked, 'Good Teacher, what must I do to win eternal life?' Jesus said to him, 'Why do you call me good? No one is good except God alone. You know the commandments: "Do not murder; do not commit adultery; do not steal; do not give false evidence; do not defraud; honour your father and mother."' 'But Teacher,' he replied, 'I have kept all these since I was a boy.' As Jesus looked at him, his heart warmed to him. 'One thing you lack,' he said. 'Go, sell everything you have, and give to the poor, and you will have treasure in heaven; then come and follow me.' At these words his face fell and he went away with a heavy heart; for he was a man of great wealth.

Whatever I am and whatever I possess,
you have given to me;
I restore it all to you again,
to be at your disposal, according to your will.
Give me only a love for you,
and the gift of your grace;
then I am rich enough,
and ask for nothing more.

Ignatius Loyola, 1491–1556

Day 7

The Servants and the Money

WHILE THEY WERE listening to this, he went on to tell them a parable, because he was now close to Jerusalem and they thought the kingdom of God might dawn at any moment. He said, 'A man of noble birth went on a long journey abroad, to have himself appointed king and then return. But first he called ten of his servants and gave them each a sum of money, saying, "Trade with this while I am away." His fellow citizens hated him and sent a delegation after him to say, "We do not want this man as our king." He returned however as king, and sent for the servants to whom he had given the money, to find out what profit each had made. The first came and said, "Your money, sir, has increased tenfold." "Well done," he replied; "you are a good servant. Because you have shown yourself trustworthy in a very small matter, you shall have charge of ten cities." The second came and said, "Your money, sir, has increased fivefold"; and he was told, "You shall be in charge of five cities." The third came and said, "Here is your money, sir; I kept it wrapped up in a handkerchief. I was afraid of you, because you are a hard man: you draw out what you did not put in and reap what you did not sow." "You scoundrel!" he replied. "I will condemn you out of your own mouth. You knew me to be a hard man, did you, drawing out what I never put in, and reaping what I did not sow? Then why did you not put my money on deposit, and I could have claimed it with interest when I came back?" Turning to his attendants he said, "Take the money from him and give it to the man with the most." "But, sir," they replied, "he has ten times as much already." "I tell you," he said, "everyone who has will be given more; but whoever has nothing will forfeit even what he has. But as for those enemies of mine who did not want me for their king, bring them here and slaughter them in my presence.'"

O God, who has commanded that no man should be idle, but that we should all work with our hands the thing that is good; grant that I may diligently do my duty in that station of life to whih thou hast been pleased to call me. Give me grace, that I may honestly improve the talents thou has committed to my trust, and that no worldly pleasures may ever divert me from the thoughts of the life to come, through Jesus Christ our Lord.

Sabine Baring-Gould, 1834–1924

WEEK 32

The Darkness Gathers

Day 1

Jesus Causes a Division

✤

Jᴇsᴜs ᴡᴇɴᴛ ᴜᴘ to the temple and began to teach. The Jews were astonished: 'How is it', they said, 'that this untrained man has such learning?' Jesus replied, 'I was sent by one who is true, and him you do not know. I know him because I come from him, and he it is who sent me.' At this they tried to seize him, but no one could lay hands on him because his appointed hour had not yet come. Among the people many believed in him. 'When the Messiah comes,' they said, 'is it likely that he will perform more signs than this man?'

The Pharisees overheard these mutterings about him among the people, so the chief priests and the Pharisees sent temple police to arrest him. Then Jesus said, 'For a little longer I shall be with you; then I am going away to him who sent me. You will look for me, but you will not find me; and where I am, you cannot come.' So the Jews said to one another, 'Where does he intend to go, that we should not be able to find him? Will he go to the Dispersion among the Gentiles, and teach Gentiles? What does he mean by saying, "You will look for me, but you will not find me; and where I am, you cannot come"?'

On the last and greatest day of the festival Jesus stood and declared, 'If anyone is thirsty, let him come to me and drink. Whoever believes in me, as scripture says, "Streams of living water shall flow from within him."' He was speaking of the Spirit which believers in him would later receive; for the Spirit had not yet been given, because Jesus had not yet been glorified.

On hearing his words some of the crowd said, 'This must certainly be the Prophet.' Others said, 'This is the Messiah.' But others argued, 'Surely the Messiah is not to come from Galilee? Does not scripture say that the Messiah is to be of the family of David, from David's village of Bethlehem?' Thus he was the cause of a division among the people. Some were for arresting him, but no one laid hands on him.

I beseech you, merciful God, to allow me to drink from the stream which flows from your fountain of life. May I taste the sweet beauty of its waters, which sprang from the very depths of your truth. O Lord, you are that fountain from which I desire with all my heart to drink. Give me, Lord Jesus, this water, that it may quench the burning spiritual thirst within my soul and purify me from all sin.

Columbanus, c.550–615

Day 2

Jesus and the Woman Caught in Adultery

A T DAYBREAK HE appeared again in the temple, and all the people gathered round him. He had taken his seat and was engaged in teaching them when the scribes and the Pharisees brought in a woman caught committing adultery. Making her stand in the middle they said to him, 'Teacher, this woman was caught in the very act of adultery. In the law Moses has laid down that such women are to be stoned. What do you say about it?' They put the question as a test, hoping to frame a charge against him. Jesus bent down and wrote with his finger on the ground. When they continued to press their question he sat up straight and said, 'Let whichever of you is free from sin throw the first stone at her.' Then once again he bent down and wrote on the ground. When they heard what he said, one by one they went away, the eldest first; and Jesus was left alone, with the woman still standing there. Jesus again sat up and said to the woman, 'Where are they? Has no one condemned you?' She answered, 'No one, sir.' 'Neither do I condemn you,' Jesus said. 'Go; do not sin again.'

> *Father you never forget us or turn away from us*
> *even when we fail you.*
> *You sent your Son Jesus who gave his life for us,*
> *cured those who were sick,*
> *cared for those who were poor*
> *and cried with those who were sad.*
> *He forgave sinners and taught us to forgive each other.*
>
> Scottish Liturgy

Day 3

The Light of the World

ONCE AGAIN JESUS addressed the people: 'I am the light of the world. No follower of mine shall walk in darkness; he shall have the light of life.' The Pharisees said to him, 'You are witness in your own cause; your testimony is not valid.' Jesus replied, 'My testimony is valid, even though I do testify on my own behalf; because I know where I come from, and where I am going. But you know neither where I come from nor where I am going. I have much to say about you – and in judgement. But he who sent me speaks the truth, and what I heard from him I report to the world.'

They did not understand that he was speaking to them about the Father. So Jesus said to them, 'When you have lifted up the Son of Man you will know that I am what I am. I do nothing on my own authority, but in all I say, I have been taught by my Father. He who sent me is present with me, and has not left me on my own; for I always do what is pleasing to him.' As he said this, many put their faith in him.

Shine into our hearts, O loving Master, by the pure light of the knowledge of yourself and open the eyes of our minds to your teaching: that in all things we may both think and act according to your good pleasure, and meditating on those things that are holy, may continually live in your light.

From the Dawn Office of the Eastern and Leonine Churches

Day 4

Before Abraham Was Born, I Am

Turning to the Jews who had believed him, Jesus said, 'If you stand by my teaching, you are truly my disciples; you will know the truth, and the truth will set you free.' 'We are Abraham's descendants,' they replied; 'we have never been in slavery to anyone. What do you mean by saying, "You will become free"?' 'In very truth I tell you,' said Jesus, 'that everyone who commits sin is a slave. The slave has no permanent standing in the household, but the son belongs to it for ever. If then the Son sets you free, you will indeed be free.

'I know that you are descended from Abraham, yet you are bent on killing me because my teaching makes no headway with you. I tell what I have seen in my Father's presence. But because I speak the truth, you do not believe me. Which of you can convict me of sin? If what I say is true, why do you not believe me? He who has God for his father listens to the words of God. You are not God's children, and that is why you do not listen.'

The Jews answered, 'Are you greater than our father Abraham? He is dead and the prophets too are dead. Who do you claim to be?' Jesus replied, 'In very truth I tell you, before Abraham was born, I am.' They took up stones to throw at him, but he was not to be seen; and he left the temple.

Lord Jesus, Redeemer and Saviour of humanity, Only Begotten of the Father, shining Morning Star, Sun of Righteousness, we thank thee that thou hast appeared in our darkness and that thy radiant splendour will never set. The patriarchs hoped in thee; Abraham rejoiced to see thy day; the sages awaited thee; the holy prophets foretold thy coming.

Thy compassion be praised. Thy mercy be praised. Thy grace be praised for ever.

J. H. Gunning, 1829–1905

Day 5

The Healing of a Man Born Blind

A S HE WENT on his way Jesus saw a man who had been blind from birth. His disciples asked him, 'Rabbi, why was this man born blind? Who sinned, this man or his parents?' 'It is not that he or his parents sinned,' Jesus answered; 'he was born blind so that God's power might be displayed in curing him. While daylight lasts we must carry on the work of him who sent me; night is coming, when no one can work. While I am in the world I am the light of the world.'

With these words he spat on the ground and made a paste with the spittle; he spread it on the man's eyes, and said to him, 'Go and wash in the pool of Siloam.' (The name means 'Sent'.) The man went off and washed, and came back able to see.

The man who had been blind was brought before the Pharisees. As it was a sabbath day when Jesus made the paste and opened his eyes, the Pharisees too asked him how he had gained his sight. The man told them, 'He spread a paste on my eyes; then I washed, and now I can see.' Some of the Pharisees said, 'This man cannot be from God; he does not keep the sabbath.' Others said, 'How could such signs come from a sinful man?' So they took different sides. Then they continued to question him: 'What have you to say about him? Speak the truth before God. We know that this man is a sinner.' 'Whether or not he is a sinner, I do not know,' the man replied. 'All I know is this: I was blind and now I can see.' 'What did he do to you?' they asked. 'How did he open your eyes?' 'I have told you already,' he retorted, 'but you took no notice. Why do you want to hear it again? Do you also want to become his disciples?' Then they became abusive. 'You are that man's disciple,' they said, 'but we are disciples of Moses. We know that God spoke to Moses, but as for this man, we do not know where he comes from.' Then they turned him out.

Hearing that they had turned him out, Jesus found him and asked, 'Have you faith in the Son of Man?' The man answered, 'Tell me who he is, sir, that I may put my faith in him.' 'You have seen him,' said Jesus; 'indeed, it is he who is speaking to you.' 'Lord, I believe,' he said, and fell on his knees before him.

Jesus said, 'It is for judgement that I have come into this world – to give sight to the sightless and to make blind those who see.' Some Pharisees who were present asked, 'Do you mean that we are blind?' 'If you were blind,' said Jesus, 'you would not be guilty, but because you claim to see, your guilt remains.'

> *O God, our Judge and Saviour, set before us the vision of your purity and let us see our sins in the light of your holiness. Pierce our self-contentment with the shafts of your burning love and let love consume in us all that hinders us from perfect service of your cause; for your holiness is our judgement, so are your wounds our salvation.*
>
> William Temple, 1881–1944

Day 6

The Good Shepherd

I N VERY TRUTH I tell you, the man who does not enter the sheepfold by the door, but climbs in some other way, is nothing but a thief and a robber. He who enters by the door is the shepherd in charge of the sheep. The door-keeper admits him, and the sheep hear his voice; he calls his own sheep by name, and leads them out. When he has brought them all out, he goes ahead of them and the sheep follow, because they know his voice. They will not follow a stranger; they will run away from him, because they do not recognize the voice of strangers.

'A thief comes only to steal, kill, and destroy; I have come that they may have life, and may have it in all its fullness. I am the good shepherd; the good shepherd lays down his life for the sheep. The hired man, when he sees the wolf coming, abandons the sheep and runs away, because he is not the shepherd and the sheep are not his. Then the wolf harries the flock and scatters the sheep. The man runs away because he is a hired man and cares nothing for the sheep.

'I am the good shepherd; I know my own and my own know me, as the Father knows me and I know the Father; and I lay down my life for the sheep. But there are other sheep of mine, not belonging to this fold; I must lead them as well, and they too will listen to my voice. There will then be one flock, one shepherd. My Father who has given them to me is greater than all, and no one can snatch them out of the Father's care. The Father and I are one.'

Thou art the good shepherd, who hast laid down thy life for thy sheep. Behold, I am that sheep that was lost. Take me on thy shoulders, and carry me in thy bosom. What cast thou deny to me, who has given thyself to me? Lead thou me, and I shall lack nothing in the green pastures wherein thou feedest thy flock until I am brought to the pastures of eternal life.

Sabine Baring-Gould, 1834–1924

Day 7

The Raising of Lazarus

THERE WAS A MAN named Lazarus who had fallen ill. His home was at Bethany, the village of Mary and her sister Martha. When Jesus heard this he said to his disciples, 'Let us go back to Judaea. Our friend Lazarus has fallen asleep, but I shall go and wake him.'

As soon as Martha heard that Jesus was on his way, she went to meet him, and left Mary sitting at home.

Martha said to Jesus, 'Lord, if you had been here my brother would not have died. Even now I know that God will grant you whatever you ask of him.' Jesus said, 'Your brother will rise again.' 'I know that he will rise again', said Martha, 'at the resurrection on the last day.' Jesus said, 'I am the resurrection and the life. Whoever has faith in me shall live, even though he dies; and no one who lives and has faith in me shall ever die. Do you believe this?' 'I do, Lord,' she answered; 'I believe that you are the Messiah, the Son of God who was to come into the world.'

So saying she went to call her sister Mary and, taking her aside, she said, 'The Master is here and is asking for you.' As soon as Mary heard this she rose and went to him. When Jesus saw her weeping and the Jews who had come with her weeping, he was moved with indignation and deeply distressed. 'Where have you laid him?' he asked. They replied, 'Come and see.' Jesus wept.

Jesus, again deeply moved, went to the tomb. It was a cave, with a stone placed against it. Jesus said, 'Take away the stone.' Martha, the dead man's sister, said to him, 'Sir, by now there will be a stench; he has been there four days.' Jesus said, 'Did I not tell you that if you have faith you will see the glory of God?' Then they removed the stone.

Then he raised his voice in a great cry: 'Lazarus, come out.' The dead man came out, his hands and feet bound with linen bandages, his face wrapped in a cloth. Jesus said, 'Loose him; let him go.'

Our Father in heaven, I thank thee that thou has led me into the light. I thank thee for sending the Saviour to call me from death to life. I confess that I was dead in sin before I heard his call, but when I heard him, like Lazarus, I arose. But, O my Father, the grave clothes bind me still. Old habits that I cannot throw off, old customs that are so much a part of my life I am helpless to live the new life that Christ calls me to live. Give me strength, O Father, to break the bonds; give me courage to live a new life in thee; give me faith, to believe that with thy help I cannot fail. And this I ask in the Saviour's name who has taught me to come to thee.

Source unknown, Taiwan

Jesus' Final Teachings

Day 1

The Triumphal Entry

JESUS SET OUT on the ascent to Jerusalem. As he approached Bethphage and Bethany at the hill called Olivet, he sent off two of the disciples, telling them: 'Go into the village opposite; as you enter it you will find tethered there a colt which no one has yet ridden. Untie it and bring it here. If anyone asks why you are untying it, say, "The Master needs it."' The two went on their errand and found everything just as he had told them. As they were untying the colt, its owners asked, 'Why are you untying that colt?' They answered, 'The Master needs it.'

So they brought the colt to Jesus, and threw their cloaks on it for Jesus to mount. As he went along, people laid their cloaks on the road. And when he reached the descent from the mount of Olives, the whole company of his disciples in their joy began to sing aloud the praises of God for all the great things they had seen:

'Blessed is he who comes as king in the name of the Lord!
Peace in heaven, glory in highest heaven!'

Some Pharisees in the crowd said to him, 'Teacher, restrain your disciples.' He answered, 'I tell you, if my disciples are silent the stones will shout aloud.'

When he came in sight of the city, he wept over it and said, 'If only you had known this day the way that leads to peace! But no; it is hidden from your sight. For a time will come upon you, when your enemies will set up siege-works against you; they will encircle you and hem you in at every point; they will bring you to the ground, you and your children within your walls, and not leave you one stone standing on another, because you did not recognize the time of God's visitation.'

As we keep the special memory of our Redeemer's entry into the city, so grant, O Lord, that now and ever, he may triumph in our hearts. Let the King of grace and glory enter in, and let us lay ourselves and all we are in full and joyful homage before him; through the same Jesus Christ our Lord. Amen.

H. C. G. Moule, 1841–1920

Day 2

The Cleansing of the Temple

H E ENTERED JERUSALEM and went into the temple. He looked round at everything and began to drive out those who bought and sold there. He upset the tables of the money-changers and the seats of the dealers in pigeons; and he would not allow anyone to carry goods through the temple court. Then he began to teach them, and said, 'Does not scripture say, "My house shall be called a house of prayer for all nations"? But you have made it a robbers' cave.' The chief priests and the scribes heard of this and looked for a way to bring about his death; for they were afraid of him, because the whole crowd was spellbound by his teaching. And when evening came they went out of the city.

O my dear and blessed Saviour, who with so much zeal didst drive out those who turned thy house of prayer into a den of thieves, clear at this time the temple of my soul from vain and sinful thoughts, cast out all wandering imaginations, leave nothing behind, that may either disturb or distract me in the performance of this my duty, that my prayers may ascend as incense, and thy grace and mercy may descend as dew to the saving of my soul, and to the glory of thy name.

Bryan Duppa, 1588–1662

Day 3

The Two Sons

BUT WHAT DO you think about this? There was a man who had two sons. He went to the first, and said, "My son, go and work today in the vineyard." "I will, sir," the boy replied; but he did not go. The father came to the second and said the same. "I will not," he replied; but afterwards he changed his mind and went. Which of the two did what his father wanted?' 'The second,' they replied. Then Jesus said, 'Truly I tell you: tax-collectors and prostitutes are entering the kingdom of God ahead of you. For when John came to show you the right way to live, you did not believe him, but the tax-collectors and prostitutes did; and even when you had seen that, you did not change your minds and believe him.'

In full and glad surrender
I give myself to thee
Thine utterly and only
And evermore to be

O come and reign, Lord Jesus;
Rule over everything!
And keep me always loyal
And true to thee, my King.

Frances Ridley Havergal, 1836–79

Day 4

Pay Caesar What Belongs to Caesar

A NUMBER OF Pharisees and men of Herod's party were sent to trap him
with a question. They came and said, 'Teacher, we know you are a sincere
man and court no one's favour, whoever he may be; you teach in all sincerity
the way of life that God requires. Are we or are we not permitted to pay taxes to
the Roman emperor? Shall we pay or not?' He saw through their duplicity, and
said, 'Why are you trying to catch me out? Fetch me a silver piece, and let me
look at it.' They brought one, and he asked them, 'Whose head is this, and
whose inscription?' 'Caesar's,' they replied. Then Jesus said, 'Pay Caesar what
belongs to Caesar, and God what belongs to God.' His reply left them com-
pletely taken aback.

> *O Lord, take full possession of my heart, raise there your throne,*
> *and command there as you do in heaven.*
> *Being created by you, let me live for you;*
> *being created for you, let me always act for your glory;*
> *being redeemed by you, let me give to you what is yours;*
> *and let my spirit cling to you alone, for your name's sake.*
>
> John Wesley, 1703–91

Day 5

Warnings about the End

A S HE WAS leaving the temple, one of his disciples exclaimed, 'Look, Teacher, what huge stones! What fine buildings!' Jesus said to him, 'You see these great buildings? Not one stone will be left upon another; they will all be thrown down.'

As he sat on the mount of Olives opposite the temple he was questioned privately by Peter, James, John, and Andrew. 'Tell us,' they said, 'when will this happen? What will be the sign that all these things are about to be fulfilled?'

Jesus began: 'Be on your guard; let no one mislead you. Many will come claiming my name, and saying, "I am he"; and many will be misled by them. When you hear of wars and rumours of wars, do not be alarmed. Such things are bound to happen; but the end is still to come. For nation will go to war against nation, kingdom against kingdom; there will be earthquakes in many places; there will be famines. These are the first birth-pangs of the new age.

'If anyone says to you then, "Look, here is the Messiah," or, "Look, there he is," do not believe it. Impostors will come claiming to be messiahs or prophets, and they will produce signs and wonders to mislead, if possible, God's chosen.

'Be on your guard, keep watch. You do not know when the moment is coming. It is like a man away from home: he has left his house and put his servants in charge, each with his own work to do, and he has ordered the door-keeper to stay awake. Keep awake, then, for you do not know when the master of the house will come. Evening or midnight, cock-crow or early dawn – If he comes suddenly, do not let him find you asleep. And what I say to you, I say to everyone: Keep awake.'

O thou, who hast foretold that thou wilt return to judgement in an hour that we are not aware of: grant us grace to watch and pray always; that whether thou shalt come at even, or at midnight, or in the morning, we may be found among the number of those servants who shall be blessed in watching for their Lord; to whom be all glory, now and for evermore.

From the Non-jurors Prayer Book, 1734

Day 6

The Ten Girls

WHEN THE DAY comes, the kingdom of Heaven will be like this. There were ten girls, who took their lamps and went out to meet the bridegroom. Five of them were foolish, and five prudent; when the foolish ones took their lamps, they took no oil with them, but the others took flasks of oil with their lamps. As the bridegroom was a long time in coming, they all dozed off to sleep. But at midnight there came a shout: "Here is the bridegroom! Come out to meet him." Then the girls all got up and trimmed their lamps. The foolish said to the prudent, "Our lamps are going out; give us some of your oil." "No," they answered; "there will never be enough for all of us. You had better go to the dealers and buy some for yourselves." While they were away the bridegroom arrived; those who were ready went in with him to the wedding banquet; and the door was shut. Later the others came back. "Sir, sir, open the door for us," they cried. But he answered, "Truly I tell you: I do not know you." Keep awake then, for you know neither the day nor the hour.'

Keep us, O Lord, while we tarry on this earth, in a serious seeking after thee, and in an affectionate walking with thee, every day of our lives; that when thou comest, we may be found not hiding our talent, nor serving the flesh, nor yet asleep with our lamp unfurnished, but waiting and longing for our Lord, our glorious King, for ever and ever.

Richard Baxter, 1615–91

Day 7

The Sheep and the Goats

When the Son of Man comes in his glory and all the angels with him, he will sit on his glorious throne, with all the nations gathered before him. He will separate people into two groups, as a shepherd separates the sheep from the goats; he will place the sheep on his right hand and the goats on his left. Then the king will say to those on his right, "You have my Father's blessing; come, take possession of the kingdom that has been ready for you since the world was made. For when I was hungry, you gave me food; when thirsty, you gave me drink; when I was a stranger, you took me into your home; when naked, you clothed me; when I was ill, you came to my help; when in prison, you visited me." Then the righteous will reply, "Lord, when was it that we saw you hungry and fed you, or thirsty and gave you drink, a stranger and took you home, or naked and clothed you? When did we see you ill or in prison, and come to visit you?" And the king will answer, "Truly I tell you: anything you did for one of my brothers here, however insignificant, you did for me." Then he will say to those on his left, "A curse is on you; go from my sight to the eternal fire that is ready for the devil and his angels. For when I was hungry, you gave me nothing to eat; when thirsty, nothing to drink; when I was a stranger, you did not welcome me; when I was naked, you did not clothe me; when I was ill and in prison, you did not come to my help." And they in their turn will reply, "Lord, when was it that we saw you hungry or thirsty or a stranger or naked or ill or in prison, and did nothing for you?" And he will answer, "Truly I tell you: anything you failed to do for one of these, however insignificant, you failed to do for me." And they will go away to eternal punishment, but the righteous will enter eternal life.'

O Lord, who though you were rich yet for our sakes became poor, and has promised in your holy gospel that whatever is done for the least of your brethren you will receive as done to you: give us grace, we humbly beseech you, to be always willing and ready to minister, as you enable us, to the needs of others, and to extend the blessings of your kingdom over all the world; to your praise and glory, who are God over all, blessed for ever.

Augustine of Hippo, 354–430

WEEK 34

The Last Supper

Day 1

Jesus Anticipates His Death

AMONG THOSE WHO went up to worship at the festival were some Gentiles. They approached Philip, who was from Bethsaida in Galilee, and said to him, 'Sir, we should like to see Jesus.' Philip went and told Andrew, and the two of them went to tell Jesus. Jesus replied: 'The hour has come for the Son of Man to be glorified. In very truth I tell you, unless a grain of wheat falls into the ground and dies, it remains that and nothing more; but if it dies, it bears a rich harvest. Whoever loves himself is lost, but he who hates himself in this world will be kept safe for eternal life. If anyone is to serve me, he must follow me; where I am, there will my servant be. Whoever serves me will be honoured by the Father.

'Now my soul is in turmoil, and what am I to say? "Father, save me from this hour"? No, it was for this that I came to this hour. Father, glorify your name.' A voice came from heaven: 'I have glorified it, and I will glorify it again.' The crowd standing by said it was thunder they heard, while others said, 'An angel has spoken to him.' Jesus replied, 'This voice spoke for your sake, not mine. Now is the hour of judgement for this world; now shall the prince of this world be driven out. And when I am lifted up from the earth I shall draw everyone to myself.' This he said to indicate the kind of death he was to die.

Then one of the Twelve, the man called Judas Iscariot, went to the chief priests and said, 'What will you give me to betray him to you?' They weighed him out thirty silver pieces. From that moment he began to look for an opportunity to betray him.

Just as a grain of wheat must die in the earth in order to bring forth a rich harvest, so your Son died on the cross to bring a rich harvest of love. Just as the harvest of wheat must be ground into flour to make bread so the suffering of your Son brings us the bread of live. Just as bread gives our bodies strength for our daily work, so the risen body of your Son gives us strength to obey your laws.

Thomas Münzer, c.1490–1525

Day 2

Belief in the Son

I N SPITE OF the many signs which Jesus had performed in their presence they would not believe in him, for the prophet Isaiah's words had to be fulfilled: 'Lord, who has believed what we reported, and to whom has the power of the Lord been revealed?' And there is another saying of Isaiah which explains why they could not believe: 'He has blinded their eyes and dulled their minds, lest they should see with their eyes, and perceive with their minds, and turn to me to heal them.' Isaiah said this because he saw his glory and spoke about him.

For all that, even among those in authority many believed in him, but would not acknowledge him on account of the Pharisees, for fear of being banned from the synagogue. For they valued human reputation rather than the honour which comes from God.

Jesus proclaimed: 'To believe in me, is not to believe in me but in him who sent me; to see me, is to see him who sent me. I have come into the world as light, so that no one who has faith in me should remain in darkness. But if anyone hears my words and disregards them, I am not his judge; I have not come to judge the world, but to save the world. There is a judge for anyone who rejects me and does not accept my words; the word I have spoken will be his judge on the last day. I do not speak on my own authority, but the Father who sent me has himself commanded me what to say and how to speak. I know that his commands are eternal life. What the Father has said to me, therefore that is what I speak.'

God the Father, who said in the beginning, 'Let there be light', and there was light; enlighten mine eyes that I may never sleep in sin, lest at any time the deceits of the enemy, or my own corrupt nature, prevail against me.

O God the Son, the true and only light, shinning in darkness and lightening everyone that cometh into the world; dispel the clouds of ignorance, and give me a right understanding, that in thee, and through thee, I may see and know the Father; whom to know is life, and whom to serve is to reign for ever.

Sabine Baring-Gould, 1834–1924

Day 3

Jesus Washes his Disciples' Feet

O N THE FIRST DAY of Unleavened Bread the disciples came and asked Jesus, 'Where would you like us to prepare the Passover for you?' He told them to go to a certain man in the city with this message: 'The Teacher says, "My appointed time is near; I shall keep the Passover with my disciples at your house."' The disciples did as Jesus directed them and prepared the Passover.

During supper, Jesus, well aware that the Father had entrusted everything to him, and that he had come from God and was going back to God, rose from the supper table, took off his outer garment and, taking a towel, tied it round him. Then he poured water into a basin, and began to wash his disciples' feet and to wipe them with the towel.

When he came to Simon Peter, Peter said to him, 'You, Lord, washing my feet?' Jesus replied, 'You do not understand now what I am doing, but one day you will.' Peter said, 'I will never let you wash my feet.' 'If I do not wash you,' Jesus replied, 'you have no part with me.' 'Then, Lord,' said Simon Peter, 'not my feet only; wash my hands and head as well!'

Jesus said to him, 'Anyone who has bathed needs no further washing; he is clean all over; and you are clean, though not every one of you.' He added the words 'not every one of you' because he knew who was going to betray him.

After washing their feet he put on his garment and sat down again. 'Do you understand what I have done for you?' he asked. 'You call me Teacher and Lord, and rightly so, for that is what I am. Then if I, your Lord and Teacher, have washed your feet, you also ought to wash one another's feet. I have set you an example: you are to do as I have done for you. In very truth I tell you, a servant is not greater than his master, nor a messenger than the one who sent him. If you know this, happy are you if you act upon it.'

Lord Jesus Christ, who when thou wast able to institute the holy sacrament at the Last Supper, didst wash the feet of the apostles, and teach us by thy example the grace of humility: cleanse us, we beseech thee, from all stain of sin, that we may be worthy partakers of thy holy mysteries; who livest and reignest with the Father and the Holy Ghost, one God, world without end.

Office of the Royal Maundy, Westminster Abbey

Day 4

This Is my Body

D URING SUPPER JESUS took bread, and having said the blessing he broke it and gave it to the disciples with the words: 'Take this and eat; this is my body.' Then he took a cup, and having offered thanks to God he gave it to them with the words: 'Drink from it, all of you. For this is my blood, the blood of the covenant, shed for many for the forgiveness of sins. I tell you, never again shall I drink from this fruit of the vine until that day when I drink it new with you in the kingdom of my Father.'

After singing the Passover hymn, they went out to the mount of Olives. Then Jesus said to them, 'Tonight you will all lose faith because of me; for it is written: "I will strike the shepherd and the sheep of his flock will be scattered." But after I am raised, I shall go ahead of you into Galilee.' Peter replied, 'Everyone else may lose faith because of you, but I never will.' Jesus said to him, 'Truly I tell you: tonight before the cock crows you will disown me three times.'

O God, who dost govern the thoughts of men: bring to my mind the upper room where the Lord Jesus broke the bread with his disciples in the night before he was crucified; grant to me that, being of that company, I may look into the face of him who gave himself for the world.

While I eat of his bread and drink of his cup, fill my life with his life, and send me forth to think his thoughts, to say his words, and to do his deeds; and so, O blessed Father, grant me that, though I know it not, the light of his face may shine in my face, and all men may take note that I have been with Jesus; who liveth and reigneth with thee and the Holy Spirit, the God of everlasting love.

Charles Lewis Slattery, 1867–1930

Day 5

Always with Christ

S ET YOUR TROUBLED hearts at rest. Trust in God always; trust also in me. There are many dwelling-places in my Father's house; if it were not so I should have told you; for I am going to prepare a place for you. And if I go and prepare a place for you, I shall come again and take you to myself, so that where I am you may be also; and you know the way I am taking.' Thomas said, 'Lord, we do not know where you are going, so how can we know the way?' Jesus replied, 'I am the way, the truth, and the life; no one comes to the Father except by me.'

> *Jesus our Master*
> *meet us while we walk in the way,*
> *longing to reach your country.*
> *So that following your light,*
> *we may keep the way of righteousness,*
> *and never wander away*
> *into the horrible darkness of the world's night,*
> *while you,*
> *who are the Way, the Truth and the Life,*
> *are shining within us.*
>
> Gelesian Sacramentary, 5th century

Day 6

The Peace of God

ANYONE WHO LOVES ME will heed what I say; then my Father will love him, and we will come to him and make our dwelling with him; but whoever does not love me does not heed what I say. And the word you hear is not my own: it is the word of the Father who sent me. I have told you these things while I am still with you; but the advocate, the Holy Spirit whom the Father will send in my name, will teach you everything and remind you of all that I have told you.

'Peace is my parting gift to you, my own peace, such as the world cannot give. Set your troubled hearts at rest, and banish your fears. You heard me say, I am going away, and I am coming back to you. If you loved me you would be glad that I am going to the Father; for the Father is greater than I am. I have told you now, before it happens, so that when it does happen you may have faith.

'I shall not talk much longer with you, for the prince of this world approaches. He has no rights over me; but the world must be shown that I love the Father and am doing what he commands.'

Calm my troubled heart; give me peace.
O Lord, calm the waves of this heart, calm its tempests!
Calm thyself, O my soul, so that the divine can act in thee!
Calm thyself, O my soul, do that God is able to repose in thee,
so that his peace may cover thee!
Yes, Father in heaven, often have we found that the world cannot
give us peace, but make us feel that thou art able to give peace; let
us know the truth of thy promise: that the whole world may not
be able to take away thy peace.

Søren Kierkergaard, 1813–55

Day 7

The True Vine

I AM THE TRUE VINE, and my Father is the gardener. Any branch of mine that is barren he cuts away; and any fruiting branch he prunes clean, to make it more fruitful still. You are already clean because of the word I have spoken to you. Dwell in me, as I in you. No branch can bear fruit by itself, but only if it remains united with the vine; no more can you bear fruit, unless you remain united with me.

'I am the vine; you are the branches. Anyone who dwells in me, as I dwell in him, bears much fruit; apart from me you can do nothing. Anyone who does not dwell in me is thrown away like a withered branch. The withered branches are gathered up, thrown on the fire, and burnt.

'If you dwell in me, and my words dwell in you, ask whatever you want, and you shall have it. This is how my Father is glorified: you are to bear fruit in plenty and so be my disciples. As the Father has loved me, so I have loved you. Dwell in my love. If you heed my commands, you will dwell in my love, as I have heeded my Father's commands and dwell in his love.'

Lord! Grant me a simple, kind, open, believing, loving and generous heart, worthy of being your dwelling place, O most gracious one.

John of Kronstadt, 1829–1908

WEEK 35

The Willing Sacrifice

Day 1

Jesus Encourages His Disciples

I HAVE SPOKEN thus to you, so that my joy may be in you, and your joy complete. This is my commandment: love one another, as I have loved you. There is no greater love than this, that someone should lay down his life for his friends. You are my friends, if you do what I command you.

'There is much more that I could say to you, but the burden would be too great for you now. However, when the Spirit of truth comes, he will guide you into all the truth; for he will not speak on his own authority, but will speak only what he hears; and he will make known to you what is to come.

'In very truth I tell you, you will weep and mourn, but the world will be glad. But though you will be plunged in grief, your grief will be turned to joy. A woman in labour is in pain because her time has come; but when her baby is born she forgets the anguish in her joy that a child has been born into the world. So it is with you: for the moment you are sad; but I shall see you again, and then you will be joyful, and no one shall rob you of your joy.

'I have told you all this so that in me you may find peace. In the world you will have suffering. But take heart! I have conquered the world.'

Almighty God, who has sent the spirit of truth unto us to guide us into all truth, so rule our lives by thy power, that we may be truthful in word, deed and thought. O keep us, most merciful Saviour, with thy gracious protection, that no fear or hope may ever make us false in act or speech. Cast out from us whatsoever loveth or maketh a lie, and bring us all to the perfect freedom of thy truth; through Jesus Christ our Lord. Amen.

Brooke Foss Westcott, 1825–1901

Day 2

Jesus Prays for His Disciples

Then Jesus looked up to heaven and said: 'Father, the hour has come. Glorify your Son, that the Son may glorify you. For you have made him sovereign over all mankind, to give eternal life to all whom you have given him. This is eternal life: to know you – the only true God, and Jesus Christ whom you have sent.

'I have glorified you on earth by finishing the work which you gave me to do; and now, Father, glorify me in your own presence with the glory which I had with you before the world began.

'I have made your name known to the men whom you gave me out of the world. They were yours and you gave them to me, and they have obeyed your command. Now they know that all you gave me has come from you; for I have taught them what I learned from you, and they have received it.

'It is not for these alone that I pray, but for those also who through their words put their faith in me. May they all be one; as you, Father, are in me, and I in you, so also may they be in us, that the world may believe that you sent me.'

Lord Jesus Christ, who prayed for your disciples that they might be one, even as you are one with the Father; draw us to yourself, that in common love and obedience to you we may be united to one another, that the world may believe that you are Lord, to the glory of God the Father.

William Temple, 1881–1944

Day 3

The Agony in the Garden

WHEN THEY REACHED a place called Gethsemane, he said to his disciples, 'Sit here while I pray.' And he took Peter and James and John with him. Horror and anguish overwhelmed him, and he said to them, 'My heart is ready to break with grief; stop here, and stay awake.' Then he went on a little farther, threw himself on the ground, and prayed that if it were possible this hour might pass him by. 'Abba, Father,' he said, 'all things are possible to you; take this cup from me. Yet not my will but yours.'

He came back and found them asleep; and he said to Peter, 'Asleep, Simon? Could you not stay awake for one hour? Stay awake, all of you; and pray that you may be spared the test. The spirit is willing, but the flesh is weak.' Once more he went away and prayed. On his return he found them asleep again, for their eyes were heavy; and they did not know how to answer him.

He came a third time and said to them, 'Still asleep? Still resting? Enough! The hour has come. The Son of Man is betrayed into the hands of sinners. Up, let us go! The traitor is upon us.'

While he was still speaking a crowd appeared with the man called Judas, one of the Twelve, at their head. He came up to Jesus to kiss him; but Jesus said, 'Judas, would you betray the Son of Man with a kiss?'

When his followers saw what was coming, they said, 'Lord, shall we use our swords?' And one of them struck at the high priest's servant, cutting off his right ear. But Jesus answered, 'Stop! No more of that!' Then he touched the man's ear and healed him.

Turning to the chief priests, the temple guards, and the elders, who had come to seize him, he said, 'Do you take me for a robber, that you have come out with swords and cudgels? Day after day, I have been with you in the temple, and you did not raise a hand against me. But this is your hour – when darkness reigns.'

O Jesus, in thy great loneliness on the Mount of Olives, and in thy agony, thou didst pray to the heavenly Father for comfort. Thou knowest that there are souls on earth who are without support and without comforters. Send them an angel to give them joy.

Source unknown, German

Day 4

Peter Denies his Master

T HEN THEY ARRESTED him and led him away. They brought him to the
high priest's house, and Peter followed at a distance. They lit a fire in the
middle of the courtyard and sat round it, and Peter sat among them. A serving-
maid who saw him sitting in the firelight stared at him and said, 'This man was
with him too.' But he denied it: 'I do not know him,' he said. A little later a man
noticed him and said, 'You also are one of them.' But Peter said to him, 'No, I
am not.' About an hour passed and someone else spoke more strongly still: 'Of
course he was with him. He must have been; he is a Galilean.' But Peter said, 'I
do not know what you are talking about.' At that moment, while he was still
speaking, a cock crowed; and the Lord turned and looked at Peter. Peter
remembered the Lord's words, 'Tonight before the cock crows you will disown
me three times.' And he went outside, and wept bitterly.

> *O merciful God, give us the well of blessed tears, that from the bottom of
> our hearts we may with Peter bewail our sins. O with how great and griev-
> ous sins are we laden and entangled! O suffer us not to lie under the heavy
> burden; let us not sink down in heaviness and desperation. Set thou us up
> again, and convert us thoroughly: send grace of thy holy repentance into
> our heart; wash away all our sins and negligence; grant us the light of new
> graces and gifts; let not the souls perish, for whom thou didst submit thyself
> into so many pains and rebukes, and at the last didst suffer the terrible
> bitter death of the cross.*
>
> Miles Coverdale, 1488–1568

Day 5

The Trial before the High Priest

T HE CHIEF PRIESTS and the whole Council tried to find some allegation against Jesus that would warrant a death sentence; but they failed to find one, though many came forward with false evidence. Finally two men alleged that he had said, 'I can pull down the temple of God, and rebuild it in three days.' At this the high priest rose and said to him, 'Have you no answer to the accusations that these witnesses bring against you?' But Jesus remained silent. The high priest then said, 'By the living God I charge you to tell us: are you the Messiah, the Son of God?' Jesus replied, 'The words are yours. But I tell you this: from now on you will see the Son of Man seated at the right hand of the Almighty and coming on the clouds of heaven.' At these words the high priest tore his robes and exclaimed, 'This is blasphemy! Do we need further witnesses? You have just heard the blasphemy. What is your verdict?' 'He is guilty,' they answered; 'he should die.'

Then they spat in his face and struck him with their fists; some said, as they beat him, 'Now, Messiah, if you are a prophet, tell us who hit you.'

O God, give us patience when those who are wicked hurt us. O how impatient and angry we are when we think ourselves unjustly slandered, reviled, and hurt! Christ suffers blows upon his cheek, the innocent for the guilty; yet we may not abide one rough word for his sake. O Lord, grant us virtue and patience, power and strength, that we may take all adversity with goodwill, and with a gentle mind overcome it. And if necessity and the honour require us to speak, grant that we may do so with meekness and patience, that the truth and thy glory may be defended, and our patience and steadfast continuance perceived.

Miles Coverdale, 1488–1568

Day 6

The Trial before Pilate

Fʀoм Caɪaphas Jesus was led into the governor's headquarters. It was now early morning, and the Jews themselves stayed outside the headquarters to avoid defilement, so that they could eat the Passover meal. So Pilate came out to them and asked, 'What charge do you bring against this man?' 'If he were not a criminal,' they replied, 'we would not have brought him before you.' Pilate said, 'Take him yourselves and try him by your own law.' The Jews answered, 'We are not allowed to put anyone to death.' Thus they ensured the fulfilment of the words by which Jesus had indicated the kind of death he was to die.

Pilate then went back into his headquarters and summoned Jesus. 'So you are the king of the Jews?' he said. Jesus replied, 'Is that your own question, or have others suggested it to you?' 'Am I a Jew?' said Pilate. 'Your own nation and their chief priests have brought you before me. What have you done?' Jesus replied, 'My kingdom does not belong to this world. If it did, my followers would be fighting to save me from the clutches of the Jews. My kingdom belongs elsewhere.' 'You are a king, then?' said Pilate. Jesus answered, '"King" is your word. My task is to bear witness to the truth. For this I was born; for this I came into the world, and all who are not deaf to truth listen to my voice.' Pilate said, 'What is truth?'

Lord, help me not to despise or oppose what I do not understand.

William Penn, 1644–1718

Day 7

Jesus Is Sent to Herod

PILATE THEN SAID to the chief priests and the crowd, 'I find no case for this man to answer.' But they insisted: 'His teaching is causing unrest among the people all over Judaea. It started from Galilee and now has spread here.'

When Pilate heard this, he asked if the man was a Galilean, and on learning that he belonged to Herod's jurisdiction he remitted the case to him, for Herod was also in Jerusalem at that time. When Herod saw Jesus he was greatly pleased; he had heard about him and had long been wanting to see him in the hope of witnessing some miracle performed by him. He questioned him at some length without getting any reply; but the chief priests and scribes appeared and pressed the case against him vigorously. Then Herod and his troops treated him with contempt and ridicule, and sent him back to Pilate dressed in a gorgeous robe. That same day Herod and Pilate became friends; till then there had been a feud between them.

> *Thanks be to thee,*
> *O Lord Christ,*
> *for all the benefits which thou has given us;*
> *for all the pains and insults which thou has borne for us.*
>
> *O most merciful redeemer,*
> *friend*
> *and brother,*
> *may we know thee more clearly,*
> *love thee more dearly,*
> *and follow thee more nearly;*
> *for thine own sake.*
> Richard of Chichester, 1197–1253

Jesus' Final Hours

Day 1

Pilate Washes his Hands of Jesus

PILATE NOW SUMMONED the chief priests, councillors, and people, and said to them, 'You brought this man before me on a charge of subversion. But, as you see, I have myself examined him in your presence and found nothing in him to support your charges. No more did Herod, for he has referred him back to us. Clearly he has done nothing to deserve death. I therefore propose to flog him and let him go.'

At the festival season it was customary for the governor to release one prisoner chosen by the people. There was then in custody a man of some notoriety, called Jesus Barabbas. When the people assembled, Pilate said to them, 'Which would you like me to release to you – Jesus Barabbas, or Jesus called Messiah?' For he knew it was out of malice that Jesus had been handed over to him.

While Pilate was sitting in court a message came to him from his wife: 'Have nothing to do with that innocent man; I was much troubled on his account in my dreams last night.'

Meanwhile the chief priests and elders had persuaded the crowd to ask for the release of Barabbas and to have Jesus put to death. So when the governor asked, 'Which of the two would you like me to release to you?' they said, 'Barabbas.' 'Then what am I to do with Jesus called Messiah?' asked Pilate; and with one voice they answered, 'Crucify him!' 'Why, what harm has he done?' asked Pilate; but they shouted all the louder, 'Crucify him!'

When Pilate saw that he was getting nowhere, and that there was danger of a riot, he took water and washed his hands in full view of the crowd. 'My hands are clean of this man's blood,' he declared. 'See to that yourselves.'

O thou who in almighty power wast weak, and in perfect excellency wast lowly, grant unto us the same mind.

Since thou, the Lord of heaven and earth, didst humble thyself, grant unto us true humility, and make us like thyself.
Thomas Cranmer, 1489–1556

Day 2

Jesus Is Flogged and Condemned to Death

P ILATE NOW TOOK Jesus and had him flogged; and the soldiers plaited a crown of thorns and placed it on his head, and robed him in a purple cloak. Then one after another they came up to him, crying, 'Hail, king of the Jews!' and struck him on the face.

Once more Pilate came out and said to the Jews, 'Here he is; I am bringing him out to let you know that I find no case against him'; and Jesus came out, wearing the crown of thorns and the purple cloak. 'Here is the man,' said Pilate. At the sight of him the chief priests and the temple police shouted, 'Crucify! Crucify!' 'Take him yourselves and crucify him,' said Pilate; 'for my part I find no case against him.' The Jews answered, 'We have a law; and according to that law he ought to die, because he has claimed to be God's Son.'

When Pilate heard that, he was more afraid than ever, and going back into his headquarters he asked Jesus, 'Where have you come from?' But Jesus gave him no answer. 'Do you refuse to speak to me?' said Pilate. 'Surely you know that I have authority to release you, and authority to crucify you?' 'You would have no authority at all over me,' Jesus replied, 'if it had not been granted you from above; and therefore the deeper guilt lies with the one who handed me over to you.'

From that moment Pilate tried hard to release him; but the Jews kept shouting, 'If you let this man go, you are no friend to Caesar; anyone who claims to be a king is opposing Caesar.' When Pilate heard what they were saying, he brought Jesus out and took his seat on the tribunal at the place known as The Pavement (in Hebrew, 'Gabbatha'). It was the day of preparation for the Passover, about noon. Pilate said to the Jews, 'Here is your king.' They shouted, 'Away with him! Away with him! Crucify him!' 'Am I to crucify your king?' said Pilate. 'We have no king but Caesar,' replied the chief priests. Then at last, to satisfy them, he handed Jesus over to be crucified.

O Jesu Christ, the mirror of all gentleness of mind, the example of highest obedience and patience, grant us thy servants with true devotion to con-sider, how thou, Innocent and undefiled Lamb, went bound, taken and hauled away unto death for our sins; how well content thou wast to suffer such things, not opening thy mouth in unpatience, but willingly offering up thyself unto death.

Miles Coverdale, 1488–1568

Day 3

Jesus Forgives his Enemies

AS THEY LED him away to execution they took hold of a man called Simon, from Cyrene, on his way in from the country; putting the cross on his back they made him carry it behind Jesus.

Great numbers of people followed, among them many women who mourned and lamented over him. Jesus turned to them and said, 'Daughters of Jerusalem, do not weep for me; weep for yourselves and your children. For the days are surely coming when people will say, "Happy are the barren, the wombs that never bore a child, the breasts that never fed one." Then they will begin to say to the mountains, "Fall on us," and to the hills, "Cover us." For if these things are done when the wood is green, what will happen when it is dry?'

There were two others with him, criminals who were being led out to execution; and when they reached the place called The Skull, they crucified him there, and the criminals with him, one on his right and the other on his left. Jesus said, 'Father, forgive them; they do not know what they are doing.'

> *O thou Prince of Peace, who, when thou was reviled reviledst not again, and on the cross didst pray for thy murderers, implant in our hearts the virtues of gentleness and patience, that we may overcome evil with good, for thy sake love our enemies, and as children of our heavenly Father seek thy peace, and evermore rejoice in thy love; through Jesus Christ our Saviour.*

Treasury of Devotion, 1869

Day 4

The Crucifixion

P ILATE HAD AN inscription written and fastened to the cross; it read, 'Jesus of Nazareth, King of the Jews'. This inscription, in Hebrew, Latin, and Greek, was read by many Jews, since the place where Jesus was crucified was not far from the city. So the Jewish chief priests said to Pilate, 'You should not write "King of the Jews", but rather "He claimed to be king of the Jews".' Pilate replied, 'What I have written, I have written.'

When the soldiers had crucified Jesus they took his clothes and, leaving aside the tunic, divided them into four parts, one for each soldier. The tunic was seamless, woven in one piece throughout; so they said to one another, 'We must not tear this; let us toss for it.' Thus the text of scripture came true: 'They shared my garments among them, and cast lots for my clothing.'

That is what the soldiers did. Meanwhile near the cross on which Jesus hung, his mother was standing with her sister, Mary wife of Clopas, and Mary of Magdala. Seeing his mother, with the disciple whom he loved standing beside her, Jesus said to her, 'Mother, there is your son'; and to the disciple, 'There is your mother'; and from that moment the disciple took her into his home.

When I survey the wondrous cross.
On which the Prince of Glory died,
My richest gain I count but loss,
And pour contempt on all my pride.

Forbid it, Lord, that I should boast
Save in the death of Christ my God;
All the vain things that charm me most,
I sacrifice them to his blood.

See from his head, his hands, his feet,
Sorrow and love flow mingled down;
Did e'er such love and sorrow meet,
Or thorns compose so rich a crown?

His dying crimson, like a robe,
Spread o'er his body on the tree;
Then am I dead to all the globe,
And all the globe is dead to me.

Were the whole realm of nature mine,
That were a present far too small;
Love so amazing, so divine,
Demands my soul, my life, my all.

Isaac Watts, 1674–1748

Day 5

The Repentant Criminal

THE PASSERS-BY wagged their heads and jeered at him, crying, 'So you are the man who was to pull down the temple and rebuild it in three days! If you really are the Son of God, save yourself and come down from the cross.' The chief priests with the scribes and elders joined in the mockery: 'He saved others,' they said, 'but he cannot save himself. King of Israel, indeed! Let him come down now from the cross, and then we shall believe him. He trusted in God, did he? Let God rescue him, if he wants him – for he said he was God's Son.'

One of the criminals hanging there taunted him: 'Are not you the Messiah? Save yourself, and us.' But the other rebuked him: 'Have you no fear of God? You are under the same sentence as he is. In our case it is plain justice; we are paying the price for our misdeeds. But this man has done nothing wrong.' And he said, 'Jesus, remember me when you come to your throne.' Jesus answered, 'Truly I tell you: today you will be with me in Paradise.'

Eternal God, you have broken the fiery sword and restored to Paradise the thief who was crucified with you and implored your mercy: remember me also in your kingdom. Let not the dread abyss separate me from your elect. Let not the envious one bar the way before me. But forgive me and accept my soul into your hands, spotless and undefiled, as incense in your sight.

Macrina, 4th century

Day 6

The Darkest Hour

F ROM MIDDAY A darkness fell over the whole land, which lasted until three in the afternoon; and about three Jesus cried aloud, '*Eli, Eli, lema sabachthani?*' which means, 'My God, my God, why have you forsaken me?' Hearing this, some of the bystanders said, 'He is calling Elijah.'

After this, Jesus, aware that all had now come to its appointed end, said in fulfilment of scripture, 'I am thirsty.' A jar stood there full of sour wine; so they soaked a sponge with the wine, fixed it on hyssop, and held it up to his lips. Having received the wine, he said, 'It is accomplished!'

Then Jesus uttered a loud cry and said, 'Father, into your hands I commit my spirit'; and with these words he died.

O Jesus, poor and abject, unknown and despised, have mercy upon me, and let me not be ashamed to follow thee.

O Jesus, hated, calumniated, and persecuted, have mercy upon me, and make me content to be as my master.

O Jesus, blasphemed, accused, and wrongfully condemned, have mercy upon me, and teach me to endure the contradiction of sinners.

O Jesus, clothed with a habit of reproach and shame, have mercy upon me, and let me not seek my own glory.

O Jesus, insulted, mocked, and spit upon, have mercy upon me, and let me not faint in fiery trial.

O Jesus, crowned with thorn and hailed in derision;

O Jesus, burdened with our sins and the curses of people;

O Jesus, affronted, outraged, buffeted, overwhelmed with injuries, griefs and humiliations;

O Jesus, hanging on the accursed tree, bowing the head, giving up the ghost, have mercy upon me, and conform my whole soul to thy holy, humble, suffering Spirit.

John Wesley, 1703–91

Day 7

The Burial

B ECAUSE IT WAS the eve of the sabbath, the Jews were anxious that the bodies should not remain on the crosses, since that sabbath was a day of great solemnity; so they requested Pilate to have the legs broken and the bodies taken down. The soldiers accordingly came to the men crucified with Jesus and broke the legs of each in turn, but when they came to Jesus and found he was already dead, they did not break his legs. But one of the soldiers thrust a lance into his side, and at once there was a flow of blood and water. This is vouched for by an eyewitness, whose evidence is to be trusted. He knows that he speaks the truth, so that you too may believe; for this happened in fulfilment of the text of scripture: 'No bone of his shall be broken.' And another text says, 'They shall look on him whom they pierced.'

After that, Joseph of Arimathaea, a disciple of Jesus, but a secret disciple for fear of the Jews, asked Pilate for permission to remove the body of Jesus. He consented; so Joseph came and removed the body. He was joined by Nicodemus (the man who had visited Jesus by night), who brought with him a mixture of myrrh and aloes, more than half a hundredweight. They took the body of Jesus and following Jewish burial customs they wrapped it, with the spices, in strips of linen cloth. Near the place where he had been crucified there was a garden, and in the garden a new tomb, not yet used for burial; and there, since it was the eve of the Jewish sabbath and the tomb was near at hand, they laid Jesus.

O my God Jesus, I am in every way unworthy of you. Yet, like Joseph of Arimathaea, I want to offer a space for you. He offered his own tomb, I offer my heart.

Enter the darkness of my heart, as your body entered that darkness of Joseph's tomb. And make me worthy to receive you, driving out all sin that I may be filled with your spiritual light.

Source unknown

WEEK 37

Resurrection and Ascension

Day 1

The Empty Tomb

E ARLY ON THE FIRST DAY of the week, while it was still dark, Mary of Magdala came to the tomb. She saw that the stone had been moved away from the entrance, and ran to Simon Peter and the other disciple, the one whom Jesus loved. 'They have taken the Lord out of the tomb,' she said, 'and we do not know where they have laid him.' So Peter and the other disciple set out and made their way to the tomb. They ran together, but the other disciple ran faster than Peter and reached the tomb first. He peered in and saw the linen wrappings lying there, but he did not enter. Then Simon Peter caught up with him and went into the tomb. He saw the linen wrappings lying there, and the napkin which had been round his head, not with the wrappings but rolled up in a place by itself. Then the disciple who had reached the tomb first also went in, and he saw and believed; until then they had not understood the scriptures, which showed that he must rise from the dead.

> *Christ is risen:*
> *the world below lies desolate.*
> *Christ is risen:*
> *the spirits of evil are fallen.*
> *Christ is risen:*
> *the angels of God are rejoicing.*
> *Christ is risen:*
> *the tombs of the dead are empty.*
> *Christ is risen indeed from the dead,*
> *the first of the sleepers.*
> *Glory and power are his for ever and ever.*
> Hippolytus of Rome, c.190–c.236

Day 2

Jesus Appears to Mary

THE DISCIPLES WENT home again; but Mary stood outside the tomb weeping. And as she wept, she peered into the tomb, and saw two angels in white sitting there, one at the head, and one at the feet, where the body of Jesus had lain. They asked her, 'Why are you weeping?' She answered, 'They have taken my Lord away, and I do not know where they have laid him.' With these words she turned round and saw Jesus standing there, but she did not recognize him. Jesus asked her, 'Why are you weeping? Who are you looking for?' Thinking it was the gardener, she said, 'If it is you, sir, who removed him, tell me where you have laid him, and I will take him away.' Jesus said, 'Mary!' She turned and said to him, 'Rabbuni!' (which is Hebrew for 'Teacher'). 'Do not cling to me,' said Jesus, 'for I have not yet ascended to the Father. But go to my brothers, and tell them that I am ascending to my Father and your Father, to my God and your God.' Mary of Magdala went to tell the disciples. 'I have seen the Lord!' she said, and gave them his message.

O risen Lord, who in your first appearance to Mary was mistaken for the gardener: be present with us, and show yourself to us in all our mistakes and uncertainties.

Church of South India, adapted

Day 3

The Supper at Emmaus

THAT SAME DAY two of them were on their way to a village called Emmaus, about seven miles from Jerusalem, talking together about all that had happened. As they talked and argued, Jesus himself came up and walked with them; but something prevented them from recognizing him. He asked them, 'What is it you are debating as you walk?' They stood still, their faces full of sadness, and one, called Cleopas, answered, 'Are you the only person staying in Jerusalem not to have heard the news of what has happened there in the last few days?' 'What news?' he said. 'About Jesus of Nazareth,' they replied, 'who, by deeds and words of power, proved himself a prophet in the sight of God and the whole people; and how our chief priests and rulers handed him over to be sentenced to death, and crucified him. But we had been hoping that he was to be the liberator of Israel.'

'How dull you are!' he answered. 'How slow to believe all that the prophets said! Was not the Messiah bound to suffer in this way before entering upon his glory?' Then, starting from Moses and all the prophets, he explained to them in the whole of scripture the things that referred to himself.

By this time they had reached the village to which they were going, and he made as if to continue his journey. But they pressed him: 'Stay with us, for evening approaches, and the day is almost over.' So he went in to stay with them. And when he had sat down with them at table, he took bread and said the blessing; he broke the bread, and offered it to them. Then their eyes were opened, and they recognized him; but he vanished from their sight. They said to one another, 'Were not our hearts on fire as he talked with us on the road and explained the scriptures to us?'

Without a moment's delay they set out and returned to Jerusalem. There they found that the eleven and the rest of the company had assembled. Then they described what had happened on their journey and told how he had made himself known to them in the breaking of the bread.

O God, whose blessed Son did manifest himself to his disciples in the breaking of bread: open, we pray thee, the eyes of our faith, that we may behold thee in all thy works; through the same Jesus Christ our Lord.

William Reed Huntingdon, 1839–1909

Day 4

Doubting Thomas

A S THEY WERE talking about all this, there he was, standing among them. Startled and terrified, they thought they were seeing a ghost. But he said, 'Why are you so perturbed? Why do doubts arise in your minds? Look at my hands and feet. It is I myself. Touch me and see; no ghost has flesh and bones as you can see that I have.' They were still incredulous, still astounded, for it seemed too good to be true. So he asked them, 'Have you anything here to eat?' They offered him a piece of fish they had cooked, which he took and ate before their eyes.

And he said to them, 'This is what I meant by saying, while I was still with you, that everything written about me in the law of Moses and in the prophets and psalms was bound to be fulfilled.' Then he opened their minds to understand the scriptures. 'So you see', he said, 'that scripture foretells the sufferings of the Messiah and his rising from the dead on the third day, and declares that in his name repentance bringing the forgiveness of sins is to be proclaimed to all nations beginning from Jerusalem. You are to be witnesses to it all. I am sending on you the gift promised by my Father. As the Father sent me, so I send you.' Then he breathed on them, saying, 'Receive the Holy Spirit! If you forgive anyone's sins, they are forgiven; if you pronounce them unforgiven, unforgiven they remain.'

One of the Twelve, Thomas the Twin, was not with the rest when Jesus came. So the others kept telling him, 'We have seen the Lord.' But he said, 'Unless I see the mark of the nails on his hands, unless I put my finger into the place where the nails were, and my hand into his side, I will never believe it.'

A week later his disciples were once again in the room, and Thomas was with them. Although the doors were locked, Jesus came and stood among them, saying, 'Peace be with you!' Then he said to Thomas, 'Reach your finger here; look at my hands. Reach your hand here and put it into my side. Be unbelieving no longer, but believe.' Thomas said, 'My Lord and my God!' Jesus said to him, 'Because you have seen me you have found faith. Happy are they who find faith without seeing me.'

Lord God, in whom we live, and move, and have our being, open our eyes that we may behold thy fatherly presence ever about us. Take from us all doubt and distrust. Lift our thoughts up to thee in heaven, and make us to know that all things are possible to us through thy Son, our Redeemer.

Brooke Foss Westcott, 1825–1901

Day 5

Follow Me

S OME TIME LATER, Jesus showed himself to his disciples once again, by the sea of Tiberias. This is how it happened. Simon Peter was with Thomas the Twin, Nathanael from Cana-in-Galilee, the sons of Zebedee, and two other disciples. 'I am going out fishing,' said Simon Peter. 'We will go with you,' said the others. So they set off and got into the boat; but that night they caught nothing.

Morning came, and Jesus was standing on the beach, but the disciples did not know that it was Jesus. He called out to them, 'Friends, have you caught anything?' 'No,' they answered. He said, 'Throw out the net to starboard, and you will make a catch.' They did so, and found they could not haul the net on board, there were so many fish in it. Then the disciple whom Jesus loved said to Peter, 'It is the Lord!' As soon as Simon Peter heard him say, 'It is the Lord,' he fastened his coat about him (for he had stripped) and plunged into the sea. The rest of them came on in the boat, towing the net full of fish. They were only about a hundred yards from land.

When they came ashore, they saw a charcoal fire there with fish laid on it, and some bread. Jesus said, 'Bring some of the fish you have caught.' Simon Peter went on board and hauled the net to land; it was full of big fish, a hundred and fifty-three in all; and yet, many as they were, the net was not torn. Jesus said, 'Come and have breakfast.' None of the disciples dared to ask 'Who are you?' They knew it was the Lord.

After breakfast Jesus said to Simon Peter, 'Simon son of John, do you love me more than these others?' 'Yes, Lord,' he answered, 'you know that I love you.' 'Then feed my lambs,' he said. A second time he asked, 'Simon son of John, do you love me?' 'Yes, Lord, you know I love you.' 'Then tend my sheep.' A third time he said, 'Simon son of John, do you love me?' Peter was hurt that he asked him a third time, 'Do you love me?' 'Lord,' he said, 'you know everything; you know I love you.' Jesus said, 'Then feed my sheep.'

'In very truth I tell you: when you were young you fastened your belt about you and walked where you chose; but when you are old you will stretch out your arms, and a stranger will bind you fast, and carry you where you have no wish to go.' He said this to indicate the manner of death by which Peter was to glorify God.

Then he added, 'Follow me.'

O Saviour Christ, who leads to eternal blessedness those who commit them-selves to you: grant that we, being weak, may not presume to trust in ourselves, but may always have you before our eyes to follow as our guide: that you, who alone knows the way, may lead us to our heavenly desires. To you, with the Father and the Holy Ghost, be glory for ever.

Miles Coverdale, 1488–1568

Day 6

The Great Commission

T HE ELEVEN DISCIPLES made their way to Galilee, to the mountain where Jesus had told them to meet him. When they saw him, they knelt in worship, though some were doubtful. Jesus came near and said to them: 'Full authority in heaven and on earth has been committed to me. Go therefore to all nations and make them my disciples; baptize them in the name of the Father and the Son and the Holy Spirit, and teach them to observe all that I have commanded you. I will be with you always, to the end of time.'

O risen Lord, who in your final appearance on the Mount of Olives, lifted up hands of blessing on all people: be present with us, and grant that our prayers today may be taken up into yours on behalf of he whole world.

Church of South India, adapted

Day 7

The Ascension

A FTER HIS DEATH Jesus was seen by the apostles over a period of forty days and spoke to them about the kingdom of God.

When they were all together, they asked him, 'Lord, is this the time at which you are to restore sovereignty to Israel?' He answered, 'It is not for you to know about dates or times which the Father has set within his own control. But you will receive power when the Holy Spirit comes upon you; and you will bear witness for me in Jerusalem, and throughout all Judaea and Samaria, and even in the farthest corners of the earth.'

After he had said this, he was lifted up before their very eyes, and a cloud took him from their sight.

They were gazing intently into the sky as he went, and all at once there stood beside them two men robed in white, who said, 'Men of Galilee, why stand there looking up into the sky? This Jesus who has been taken from you up to heaven will come in the same way as you have seen him go.'

O Lord Jesus Christ, who after your resurrection from the dead did gloriously ascend into heaven, grant us the aid of your loving-kindness, that according to your promise you may ever dwell with us on earth, and we with you in heaven, where with the Father and the Holy Spirit, you live and reign one God for ever and ever. Amen.

Gelasian Sacramentary, 5th century

WEEK 38

God with Us

Day 1

God Was in Christ

THE LOVE OF CHRIST controls us, once we have reached the conclusion that one man died for all and therefore all mankind has died. He died for all so that those who live should cease to live for themselves, and should live for him who for their sake died and was raised to life. With us therefore worldly standards have ceased to count in our estimate of anyone; even if once they counted in our understanding of Christ, they do so now no longer. For anyone united to Christ, there is a new creation: the old order has gone; a new order has already begun.

All this has been the work of God. He has reconciled us to himself through Christ, and has enlisted us in this ministry of reconciliation: God was in Christ reconciling the world to himself, no longer holding peoples misdeeds against them, and has entrusted us with the message of reconciliation. We are therefore Christ's ambassadors. It is as if God were appealing to you through us: we implore you in Christ's name, be reconciled to God! Christ was innocent of sin, and yet for our sake God made him one with human sinfulness, so that in him we might be made one with the righteousness of God.

> *We praise you, Father, invisible, giver of immortality. You are the source of life and light, the source of all grace and truth; you love us all and you love the poor, you seek reconciliation with all and draw them all to you by sending your dear Son to visit them, who now lives and reigns, with you, Father and the Holy Spirit, one God for ever and ever.*
>
> Serapion, d. after 360

Day 2

God's Gracious Gift

B LESSED BE THE GOD and Father of our Lord Jesus Christ, who has conferred on us in Christ every spiritual blessing in the heavenly realms.
Before the foundation of the world he chose us in Christ to be his people, to be
without blemish in his sight, to be full of love; and he predestined us to be
adopted as his children through Jesus Christ. This was his will and pleasure in
order that the glory of his gracious gift, so graciously conferred on us in his
Beloved, might redound to his praise. In Christ our release is secured and our
sins forgiven through the shedding of his blood.

*Blessed are you, O Lord, for coming to earth as man, You were born that
you might die, and in dying that you might procure our salvation. O mar-
vellous and indescribable love! In you is all sweetness and joy! To contem-
plate your love is to exalt the soul above the world and enable it to abide
alone in joy and rest and tranquillity.*

Angela of Foligno, 1248–1309

Day 3

The Form of God

T AKE TO HEART among yourselves what you find in Christ Jesus: he was in the form of God; yet he laid no claim to equality with God, but made himself nothing, assuming the form of a slave. Bearing the human likeness, sharing the human lot, he humbled himself, and was obedient, even to the point of death, death on a cross! Therefore God raised him to the heights and bestowed on him the name above all names, that at the name of Jesus every knee should bowin heaven, on earth, and in the depths and every tongue acclaim, 'Jesus Christ is Lord,' to the glory of God the Father.

O Lord Jesus Christ, make me worthy to understand the profound mystery of your holy incarnation, which you have worked for our sake and for our salvation. Truly there is nothing so great and wonderful as this, that you, my God, who are the creator of all things, should become a creature, so that we should become like God. You have humbled yourself small that we might be made mighty. You have taken the form of a servant, so that you might confer upon us a royal and divine beauty.

You, who are beyond our understanding, have made yourself understandable to us in Jesus Christ. You, who are the uncreated God, have made yourself a creature for us. You, who are the untouchable One, have made yourself touchable to us. You, who are most high, make us capable of understanding your amazing love and the wonderful things you have done for us. Make us able to understand the mystery of your incarnation, the mystery of your life, example and doctrine, they mystery of your cross and Passion, the mystery of your resurrection and ascension.

Angela of Foligno, 1248–1309

Day 4

The Supremacy of Christ

W<small>E PRAY THAT</small> you may bear fruit in active goodness of every kind, and grow in knowledge of God. He rescued us from the domain of darkness and brought us into the kingdom of his dear Son, through whom our release is secured and our sins are forgiven. He is the image of the invisible God; his is the primacy over all creation. In him everything in heaven and on earth was created, not only things visible but also the invisible orders of thrones, sovereignties, authorities, and powers: the whole universe has been created through him and for him. He exists before all things, and all things are held together in him. He is the head of the body, the church. He is its origin, the first to return from the dead, to become in all things supreme. For in him God in all his fullness chose to dwell, and through him to reconcile all things to himself, making peace through the shedding of his blood on the cross – all things, whether on earth or in heaven.

Thou art the Everlasting Word,
The Father's only Son;
God manifestly seen and heard,
And heaven's beloved One

In thee, most perfectly expressed,
The Father's glories shine:
Of the full Deity possessed,
Eternally divine:

True image of the Infinite,
Whose essence is concealed;
Brightness of uncreated light;
The heart of God revealed.

Josiah Condor, 1789–1855

Day 5

The Fullness of God

S INCE YOU HAVE accepted Christ Jesus as Lord, live in union with him. Be rooted in him, be built in him, grow strong in the faith as you were taught; let your hearts overflow with thankfulness. Be on your guard; let no one capture your minds with hollow and delusive speculations, based on traditions of human teaching and centred on the elemental spirits of the universe and not on Christ.

For it is in Christ that the Godhead in all its fullness dwells embodied, it is in him you have been brought to fulfilment. Every power and authority in the universe is subject to him as head.

O God, my heart is full of thanks that in Christ you have shown me the embodiment of your purpose. Guard my heart against the hollow and delusive spirits of this world, and fill it instead with a strong and satisfying faith in the universal heart of Jesus.

Philip Law

Day 6

Our Great God and Saviour

F OR THE GRACE of God has dawned upon the world with healing for all mankind; and by it we are disciplined to renounce godless ways and worldly desires, and to live a life of temperance, honesty, and godliness in the present age, looking forward to the happy fulfilment of our hope when the splendour of our great God and Saviour Christ Jesus will appear. He it is who sacrificed himself for us, to set us free from all wickedness and to make us his own people, pure and eager to do good.

There was a time when we too were lost in folly and disobedience and were slaves to passions and pleasures of every kind. Our days were passed in malice and envy; hateful ourselves, we loathed one another. But when the kindness and generosity of God our Saviour dawned upon the world, then, not for any good deeds of our own, but because he was merciful, he saved us through the water of rebirth and the renewing power of the Holy Spirit, which he lavished upon us through Jesus Christ our Saviour, so that, justified by his grace, we might in hope become heirs to eternal life.

> *O God,*
> *maker of time and creator of all things,*
> *we your helpless servants*
> *bow our heads before you and so we pray:*
> *send us the blessing of your Spirit*
> *that we may live our lives in all godliness*
> *and in obedience to your commandments.*
> *For you are our God,*
> *the God of salvation and compassion,*
> *and we glorify you,*
> *Father, Son and Holy Spirit,*
> *now and for ever, to the ages of ages.*
>
> Russian Orthodox Church

Day 7

The Radiance of God's Glory

WHEN IN TIMES past God spoke to our forefathers, he spoke in many and varied ways through the prophets. But in this the final age he has spoken to us in his Son, whom he has appointed heir of all things; and through him he created the universe. He is the radiance of God's glory, the stamp of God's very being, and he sustains the universe by his word of power. When he had brought about purification from sins, he took his seat at the right hand of God's Majesty on high, raised as far above the angels as the title he has inherited is superior to theirs.

To which of the angels did God ever say, 'You are my son; today I have become your father,' or again, 'I shall be his father, and he will be my son'? Again, when he presents the firstborn to the world, he says, 'Let all God's angels pay him homage.' Of the angels he says:

He makes his angels winds,
and his ministers flames of fire;

but of the Son:

Your throne, O God, is for ever and ever,
and the sceptre of his kingdom is the sceptre of justice.
    You have loved right and hated wrong;
therefore, O God, your God has set you above your fellows
by anointing you with oil, the token of joy.

And again:

By you, Lord, were earths foundations laid of old,
and the heavens are the work of your hands.
    They will perish, but you remain;
like clothes they will all wear out.
    You will fold them up like a cloak,
they will be changed like any garment.
But you are the same, and your years will have no end.

Almighty God, who in many and various ways didst speak to thy chosen people by the prophets, and hast given us, in thy Son, our Saviour Jesus Christ, the fulfilment of the hope of Israel: hasten, we beseech thee, the coming of the day when all things shall be subject to him, who liveth and reigneth with thee and the Holy Spirit, ever one God, world without end.

Church of South India

PART THREE

Living in the Spirit

The Christian Life: I

Day 1

Controlled by the Spirit

THERE IS NOW no condemnation for those who are united with Christ Jesus. In Christ Jesus the life-giving law of the Spirit has set you free from the law of sin and death. What the law could not do, because human weakness robbed it of all potency, God has done: by sending his own Son in the likeness of our sinful nature and to deal with sin, he has passed judgement against sin within that very nature, so that the commandment of the law may find fulfilment in us, whose conduct is no longer controlled by the old nature, but by the Spirit.

Those who live on the level of the old nature have their outlook formed by it, and that spells death; but those who live on the level of the Spirit have the spiritual outlook, and that is life and peace. For the outlook of the unspiritual nature is enmity with God; it is not subject to the law of God and indeed it cannot be; those who live under its control cannot please God.

May the mind of Christ my Saviour
Live in me from day to day,
By his love and power controlling
All I do and say.

May the peace of God my Father
Rule my life in everything,
That I may be calm to comfort
Sick and sorrowing

May the love of Jesus fill me
As the waters fill the sea;
Him exalting, self abasing,
This is victory.
Katie Barclay Wilkinson, 1859–1928

Day 2

Divine Consolation

P RAISE BE TO the God and Father of our Lord Jesus Christ, the all-merciful
Father, the God whose consolation never fails us! He consoles us in all our
troubles, so that we in turn may be able to console others in any trouble of
theirs and to share with them the consolation we ourselves receive from God.
As Christ's suffering exceeds all measure and extends to us, so too it is through
Christ that our consolation has no limit. If distress is our lot, it is the price we
pay for your consolation and your salvation; if our lot is consolation, it is to
help us to bring you consolation, and strength to face with fortitude the same
sufferings we now endure. And our hope for you is firmly grounded; for we
know that if you share in the suffering, you share also in the consolation.

> *Almighty and merciful God, who art the strength of the weak, the refresh-*
> *ment of the weary, the comfort of the sad, the help of the tempted, the life of*
> *the dying, the God of patience and of all consolation; thou knowest full well*
> *the inner weakness of our nature, how we tremble and quiver before pain,*
> *and cannot bear the cross with thy divine help and support. Help me, then,*
> *O eternal and pitying God, help me to possess my soul in patience, to*
> *maintain unshaken hope in thee, to keep that childlike trust which feels a*
> *Father's heart hidden beneath the cross; so shall I be strengthened with*
> *power according to thy glorious might, in all patience and long-suffering; I*
> *shall be enabled to endure pain and temptation, and, in the very depth of*
> *my suffering, to praise thee with a joyful heart.*
>
> Johann Habermann, 1516–90

Day 3

Work out your Salvation

S O YOU TOO, my friends, must be obedient, as always; even more, now that I am absent, than when I was with you. You must work out your own salvation in fear and trembling; for it is God who works in you, inspiring both the will and the deed, for his own chosen purpose.

Do everything without grumbling or argument. Show yourselves innocent and above reproach, faultless children of God in a crooked and depraved generation, in which you shine like stars in a dark world and proffer the word of life. Then you will be my pride on the day of Christ, proof that I did not run my race in vain or labour in vain.

Almighty God, who has poured upon us the new light of your incarnate Word; grant that the same light enkindled in our hearts may shine forth in our lives; through Jesus Christ our Lord.

Mass of Christmas at dawn, Sarum Rite

Day 4

What Is your Life?

N OW A WORD with all who say, 'Today or the next day we will go off to such and such a town and spend a year there trading and making money.' Yet you have no idea what tomorrow will bring. What is your life after all? You are no more than a mist, seen for a little while and then disappearing. What you ought to say is: 'If it be the Lord's will, we shall live to do so and so.' But instead, you boast and brag, and all such boasting is wrong. What it comes to is that anyone who knows the right thing to do and does not do it is a sinner.

O God our Father, deliver us from the foolishness of self-confidence, from all boasting and vanity, from pride of energy and false notions of success. Teach us that our springs are not in ourselves but in thee, that so far from being able to do what we will, we can neither will nor do any good except by thy grace and with thy help, that it is when we are weak in ourselves that we are strong in thee, that thy power is made perfect in our conscious lack of power that compels is to lay our helplessness on thy strength. Here may we find our rest and feel, pouring through all our impotence, the tides of thy mighty Spirit, for thine is the kingdom, the power and glory.

Robert E. Speer

Day 5

The Corruption of Riches

NEXT A WORD to you who are rich. Weep and wail over the miserable fate overtaking you: your riches have rotted away; your fine clothes are moth-eaten; your silver and gold have corroded, and their corrosion will be evidence against you and consume your flesh like fire. You have piled up wealth in an age that is near its close. The wages you never paid to the men who mowed your fields are crying aloud against you, and the outcry of the reapers has reached the ears of the Lord of Hosts. You have lived on the land in wanton luxury, gorging yourselves and that on the day appointed for your slaughter. You have condemned and murdered the innocent one, who offers no resistance.

O God, the King of righteousness, lead us, we pray you, in the ways of justice and peace; inspire us to break down all tyranny and oppression, to gain for every man his due reward and from every man his due service; that each may live for all, and all may care for each, in the name of Jesus Christ.

William Temple, 1881–1944

Day 6

Live in God's Light

IT WAS THERE from the beginning; we have heard it; we have seen it with our own eyes; we looked upon it, and felt it with our own hands: our theme is the Word which gives life. This life was made visible; we have seen it and bear our testimony; we declare to you the eternal life which was with the Father and was made visible to us. It is this which we have seen and heard that we declare to you also, in order that you may share with us in a common life, that life which we share with the Father and his Son Jesus Christ. We are writing this in order that our joy may be complete.

Here is the message we have heard from him and pass on to you: God is light, and in him there is no darkness at all. If we claim to be sharing in his life while we go on living in darkness, our words and our lives are a lie. But if we live in the light as he himself is in the light, then we share a common life, and the blood of Jesus his Son cleanses us from all sin.

If we claim to be sinless, we are self-deceived and the truth is not in us. If we confess our sins, he is just and may be trusted to forgive our sins and cleanse us from every kind of wrongdoing. If we say we have committed no sin, we make him out to be a liar and his word has no place in us.

Pour into our hearts, Almighty God, the pure serene light of your truth that we may avoid the darkness of sin, who have come to know and fear you, the eternal light; through Jesus Christ our Lord.

Ambrosian Manual

Day 7

God Alone

W<small>E KNOW THAT</small> no child of God commits sin; he is kept safe by the Son of God, and the evil one cannot touch him.

We know that we are of God's family, but that the whole world lies in the power of the evil one.

We know that the Son of God has come and given us understanding to know the true God; indeed we are in him who is true, since we are in his Son Jesus Christ. He is the true God and eternal life. Children, be on your guard against idols.

> *The dearest idol I have known,*
> *Whate'er that idol be,*
> *Help me to tear it from thy throne,*
> *And worship only thee.*
> William Cowper, 1731–1800

The Christian Life: II

Day 1

Banish the Darkness!

ALWAYS REMEMBER THAT this is the hour of crisis: it is high time for you to wake out of sleep, for deliverance is nearer to us now than it was when we believed. It is far on in the night; day is near. Let us therefore throw off the deeds of darkness and put on the armour of light. Let us behave with decency as befits the day: no drunken orgies, no debauchery or vice, no quarrels or jealousies! Let Christ Jesus himself be the armour that you wear; give your unspiritual nature no opportunity to satisfy its desires.

> *Look down, O Lord, from your heavenly throne;*
> *lighten the darkness of the night*
> *with your celestial brightness;*
> *and from the children of light*
> *banish the deeds of darkness;*
> *through Jesus Christ our Lord.*
>
> The Office of Compline

Day 2

Gifts of the Spirit

THERE ARE VARIETIES of gifts, but the same Spirit. There are varieties of service, but the same Lord. There are varieties of activity, but in all of them and in everyone the same God is active. In each of us the Spirit is seen to be at work for some useful purpose. One, through the Spirit, has the gift of wise speech, while another, by the power of the same Spirit, can put the deepest knowledge into words. Another, by the same Spirit, is granted faith; another, by the one Spirit, gifts of healing, and another miraculous powers; another has the gift of prophecy, and another the ability to distinguish true spirits from false; yet another has the gift of tongues of various kinds, and another the ability to interpret them. But all these gifts are the activity of one and the same Spirit, distributing them to each individual at will.

Christ is like a single body with its many limbs and organs, which, many as they are, together make up one body; for in the one Spirit we were all brought into one body by baptism, whether Jews or Greeks, slaves or free; we were all given that one Spirit to drink.

> *Spirit of God, with your holy breath*
> *you cleanse the hearts and minds of your people;*
> *you comfort them when they are in sorrow,*
> *you lead them when they wander from the way,*
> *you kindle them when they are cold,*
> *you knit them together when they are at variance,*
> *and you enrich them with many and various gifts.*
> *We beseech you daily to increase*
> *those gifts which you have entrusted to us;*
> *that with your light before us and within us*
> *we may pass through this world*
> *without stumbling or straying.*
>
> Erasmus, 1466–1536

Day 3

Living God's Word

M AKE NO MISTAKE, my dear friends. Every good and generous action and every perfect gift come from above, from the Father who created the lights of heaven. With him there is no variation, no play of passing shadows. Of his own choice, he brought us to birth by the word of truth to be a kind of first-fruits of his creation.

Of that you may be certain, my dear friends. But everyone should be quick to listen, slow to speak, and slow to be angry. For human anger does not promote God's justice. Then discard everything sordid, and every wicked excess, and meekly accept the message planted in your hearts, with its power to save you.

Only be sure you act on the message, and do not merely listen and so deceive yourselves. Anyone who listens to the message but does not act on it is like somebody looking in a mirror at the face nature gave him; he glances at himself and goes his way, and promptly forgets what he looked like. But he who looks into the perfect law, the law that makes us free, and does not turn away, remembers what he hears; he acts on it, and by so acting he will find happiness.

> *O Lord, we most humbly beseech thee to give us grace*
> *not only to be hearers of the Word,*
> *but also doers of the same;*
> *not only to love*
> *but also to live thy Gospel;*
> *not only to profess,*
> *but also to practise thy blessed commandments,*
> *unto the honour of thy holy name.*
>
> Thomas Becon, 1512–67

Day 4

Children of Light

ABOUT DATES AND TIMES, my friends, there is no need to write to you, for you yourselves know perfectly well that the day of the Lord comes like a thief in the night. While they are saying, All is peaceful, all secure, destruction is upon them, sudden as the pangs that come on a woman in childbirth; and there will be no escape. But you, friends, are not in the dark; the day will not come upon you like a thief. You are all children of light, children of day. We do not belong to night and darkness, and we must not sleep like the rest, but keep awake and sober. Sleepers sleep at night, and drunkards get drunk at night, but we, who belong to the daylight, must keep sober, armed with the breastplate of faith and love, and the hope of salvation for a helmet. God has not destined us for retribution, but for the full attainment of salvation through our Lord Jesus Christ. He died for us so that awake or asleep we might live in company with him. Therefore encourage one another, build one another up as indeed you do.

God, the creator of both summer and winter, who causest light to shine out of the thick gloom, and bringest good out of evil: give us grace so to flee what thou forbiddest, that we may cast aside the works of darkness, and so to choose what thou commandest, that we may be children of light; but since darkness and light obey thee, give all the messengers of thy providence charge over us, that, serving thee in peace and thankfulness, we may be brought through humility to serve thee in glory.

Rowland Williams, 1817–1870

Day 5

Don't Give Up!

T HESE ARE OUR instructions to you, friends, in the name of our Lord Jesus Christ: hold aloof from every Christian who falls into idle habits, and disregards the tradition you received from us. You yourselves know how you ought to follow our example: you never saw us idling; we did not accept free hospitality from anyone; night and day in toil and drudgery we worked for a living, rather than be a burden to any of you not because we do not have the right to maintenance, but to set an example for you to follow. Already during our stay with you we laid down this rule: anyone who will not work shall not eat. We mention this because we hear that some of you are idling their time away, minding everybody's business but their own. We instruct and urge such people in the name of the Lord Jesus Christ to settle down to work and earn a living.

My friends, you must never tire of doing right.

O God, who has commanded that no one should be idle, give us grace to employ our talents and faculties in the service appointed for us, that whatever our hand finds to do, we may do it with our might.

James Martineau, 1805–1900

Day 6

Renewed in Mind and Spirit

H ERE THEN IS my word to you, and I urge it on you in the Lord's name: give up living as pagans do with their futile notions. Their minds are closed, they are alienated from the life that is in God, because ignorance prevails among them and their hearts have grown hard as stone. Dead to all feeling, they have abandoned themselves to vice, and there is no indecency that they do not practise. But that is not how you learned Christ. For were you not told about him, were you not as Christians taught the truth as it is in Jesus? Renouncing your former way of life, you must lay aside the old human nature which, deluded by its desires, is in process of decay: you must be renewed in mind and spirit, and put on the new nature created in God's likeness, which shows itself in the upright and devout life called for by the truth.

O Lord, who art full of mercy and compassion, whom I beseech to look down upon me with the eye of mercy, and for the sake of Jesus firm me for thy acceptance, by giving me a hearty and deep repentance for all my sins past; grant that I may from this moment become a new creature, utterly forsaking every evil way.

Elizabeth Percy, 1667–1722, adapted

Day 7

The New Nature

S O PUT TO DEATH those parts of you which belong to the earth: fornication, indecency, lust, evil desires, and the ruthless greed which is nothing less than idolatry; on these divine retribution falls. This is the way you yourselves once lived; but now have done with rage, bad temper, malice, slander, filthy talk: banish them all from your lips! Do not lie to one another, now that you have discarded the old human nature and the conduct that goes with it, and have put on the new nature which is constantly being renewed in the image of its Creator and brought to know God. There is no question here of Greek and Jew, circumcised and uncircumcised, barbarian, Scythian, slave and freeman; but Christ is all, and is in all.

Put on, then, garments that suit God's chosen and beloved people: compassion, kindness, humility, gentleness, patience. Be tolerant with one another and forgiving, if any of you has cause for complaint: you must forgive as the Lord forgave you. Finally, to bind everything together and complete the whole, there must be love. Let Christ's peace be arbiter in your decisions, the peace to which you were called as members of a single body. Always be thankful. Let the gospel of Christ dwell among you in all its richness; teach and instruct one another with all the wisdom it gives you.

O God the Father, origin of divinity, good beyond all that is good, fair beyond all that is fair; in whom is calmness, peace, and concord; do thou make up the dissensions which divide us from each other, and bring us back into a unity of love, which may bear some likeness to thy divine nature. And as thou art above all things, make us one by the unanimity of a good mind, that through the embrace of charity and the bonds of affection, we may be spiritually one, as well in ourselves as in each other, through that peace of thine which maketh all things peaceful, and through the grace, mercy, and tenderness of thy Son, Jesus Christ.

Liturgy of St Dionysius, 9th century

Resisting Temptation

Day 1

At God's Disposal

W E KNOW THAT our old humanity has been crucified with Christ, for the destruction of the sinful self, so that we may no longer be slaves to sin, because death cancels the claims of sin. But if we thus died with Christ, we believe that we shall also live with him, knowing as we do that Christ, once raised from the dead, is never to die again: he is no longer under the dominion of death. When he died, he died to sin, once for all, and now that he lives, he lives to God. In the same way you must regard yourselves as dead to sin and alive to God, in union with Christ Jesus.

Therefore sin must no longer reign in your mortal body, exacting obedience to the body's desires. You must no longer put any part of it at sin's disposal, as an implement for doing wrong. Put yourselves instead at the disposal of God; think of yourselves as raised from death to life, and yield your bodies to God as implements for doing right. Sin shall no longer be your master, for you are no longer under law, but under grace.

> *Speak, Lord, for your servant hears.*
> *Grant us ears to hear,*
> *eyes to see,*
> *wills to obey,*
> *hearts to love;*
> *then declare what you will,*
> *reveal what you will,*
> *command what you will,*
> *demand what you will.*
> Christina Rossetti, 1830–1894

Day 2

The Inner Battle

WE KNOW THAT the law is spiritual; but I am not: I am unspiritual, sold as a slave to sin. I do not even acknowledge my own actions as mine, for what I do is not what I want to do, but what I detest. But if what I do is against my will, then clearly I agree with the law and hold it to be admirable. This means that it is no longer I who perform the action, but sin that dwells in me. For I know that nothing good dwells in my unspiritual self, I mean for though the will to do good is there, the ability to effect it is not. The good which I want to do, I fail to do; but what I do is the wrong which is against my will; and if what I do is against my will, clearly it is no longer I who am the agent, but sin that has its dwelling in me.

I discover this principle, then: that when I want to do right, only wrong is within my reach. In my inmost self I delight in the law of God, but I perceive in my outward actions a different law, fighting against the law that my mind approves, and making me a prisoner under the law of sin which controls my conduct. Wretched creature that I am, who is there to rescue me from this state of death? Who but God? Thanks be to him through Jesus Christ our Lord! To sum up then: left to myself I serve God's law with my mind, but with my unspiritual nature I serve the law of sin.

My thoughts confuse and cloud my mind. I am in despair because my guilt is vaster than the ocean and my sins more numerous than the waves of the sea. When I remember how I have fallen, I tremble at the thought of your justice. I dare not look upwards, because my sins reach as high as the heavens. The mere sight of the earth is an accusation to me, because my offences exceed the number of its inhabitants. Have pity on me, Lord.

Rabbula of Edessa, d.435

Day 3

Exposed to the Light

FORNICATION AND INDECENCY of any kind, or ruthless greed, must not be so much as mentioned among you, as befits the people of God. No coarse, stupid, or flippant talk: these things are out of place; you should rather be thanking God. For be very sure of this: no one given to fornication or vice, or the greed which makes an idol of gain, has any share in the kingdom of Christ and of God. Let no one deceive you with shallow arguments; it is for these things that divine retribution falls on God's rebel subjects. Have nothing to do with them. Though you once were darkness, now as Christians you are light. Prove yourselves at home in the light, for where light is, there is a harvest of goodness, righteousness, and truth. Learn to judge for yourselves what is pleasing to the Lord; take no part in the barren deeds of darkness, but show them up for what they are. It would be shameful even to mention what is done in secret. But everything is shown up by being exposed to the light, and whatever is exposed to the light itself becomes light.

Cause, O Lord, we beseech thee, the pure light of thy divine knowledge to shine in our hearts, and open the eyes of our understanding, that we may comprehend the precepts of thy gospel. Plant in us the fear of thy judgements, that we, overcoming all carnal lusts, may seek a heavenly citizenship, doing always such things as shall well please thee. For thou art the illumination of our souls and bodies, Christ our God; and to thee, with the Father and the Holy Spirit, we ascribe glory, honour and power.

Sabine Baring-Gould, 1834–1924

Day 4

The Root of All Evil

W E BROUGHT NOTHING into this world, and we can take nothing out; if we have food and clothing let us rest content. Those who want to be rich fall into temptations and snares and into many foolish and harmful desires which plunge people into ruin and destruction. The love of money is the root of all evil, and in pursuit of it some have wandered from the faith and spiked themselves on many a painful thorn.

But you, man of God, must shun all that, and pursue justice, piety, integrity, love, fortitude, and gentleness. Run the great race of faith and take hold of eternal life, for to this you were called.

> *O my God, give me thy grace so that the things of this earth and things more naturally pleasing to me, may not be as close as thou art to me. Keep thou my eyes, my ears, my heart from clinging to the things of this world. Break my bonds, raise my heart. Keep my whole being fixed on thee. Let me never lose sight of thee; and while I gaze on thee, let my love of thee grow more and more every day.*
>
> John Henry Newman, 1801–90

Day 5

Perfect through Sufferings

IN BRINGING MANY sons to glory it was fitting that God, for whom and through whom all things exist, should make the pioneer of their salvation perfect through sufferings; for he who consecrates and those who are consecrated are all of one stock. That is why he does not shrink from calling men his brothers, when he says, 'I will make your fame known to my brothers; in the midst of the assembly I will praise you'; and again, 'I will keep my trust fixed on him'; and again, 'Here am I, and the children whom God has given me.' Since the children share in flesh and blood, he too shared in them, so that by dying he might break the power of him who had death at his command, that is, the devil, and might liberate those who all their life had been in servitude through fear of death. Clearly they are not angels whom he helps, but the descendants of Abraham.

Therefore he had to be made like his brothers in every way, so that he might be merciful and faithful as their high priest before God, to make expiation for the sins of the people. Because he himself has passed through the test of suffering, he is able to help those who are in the midst of their test.

Almighty God, whose most dear Son went not up to joy but he suffered pain, and entered not into glory before he was crucified; mercifully grant that we, walking in the way of the cross, may find it none other than the way of life and peace; through the same, thy Son, Jesus Christ our Lord.

William Reed Huntington, 1838–1909

Day 6

The Source of Temptation

HAPPY IS THE MAN who stands up to trial! Having passed that test he will receive in reward the life which God has promised to those who love him. No one when tempted should say, I am being tempted by God; for God cannot be tempted by evil and does not himself tempt anyone. Temptation comes when anyone is lured and dragged away by his own desires; then desire conceives and gives birth to sin, and sin when it is full-grown breeds death.

> *Truly, Lord,*
> *lead us not into temptation,*
> *but deliver us from evil;*
> *for your abundant mercy shows that we, through our great infirmity,*
> *are unable to resist it.*
> *Grant that we may find a way whereby we may be able to withstand*
> *temptation;*
> *for you have given us power to tread upon serpents and scorpions,*
> *and all power of the enemy.*
> *Amen.*
>
> Liturgy of St Mark

Day 7

Ready for Action

Y OUR MINDS MUST therefore be stripped for action and fully alert. Fix your hopes on the grace which is to be yours when Jesus Christ is revealed. Be obedient to God your Father, and do not let your characters be shaped any longer by the desires you cherished in your days of ignorance. He who called you is holy; like him, be holy in all your conduct. Does not scripture say, 'You shall be holy, for I am holy'?

> *Breathe in me, Holy Spirit,*
> *that I may think what is holy.*
> *Move me, Holy Spirit,*
> *that I may do what is holy.*
> *Attract me, Holy Spirit,*
> *that I may love what is holy.*
> *Strengthen me, Holy Spirit,*
> *that I may guard what is holy.*
> *Guard me, Holy Spirit,*
> *that I may keep what is holy.*
> Augustine of Hippo, 354–430

WEEK 42

Persisting in Prayer

Day 1

The Spirit within

IN THE SAME WAY the Spirit comes to the aid of our weakness. We do not even know how we ought to pray, but through our inarticulate groans the Spirit himself is pleading for us, and God who searches our inmost being knows what the Spirit means, because he pleads for God's people as God himself wills; and in everything, as we know, he co-operates for good with those who love God and are called according to his purpose. For those whom God knew before ever they were, he also ordained to share the likeness of his Son.

> *O my Father, I have moments of deep unrest – moments when I know not what to ask by reason of the very excess of my wants. I have in these hours no words for thee, no conscious prayers for thee.*
>
> *My cry seems purely worldly; I want only the wings of a dove that I may flee away. Yet all the time thou hast accepted my unrest as a prayer. thou hast received the nameless longings of my heart as the intercessions of thy Spirit.*
>
> *They are not yet the intercessions of my spirit; I know not what to ask. But thou knowest what I ask, O God. Thou knowest the name of that need which lies beneath my speechless groan. Thou knowest that, because I am made in thine image, I can find rest only in what gives rest to thee; therefore thou hast counted my unrest unto me for righteousness, and hast called my groaning thy Spirit's prayer.*
>
> George Matheson, 1842–1906

Day 2

The Word Is near You

B UT THE RIGHTEOUSNESS that comes by faith says, Do not say to yourself, 'Who can go up to heaven?' (that is, to bring Christ down) or, 'Who can go down to the abyss?' (to bring Christ up from the dead). And what does it say next? The word is near you: it is on your lips and in your heart; and that means the word of faith which we proclaim. If the confession Jesus is Lord is on your lips, and the faith that God raised him from the dead is in your heart, you will find salvation. For faith in the heart leads to righteousness, and confession on the lips leads to salvation.

> *Instruct my speech and touch my lips with graciousness;*
> *make me keen to understand, quick to learn,*
> *and able to remember;*
> *and keep me finely tuned*
> *to interpret your word,*
> *for you are God for ever and ever.*
>
> Thomas Aquinas, 1225–74

Day 3

Take Everything to God

THE LORD IS NEAR; do not be anxious, but in everything make your requests known to God in prayer and petition with thanksgiving. Then the peace of God, which is beyond all understanding, will guard your hearts and your thoughts in Christ Jesus.

Most loving Father, who willest us to give thanks for all things, to dread nothing but the loss of thee, and to cast all our care on thee who carest for us; preserve us from faithless fears and worldly anxieties, and grant that no clouds of this mortal life may hide from us the light of that love which is immortal, and which thou hast manifested unto us in thy Son, Jesus Christ our Lord.

William Bright, 1824–1901

Day 4

Thank God!

ALWAYS BE THANKFUL. Let the gospel of Christ dwell among you in all its richness; teach and instruct one another with all the wisdom it gives you. With psalms and hymns and spiritual songs, sing from the heart in gratitude to God. Let every word and action, everything you do, be in the name of the Lord Jesus, and give thanks through him to God the Father.

> *Thou hast given so much to me,*
> *give one thing more – a grateful heart;*
> *not thankful when it pleases me,*
> *as if thy blessings had spare days;*
> *but such a heart whose very pulse may be*
> *thy praise.*
>
> George Herbert, 1593–1633

Day 5

Pray for Everyone

FIRST OF ALL, then, I urge that petitions, prayers, intercessions, and thanksgivings be offered for everyone, for sovereigns and for all in high office so that we may lead a tranquil and quiet life, free to practise our religion with dignity. Such prayer is right, and approved by God our Saviour, whose will it is that all should find salvation and come to know the truth. For there is one God, and there is one mediator between God and man, Christ Jesus, himself man, who sacrificed himself to win freedom for all mankind.

> *Grant thy compassion to go before us, thy compassion to come behind us; before us in undertaking, behind us in our ending. And what more shall I say, unless that thy will be done, who dost will that all should be saved.*
>
> Alcuin of York, 735–804

Day 6

The Example of Jesus

I N THE COURSE of his earthly life he offered up prayers and petitions, with loud cries and tears, to God who was able to deliver him from death. Because of his devotion his prayer was heard: son though he was, he learned obedience through his sufferings, and, once perfected, he became the source of eternal salvation for all who obey him,

Almighty God, from whom every good prayer cometh, deliver us, when we draw nigh to thee, from coldness of heart and wanderings of mind, that with steadfast thought and kindled desire we may worship thee in the faith and spirit of Jesus Christ our lord.

William Bright, 1824–1901

Day 7

The Power of Prayer

IS ANYONE AMONG you in trouble? Let him pray. Is anyone in good heart? Let him sing praises. Is one of you ill? Let him send for the elders of the church to pray over him and anoint him with oil in the name of the Lord; the prayer offered in faith will heal the sick man, the Lord will restore him to health, and if he has committed sins they will be forgiven. Therefore confess your sins to one another, and pray for one another, that you may be healed. A good man's prayer is very powerful and effective. Elijah was a man just like us; yet when he prayed fervently that there should be no rain, the land had no rain for three and a half years; when he prayed again, the rain poured down and the land bore crops once more.

> *Assist me mercifully, O Lord, in all my supplications and prayers, that I may not draw near to thee with my lips while my heart is far from thee. Give me a hearty desire to pray, and grace to pray faithfully, that I may live under thy most mighty protection here, and praise thee hereafter; through Jesus Christ.*
>
> Sabine Baring-Gould, 1834–1924

WEEK 43

Courage and Confidence

Day 1

The Encouragement of Scripture

T HE SCRIPTURES WRITTEN long ago were all written for our instruction, in order that through the encouragement they give us we may maintain our hope with perseverance. And may God, the source of all perseverance and all encouragement, grant that you may agree with one another after the manner of Christ Jesus, and so with one mind and one voice may praise the God and Father of our Lord Jesus Christ.

> *Blessed Lord, which hast caused all holy scriptures to be written for our learning: grant us that we may in such wise hear them, read, mark, learn and inwardly digest them: that by patience and comfort of thy holy word, we may embrace and ever hold fast the blessed hope of everlasting life, which thou hast given us in our saviour Jesus Christ.*
>
> Thomas Cranmer, 1489–1556

Day 2

The Armour of God

FIND YOUR STRENGTH in the Lord, in his mighty power. Put on the full armour provided by God, so that you may be able to stand firm against the stratagems of the devil. For our struggle is not against human foes, but against cosmic powers, against the authorities and potentates of this dark age, against the superhuman forces of evil in the heavenly realms. Therefore, take up the armour of God; then you will be able to withstand them on the evil day and, after doing your utmost, to stand your ground.

Stand fast, I say. Fasten on the belt of truth; for a breastplate put on integrity; let the shoes on your feet be the gospel of peace, to give you firm footing; and, with all these, take up the great shield of faith, with which you will be able to quench all the burning arrows of the evil one. Accept salvation as your helmet, and the sword which the Spirit gives you, the word of God. Constantly ask God's help in prayer, and pray always in the power of the Spirit.

> *Come quickly to help me,*
> *O Lord God my salvation,*
> *for the battle is great*
> *and the adversaries are powerful.*
> *The enemy is hostile,*
> *the invisible foe fighting through visible forms.*
> *Come quickly, therefore, to help us,*
> *and assist us through your Holy Son,*
> *our Lord Jesus Christ,*
> *through whom you have redeemed us all,*
> *through whom be glory and power to you*
> *for ever and ever.*

> Origen, 185–254

Day 3

Firm in the Faith

WE ARE ALWAYS bound to thank God for you, my friends beloved by the Lord. From the beginning of time God chose you to find salvation in the Spirit who consecrates you and in the truth you believe. It was for this that he called you through the gospel we brought, so that you might come to possess the splendour of our Lord Jesus Christ.

Stand firm then, my friends, and hold fast to the traditions which you have learned from us by word or by letter. And may our Lord Jesus Christ himself and God our Father, who has shown us such love, and in his grace has given us such unfailing encouragement and so sure a hope, still encourage and strengthen you in every good deed and word.

> *O Lord, my God, to thee and to thy service I devote myself, soul, body, and spirit, with all their powers and faculties. Fill my memory with the words of thy law, enlighten my understanding with the illumination of thy Holy Ghost, and may all the wishes and desires of my will centre in what thou hast commanded. Be ever with me, and because through the weakness of my mortal nature I can do no good thing without thee, grant me the help of thy grace, that in keeping thy commandments I may please thee both in will and deed; through Jesus Christ our Lord.*
>
> Phillips Brooks, 1835–93

Day 4

Full Assurance

S INCE THEREFORE WE have a great high priest who has passed through the heavens, Jesus the Son of God, let us hold fast to the faith we profess. Ours is not a high priest unable to sympathize with our weaknesses, but one who has been tested in every way as we are, only without sinning. Let us therefore boldly approach the throne of grace, in order that we may receive mercy and find grace to give us timely help.

My friends, the blood of Jesus makes us free to enter the sanctuary with confidence by the new and living way which he has opened for us through the curtain, the way of his flesh. We have a great priest set over the household of God; so let us make our approach in sincerity of heart and the full assurance of faith, inwardly cleansed from a guilty conscience, and outwardly washed with pure water. Let us be firm and unswerving in the confession of our hope, for the giver of the promise is to be trusted.

Oh my Father, let me thank thee for thy mercies to me, that thou hast drawn me to thee by the cords of love. What shall I render to the Lord for all his goodness. I would pay my vows in his courts this day. I would dedicate my life to him. I would live with a single eye to his service. Yet, oh my Saviour, thou who hast borne our human nature knowest how weak we are, how utterly unable to do anything of ourselves. Thou wilt pity me and support me. Oh my Father in heaven enable me daily to offer up fervent supplications to that throne of mercy from which none ever went empty away. Enable me to feel that what thou hast promised thou wilt surely perform. Lord in whom shall we trust, if not in thee?

Mary Anne Randolph Custis Lee, 1807–73

Day 5

Inner Strength

D O NOT LIVE for money; be content with what you have, for God has said, I will never leave you or desert you. So we can take courage and say, The Lord is my helper, I will not fear; what can man do to me?

Remember your leaders, who spoke God's message to you. Keep before you the outcome of their life and follow the example of their faith.

Jesus Christ is the same yesterday, today, and for ever. So do not be swept off your course by all sorts of outlandish teachings; it is good that we should gain inner strength from the grace of God.

Oppressed with sin and woe,
A burdened heart I bear;
Opposed by many a mighty foe,
Yet I will not despair.

I feel that I am weak,
And prone to every sin;
But thou, who giv'st to those who seek,
Wilt give me strength within.

In my redeemer's name,
I give myself to thee;
And, all unworthy as I am,
My God will cherish me.

Anne Bronte, 1820–49

Day 6

Wait in Patience

Y OU MUST BE patient, my friends, until the Lord comes. Consider: the farmer looking for the precious crop from his land can only wait in patience until the early and late rains have fallen. You too must be patient and stout-hearted, for the coming of the Lord is near. My friends, do not blame your troubles on one another, or you will fall under judgement; and there at the door stands the Judge. As a pattern of patience under ill-treatment, take the prophets who spoke in the name of the Lord. We count those happy who stood firm. You have heard how Job stood firm, and you have seen how the Lord treated him in the end, for the Lord is merciful and compassionate.

O thou God of patience, give us patience in the time of trial, and steadfast-ness to endure to the end.

Bernhard Albrecht, 1569–1636

Day 7

A Firm Foundation

B<small>E ON THE ALERT</small>! Wake up! Your enemy the devil, like a roaring lion, prowls around looking for someone to devour. Stand up to him, firm in your faith, and remember that your fellow-Christians in this world are going through the same kinds of suffering. After your brief suffering, the God of all grace, who called you to his eternal glory in Christ, will himself restore, establish, and strengthen you on a firm foundation. All power belongs to him for ever and ever! Amen.

> *May Jesus Christ, the King of glory, help us to make the right use of all the suffering that comes to us and to offer to him the incense of a patient and trustful heart; for his name's sake.*
>
> Johannes Tauler, 1300–61

WEEK 44

Faith and Hope

Day 1

The Hope of Glory

N OW THAT WE have been justified through faith, we are at peace with God through our Lord Jesus Christ, who has given us access to that grace in which we now live; and we exult in the hope of the divine glory that is to be ours. More than this: we even exult in our present sufferings, because we know that suffering is a source of endurance, endurance of approval, and approval of hope. Such hope is no fantasy; through the Holy Spirit he has given us, God's love has flooded our hearts.

> *O Christ, our morning star,*
> *splendour of light eternal,*
> *shining with the glory of the rainbow,*
> *come and waken us*
> *from the greyness of our apathy*
> *and renew in us your gift of hope.*
>
> Bede, 672–735

Day 2

Inwardly Renewed

S CRIPTURE SAYS, I believed, and therefore I spoke out, and we too, in the same spirit of faith, believe and therefore speak out; for we know that he who raised the Lord Jesus to life will with Jesus raise us too, and bring us to his presence.

No wonder we do not lose heart! Though our outward humanity is in decay, yet day by day we are inwardly renewed. Our troubles are slight and short-lived, and their outcome is an eternal glory which far outweighs them, provided our eyes are fixed, not on the things that are seen, but on the things that are unseen; for what is seen is transient, what is unseen is eternal. We know that if the earthly frame that houses us today is demolished, we possess a building which God has provided – a house not made by human hands, eternal and in heaven.

> *Lift up our souls, O Lord,*
> *above the weary round of harassing thoughts,*
> *to your eternal presence.*
> *Lift up our minds*
> *to the pure, bright, serene*
> *atmosphere of your presence,*
> *that we may breathe freely,*
> *and rest there in your love.*
> *From there, surrounded by your peace,*
> *may we return to do or to bear*
> *whatever shall best please you,*
> *O blessed Lord.*

Edward Pusey, 1800–82

Day 3

Knowing Christ

I COUNT EVERYTHING sheer loss, far outweighed by the gain of knowing Christ Jesus my Lord, for whose sake I did in fact forfeit everything. I count it so much rubbish, for the sake of gaining Christ and finding myself in union with him, with no righteousness of my own based on the law, nothing but the righteousness which comes from faith in Christ, given by God in response to faith. My one desire is to know Christ and the power of his resurrection, and to share his sufferings in growing conformity with his death, in hope of somehow attaining the resurrection from the dead.

It is not that I have already achieved this. I have not yet reached perfection, but I press on, hoping to take hold of that for which Christ once took hold of me. My friends, I do not claim to have hold of it yet. What I do say is this: forgetting what is behind and straining towards what lies ahead, I press towards the finishing line, to win the heavenly prize to which God has called me in Christ Jesus.

> *O God, who hast commanded us to be perfect, as thou art perfect; put into my heart; I pray thee, a continual desire to obey thy holy will. Teach me day by day what thou wouldst have me do, and give me grace and power to fulfil the same. May I never from love of ease, decline the path which thou pointest out, nor, from fear of shame, turn away from it.*
> Henry Alford, 1810–71

Day 4

An Anchor of the Soul

G OD IS NOT so unjust as to forget what you have done for love of his name in rendering service to his people, as you still do. But we should dearly like each one of you to show the same keenness to the end, until your hope is fully realized. We want you not to be lax, but to imitate those who, through faith and patience, receive the promised inheritance.

When God made his promise to Abraham, because he had no one greater to swear by he swore by himself: I vow that I will bless you abundantly and multiply your descendants. Thus it was that Abraham, after patient waiting, obtained the promise. People swear by what is greater than themselves, and making a statement on oath sets a limit to what can be called in question; and so, since God desired to show even more clearly to the heirs of his promise how immutable was his purpose, he guaranteed it by an oath.

Here, then, are two irrevocable acts in which God could not possibly play us false. They give powerful encouragement to us, who have laid claim to his protection by grasping the hope set before us. We have that hope as an anchor for our lives, safe and secure.

Save us from an evil heart of unbelief. In pressing difficulties, how ready are we to distrust thy goodness! How hard we find it, to rely upon thy word and thy invisible power! May we receive thy promises in the full assurance of faith, and wait the accomplishment of them in hope, though all things seem to go contrary to them.

Henry Venn, 1725–97

Day 5

A Better Country

F AITH GIVES SUBSTANCE to our hopes and convinces us of realities we do not see. It was for their faith that the people of old won God's approval.

Although they had not received the things promised, yet they had seen them far ahead and welcomed them, and acknowledged themselves to be strangers and aliens without fixed abode on earth. Those who speak in that way show plainly that they are looking for a country of their own. If their thoughts had been with the country they had left, they could have found opportunity to return. Instead, we find them longing for a better country, a heavenly one. That is why God is not ashamed to be called their God; for he has a city ready for them.

O Lord, who by triumphing over the power of darkness, didst prepare our place in the new Jerusalem, grant us to praise thee in that city whereof thou art the light, where with the Father and the Holy Spirit thou livest and reigneth, world without end.

William Bright, 1824–1901

Day 6

Faith and Works

WHAT GOOD IS IT, my friends, for someone to say he has faith when his actions do nothing to show it? Can that faith save him? Suppose a fellow-Christian, whether man or woman, is in rags with not enough food for the day, and one of you says, 'Goodbye, keep warm, and have a good meal,' but does nothing to supply their bodily needs, what good is that? So with faith; if it does not lead to action, it is by itself a lifeless thing.

But someone may say: 'One chooses faith, another action.' To which I reply: 'Show me this faith you speak of with no actions to prove it, while I by my actions will prove to you my faith.' You have faith and believe that there is one God. Excellent! Even demons have faith like that, and it makes them tremble. Do you have to be told, you fool, that faith divorced from action is futile? Was it not by his action, in offering his son Isaac upon the altar, that our father Abraham was justified? Surely you can see faith was at work in his actions, and by these actions his faith was perfected? Here was fulfilment of the words of scripture: Abraham put his faith in God, and that faith was counted to him as righteousness, and he was called God's friend. You see then it is by action and not by faith alone that a man is justified. The same is true also of the prostitute Rahab. Was she not justified by her action in welcoming the messengers into her house and sending them away by a different route? As the body is dead when there is no breath left in it, so faith divorced from action is dead.

I pray you, O most gentle Jesus, give me lively faith, a firm hope and perfect charity, so that I may love you with all my heart and all my soul and all my strength. Make me firm and steadfast in good works and grant me perseverance in your service so that I may be able to please you always.

Clare of Assisi, 1194–1253

Day 7

Faith's Victory

E VERYONE WHO BELIEVES that Jesus is the Christ is a child of God. To love the parent means to love his child. It follows that when we love God and obey his commands we love his children too. For to love God is to keep his commands; and these are not burdensome, because every child of God overcomes the world. Now, the victory by which the world is overcome is our faith, for who is victor over the world but he who believes that Jesus is the Son of God?

> *Set my heart on fire with the love of thee, most loving Father, and then to do thy will, and to obey thy commandments, will not be grievous to me. For to him that loveth, nothing is difficult, nothing is impossible; because love is stronger than death. Oh, may love fill and rule my heart. For then there will spring up and be cherished between thee and me a likeness of character and union of will, so that I may choose and refuse what thou dost. May thy will be done in me and by me for ever.*
>
> Jacobus Horstius Merlo, 1597–1664

WEEK 45

Humility and Service

Day 1

A Living Sacrifice

I IMPLORE YOU BY God's mercy to offer your very selves to him: a living sacrifice, dedicated and fit for his acceptance, the worship offered by mind and heart. Conform no longer to the pattern of this present world, but be transformed by the renewal of your minds. Then you will be able to discern the will of God, and to know what is good, acceptable, and perfect.

By authority of the grace God has given me I say to everyone among you: do not think too highly of yourself, but form a sober estimate based on the measure of faith that God has dealt to each of you.

Stir us up to offer to you, O Lord, our bodies, our souls, our spirits, in all we love and all we learn, in all we plan and all we do, to offer our labours, our pleasures, our sorrows to you; to work through them for your kingdom, to live as those who are not their own, but bought with your blood.

Charles Kingsley, 1819–75

Day 2

Do Not Seek Revenge

D O NOT BE proud, but be ready to mix with humble people. Do not keep thinking how wise you are.

Never pay back evil for evil. Let your aims be such as all count honourable. If possible, so far as it lies with you, live at peace with all. My dear friends, do not seek revenge, but leave a place for divine retribution; for there is a text which reads,

'Vengeance is mine, says the Lord, I will repay.' But there is another text: 'If your enemy is hungry, feed him; if he is thirsty, give him a drink'; by doing this you will heap live coals on his head. Do not let evil conquer you, but use good to conquer evil.

May I be no man's enemy, and may I be the friend of that which is eternal and abides.

May I love, seek and attain only that which is good.

May I win no victory that harms either me or my opponent.

May I always keep tame that which rages within me.

May I accustom myself to be gentle, and never be angry with people because of circumstances.

May I never discuss who is wicked and what wicked things he has done, but know good men and follow in their footsteps.

Eusebius, 3rd century

Day 3

Do Not Pass Judgement

ACCEPT ANYONE WHO IS WEAK in faith without debate about his misgivings. For instance, one person may have faith strong enough to eat all kinds of food, while another who is weaker eats only vegetables. Those who eat meat must not look down on those who do not, and those who do not eat meat must not pass judgement on those who do; for God has accepted them. Who are you to pass judgement on someone else's servant? Whether he stands or falls is his own Master's business; and stand he will, because his Master has power to enable him to stand.

Again, some make a distinction between this day and that; others regard all days alike. Everyone must act on his own convictions. Those who honour the day honour the Lord, and those who eat meat also honour the Lord, since when they eat they give thanks to God; and those who abstain have the Lord in mind when abstaining, since they too give thanks to God.

For none of us lives, and equally none of us dies, for himself alone. If we live, we live for the Lord; and if we die, we die for the Lord. So whether we live or die, we belong to the Lord. This is why Christ died and lived again, to establish his lordship over both dead and living. You, then, why do you pass judgement on your fellow-Christian? And you, why do you look down on your fellow-Christian? We shall all stand before God's tribunal; for we read in scripture, 'As I live, says the Lord, to me every knee shall bow and every tongue acknowledge God.' So, you see, each of us will be answerable to God.

Let us therefore cease judging one another, but rather make up our minds to place no obstacle or stumbling block in a fellow-Christian's way.

> *Grant me, O Lord, to know what is worth knowing,*
> *to love what is worth loving,*
> *to praise what delights you most,*
> *to value what is precious in your sight,*
> *to hate what is offensive to you.*
> *Do not let me judge by what I see,*
> *not pass sentence according to what I hear,*
> *but to judge rightly between things that differ*
> *and above all to search out and to do what pleases you,*
> *through Jesus Christ our Lord.*
>
> Thomas à Kempis, 1380–1471

Day 4

Know Yourself

W E MUST NOT BE conceited, inciting one another to rivalry, jealous of one another. If anyone is caught doing something wrong, you, my friends, who live by the Spirit must gently set him right. Look to yourself, each one of you: you also may be tempted. Carry one another's burdens, and in this way you will fulfil the law of Christ.

If anyone imagines himself to be somebody when he is nothing, he is deluding himself. Each of you should examine his own conduct, and then he can measure his achievement by comparing himself with himself and not with anyone else; for everyone has his own burden to bear.

> *We confess to thee, O heavenly Father, as thy children and thy people, our hardness, our indifference, and impenitence; our grievous failures in thy faith and in pure and holy living; our trust in riches, and our misuse of them, our confidence in self, whereby we daily multiply our temptations. We confess our timorousness as thy witnesses before the world, and the sin and bitterness that every man knoweth in his own heart.*
>
> Edward White Benson, 1829–96

Day 5

A Humble Sacrifice

S OW SPARINGLY, and you will reap sparingly; sow bountifully, and you will reap bountifully. Each person should give as he has decided for himself; there should be no reluctance, no sense of compulsion; God loves a cheerful giver. And it is in God's power to provide you with all good gifts in abundance, so that, with every need always met to the full, you may have something to spare for every good cause; as scripture says: 'He lavishes his gifts on the needy; his benevolence lasts for ever.' Now he who provides seed for sowing and bread for food will provide the seed for you to sow; he will multiply it and swell the harvest of your benevolence, and you will always be rich enough to be generous. Through our action such generosity will issue in thanksgiving to God, for as a piece of willing service this is not only a contribution towards the needs of God's people; more than that, it overflows in a flood of thanksgiving to God. For with the proof which this aid affords, those who receive it will give honour to God when they see how humbly you obey him and how faithfully you confess the gospel of Christ; and they will thank him for your liberal contribution to their need and to the general good.

> *O Lord, give us more charity, more self-denial, more likeness to thee. Teach us to sacrifice our comforts to others, and our likings for the sake of doing good. Make us kindly in thought, gentle in word, generous in deed. Teach us that it is better to give than to receive; better to forget ourselves than to put ourselves forward; better to minister than to be ministered unto. And unto thee, the God of love, be glory and praise for ever.*
>
> Henry Alford, 1810–71

Day 6

Grace to the Humble

W HAT CAUSES FIGHTING and quarrels among you? Is not their origin the appetites that war in your bodies? You want what you cannot have, so you murder; you are envious, and cannot attain your ambition, so you quarrel and fight. You do not get what you want, because you do not pray for it. Or, if you do, your requests are not granted, because you pray from wrong motives, in order to squander what you get on your pleasures. Unfaithful creatures! Surely you know that love of the world means enmity to God? Whoever chooses to be the world's friend makes himself God's enemy. Or do you suppose that scripture has no point when it says that the spirit which God implanted in us is filled with envious longings? But the grace he gives is stronger; thus scripture says, God opposes the arrogant and gives grace to the humble. Submit then to God. Stand up to the devil, and he will turn and run. Come close to God, and he will draw close to you.

O Lord Jesus Christ, who didst humble thyself to become man, and to be born into the world for our salvation; teach us the grace of humility, root out of our hearts all pride and haughtiness, and so fashion us after thy holy likeness in this world, that in the world to come we may be made like unto thee; for thine own name's and mercies' sake.

William Walsh How, 1823–97

Day 7

A Sign of Grace

I T IS A SIGN of grace if, because God is in his thoughts, someone endures the pain of undeserved suffering. What credit is there in enduring the beating you deserve when you have done wrong? On the other hand, when you have behaved well and endured suffering for it, that is a sign of grace in the sight of God. It is your vocation because Christ himself suffered on your behalf, and left you an example in order that you should follow in his steps. He committed no sin, he was guilty of no falsehood. When he was abused he did not retaliate, when he suffered he uttered no threats, but delivered himself up to him who judges justly. He carried our sins in his own person on the gibbet, so that we might cease to live for sin and begin to live for righteousness.

> *I thank you, O Christ, that you suffered for me,*
> *leaving me an example, that I should follow in your steps.*
> *You committed no sin, and you were guilty of no falsehood.*
> *When you were abused you did not retaliate;*
> *when you suffered you did not threaten;*
> *but you delivered yourself up to him who judges justly.*
> *You yourself carried my sins in your own person,*
> *so that I might cease to live for sin and begin to live for righteousness.*
> 1 Peter 2.21–24, adapted

WEEK 46

Peace and Unity

Day 1

Live at Peace

L IVE AT PEACE among yourselves. We urge you, friends, to rebuke the idle, encourage the faint-hearted, support the weak, and be patient with everyone.

See to it that no one pays back wrong for wrong, but always aim at what is best for each other and for all.

Always be joyful; pray continually; give thanks whatever happens; for this is what God wills for you in Christ Jesus.

Do not stifle inspiration or despise prophetic utterances, but test them all; keep hold of what is good and avoid all forms of evil.

May God himself, the God of peace, make you holy through and through, and keep you sound in spirit, soul, and body, free of any fault when our Lord Jesus Christ comes. He who calls you keeps faith; he will do it.

O risen Lord, who gave to your distraught followers the assurance of heal-
ing and forgiveness: be present with us, and bring together all Christians in
peace and harmony.

Church of South India, adapted

Day 2

Accept One Another

L ET US, THEN, pursue the things that make for peace and build up the common life. Do not destroy the work of God for the sake of food. Everything is pure in itself, but it is wrong to eat if by eating you cause another to stumble. It is right to abstain from eating meat or drinking wine or from anything else which causes a fellow-Christian to stumble. If you have some firm conviction, keep it between yourself and God.

Anyone who can make his decision without misgivings is fortunate. But anyone who has misgivings and yet eats is guilty, because his action does not arise from conviction, and anything which does not arise from conviction is sin. Those of us who are strong must accept as our own burden the tender scruples of the weak, and not just please ourselves. Each of us must consider his neighbour and think what is for his good and will build up the common life.

O thou God of peace, unite our hearts by thy bond of peace, that we may live with one another continually in gentleness and humility, in peace and unity.

Bernhard Albrecht, 1569–1636

Day 3

For the Good of All

M AKE NO MISTAKE about this: God is not to be fooled; everyone reaps what he sows. If he sows in the field of his unspiritual nature, he will reap from it a harvest of corruption; but if he sows in the field of the Spirit, he will reap from it a harvest of eternal life. Let us never tire of doing good, for if we do not slacken our efforts we shall in due time reap our harvest. Therefore, as opportunity offers, let us work for the good of all, especially members of the household of the faith.

> *O Lord God, destroy and root out whatever the adversary plants in me,*
> *that with my sins destroyed you may sow understanding and good work in*
> *my mouth and heart; so that in act and in truth I may serve only you and*
> *know how to fulfil the commandments of Christ and to see yourself. Give*
> *me love, give me chastity, give me faith, give me all things which you know*
> *belong to the profit of my soul. O Lord, work good in me, and provide me*
> *with what you know that I need.*
>
> Columbanus, c.550–615

Day 4

Look After Others

WHEN WE BLESS the cup of blessing, is it not a means of sharing in the blood of Christ? When we break the bread, is it not a means of sharing in the body of Christ? Because there is one loaf, we, though many, are one body; for it is one loaf of which we all partake.

We are free to do anything, you say. Yes, but not everything is good for us. We are free to do anything, but not everything builds up the community. You should each look after the interests of others, not your own.

O Lord, the author and persuader of peace, love and goodwill, soften our hard and steely hearts, warm our icy and frozen hearts, that we may wish one another well and may be true disciples of Jesus Christ. And give us grace even now to begin to display that heavenly life in which there is no disagreement or hatred, but peace and love on all hands, one towards another.

Ludovicus Vives, 1492–1540

Day 5

One Body and One Spirit

C HRIST IS LIKE a single body with its many limbs and organs, which, many as they are, together make up one body; for in the one Spirit we were all brought into one body by baptism, whether Jews or Greeks, slaves or free; we were all given that one Spirit to drink.

A body is not a single organ, but many. Suppose the foot were to say, 'Because I am not a hand, I do not belong to the body,' it belongs to the body none the less. Suppose the ear were to say, 'Because I am not an eye, I do not belong to the body, it still belongs to the body.' If the body were all eye, how could it hear? If the body were all ear, how could it smell? But, in fact, God appointed each limb and organ to its own place in the body as he chose. If the whole were a single organ, there would not be a body at all; in fact, however, there are many different organs, but one body. The eye cannot say to the hand, 'I do not need you,' or the head to the feet, 'I do not need you.' Quite the contrary: those parts of the body which seem to be more frail than others are indispensable, and those parts of the body which we regard as less honourable are treated with special honour. The parts we are modest about are treated with special respect, whereas our respectable parts have no such need. But God has combined the various parts of the body, giving special honour to the humbler parts, so that there might be no division in the body, but that all its parts might feel the same concern for one another. If one part suffers, all suffer together; if one flourishes, all rejoice together.

To sum up, my friends: when you meet for worship, each of you contributing a hymn, some instruction, a revelation, an ecstatic utterance, or its interpretation, see that all of these aim to build up the church, for God is not a God of disorder but of peace.

Gracious Lord, thou art not the God of confusion or discord but the God of peace and concord; unite our hearts and affections in such sort together, that we may walk in thy house in brotherly love and as members of the body of Christ. Let the oil of sanctification that is thy Holy Spirit inflame us, and the dew of thy blessing continually fall upon us; that we may obtain eternal life through the same Jesus thy Son.

Scottish Psalter, 1595

Day 6

One in Christ

I IMPLORE YOU then I, a prisoner for the Lord's sake: as God has called you, live up to your calling. Be humble always and gentle, and patient too, putting up with one another's failings in the spirit of love. Spare no effort to make fast with bonds of peace the unity which the Spirit gives. There is one body and one Spirit, just as there is one hope held out in God's call to you; one Lord, one faith, one baptism; one God and Father of all, who is over all and through all and in all.

But each of us has been given a special gift, a particular share in the bounty of Christ. That is why scripture says:

He ascended into the heights;
he took captives into captivity;
he gave gifts to men.

Now, the word ascended implies that he also descended to the lowest level, down to the very earth. He who descended is none other than he who ascended far above all heavens, so that he might fill the universe. And it is he who has given some to be apostles, some prophets, some evangelists, some pastors and teachers, to equip God's people for work in his service, for the building up of the body of Christ, until we all attain to the unity inherent in our faith and in our knowledge of the Son of God to mature manhood, measured by nothing less than the full stature of Christ. We are no longer to be children, tossed about by the waves and whirled around by every fresh gust of teaching, dupes of cunning rogues and their deceitful schemes. Rather we are to maintain the truth in a spirit of love; so shall we fully grow up into Christ. He is the head, and on him the whole body depends. Bonded and held together by every constituent joint, the whole frame grows through the proper functioning of each part, and builds itself up in love.

O God, the Father of our Lord Jesus Christ, our only Saviour, the Prince of Peace, give us grace seriously to lay to heart the great dangers we are in by our unhappy divisions. Take away all hatred and prejudice and whatsoever else may hinder us from godly union and concord; that as there is but one body and one Spirit and one hope of our calling, one Lord, one faith, one baptism, one God and Father of us all, so we may henceforth be all of one heart and of one soul, united in one holy bond of truth and peace, of faith and charity and may with one mind and one mouth glorify you; through Jesus Christ our Lord. Amen.

Accession Service, 1715

Day 7

Seek Peace and Pursue It

F INALLY, be united, all of you, in thought and feeling; be full of brotherly affection, kindly and humble. Do not repay wrong with wrong, or abuse with abuse; on the contrary, respond with blessing, for a blessing is what God intends you to receive. As scripture says:

> If anyone wants to love life
> and see good days
> he must restrain his tongue from evil
> and his lips from deceit;
> he must turn from wrong and do good,
> seek peace and pursue it.
> The Lord has eyes for the righteous,
> and ears open to their prayers;
> but the face of the Lord is set against wrongdoers.

O God, the Father of all, inspire us, we pray, with such love, truth, and equity, that in all our dealings one with another we may remember that we are one family in thee, for the sake of Jesus Christ our Lord.

Walter Howard Frere, 1863–1938

WEEK 47

Purity and Holiness

Day 1

Pure Religion

DISCARD EVERYTHING SORDID, and every wicked excess, and meekly accept the message planted in your hearts, with its power to save you.

Only be sure you act on the message, and do not merely listen and so deceive yourselves. Anyone who listens to the message but does not act on it is like somebody looking in a mirror at the face nature gave him; he glances at himself and goes his way, and promptly forgets what he looked like.

If anyone thinks he is religious but does not bridle his tongue, he is deceiving himself; that man's religion is futile. A pure and faultless religion in the sight of God the Father is this: to look after orphans and widows in trouble and to keep oneself untarnished by the world.

We let the world overcome us. We try too much to get what we can by our own selfish wits, without considering our neighbour. We follow too much the fashions of the day, doing and saying and thinking what comes uppermost. Free us from our selfish interests, and guide us, good Lord, to see thy way and to do thy will.

Charles Kingsley, 1819–75

Day 2

Slaves of Righteousness

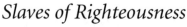

ONCE YOU WERE slaves of sin, but now, thank God, you have yielded wholehearted obedience to that pattern of teaching to which you were made subject; emancipated from sin, you have become slaves of righteousness (to use language that suits your human weakness). As you once yielded your bodies to the service of impurity and lawlessness, making for moral anarchy, so now you must yield them to the service of righteousness, making for a holy life.

When you were slaves of sin, you were free from the control of righteousness. And what gain did that bring you? Things that now make you ashamed, for their end is death. But now, freed from the commands of sin and bound to the service of God, you have gains that lead to holiness, and the end is eternal life. For sin pays a wage, and the wage is death, but God gives freely, and his gift is eternal life in union with Christ Jesus our Lord.

> *Out of my bondage, sorrow and night,*
> *Jesus, I come, Jesus, I come;*
> *Into thy freedom, gladness and light,*
> *Jesus, I come to thee.*
> *Out of my sickness into thy health,*
> *Out of my want and into thy wealth.*
> *Out of my sin and into thyself,*
> *Jesus, I come to thee.*
> William True Sleeper, 1840–1920

Day 3

Purity and Peace

L ET US THEREFORE cease judging one another, but rather make up our minds to place no obstacle or stumbling block in a fellow-Christian's way. All that I know of the Lord Jesus convinces me that nothing is impure in itself; only, if anyone considers something impure, then for him it is impure. If your fellow-Christian is outraged by what you eat, then you are no longer guided by love. Do not by your eating be the ruin of one for whom Christ died! You must not let what you think good be brought into disrepute; for the kingdom of God is not eating and drinking, but justice, peace, and joy, inspired by the Holy Spirit.

Jesus, Lord, we look to thee,
Let us in thy name agree;
Show thyself the Prince of Peace;
Bid our jarring conflicts cease.

Let us for each other care,
Each the other's burden bear,
To thy church the pattern give,
Show how true believers live.

Make us of one heart and mind,
Courteous, pitiful, and kind,
Lowly, meek in thought and word,
Altogether like our Lord.

Charles Wesley, 1707–88

Day 4

God's Holy Temple

Yᴏᴜ ᴀʀᴇ Gᴏᴅ'ꜱ ʙᴜɪʟᴅɪɴɢ. God gave me the privilege of laying the foundation like a skilled master builder; others put up the building. Let each take care how he builds. There can be no other foundation than the one already laid: I mean Jesus Christ himself. If anyone builds on that foundation with gold, silver, and precious stones, or with wood, hay, and straw, the work that each does will at last be brought to light; the day of judgement will expose it. For that day dawns in fire, and the fire will test the worth of each person's work. If anyone's building survives, he will be rewarded; if it burns down, he will have to bear the loss; yet he will escape with his life, though only by passing through the fire. Surely you know that you are God's temple, where the Spirit of God dwells. Anyone who destroys God's temple will himself be destroyed by God, because the temple of God is holy; and you are that temple.

O God, our true life, to know you is life, to serve you is freedom, to enjoy you is a kingdom, to praise you is the joy and happiness of the soul. I praise and bless and adore you, I worship you, I glorify you. I give thanks to you for your great glory. I humbly beg you to live with me, to reign in me, to make this heart of mine a holy temple, a fit habitation for your divine majesty.

Augustine of Hippo, 354–430

Day 5

Self-control

A LL OF US go wrong again and again; a man who never says anything wrong is perfect and is capable of controlling every part of his body. When we put a bit into a horse's mouth to make it obey our will, we can direct the whole animal. Or think of a ship: large though it may be and driven by gales, it can be steered by a very small rudder on whatever course the helmsman chooses. So with the tongue; it is small, but its pretensions are great.

What a vast amount of timber can be set ablaze by the tiniest spark! And the tongue is a fire, representing in our body the whole wicked world. It pollutes our whole being, it sets the whole course of our existence alight, and its flames are fed by hell. Beasts and birds of every kind, creatures that crawl on the ground or swim in the sea, can be subdued and have been subdued by man; but no one can subdue the tongue. It is an evil thing, restless and charged with deadly venom. We use it to praise our Lord and Father; then we use it to invoke curses on our fellow-men, though they are made in God's likeness. Out of the same mouth come praise and curses. This should not be so, my friends. Does a fountain flow with both fresh and brackish water from the same outlet? My friends, can a fig tree produce olives, or a grape vine produce figs? No more can salt water produce fresh.

> *O blessed Jesus, give me stillness of soul in thee.*
> *Let thy mighty calmness reign in me;*
> *rule me, O King of gentleness, King of peace.*
> *Give me control, great power of self-control,*
> *control over my words, thoughts and actions.*
> *From all irritability, want of meekness, want of gentleness,*
> *   dear Lord, deliver me.*
> *By thine own deep patience, give me patience.*
> *Make me in this and all things more and more like thee.*
>
> John of the Cross, 1542–91

Day 6

Pure and Eager to Do Good

FOR THE GRACE of God has dawned upon the world with healing for all mankind; and by it we are disciplined to renounce godless ways and worldly desires, and to live a life of temperance, honesty, and godliness in the present age, looking forward to the happy fulfilment of our hope when the splendour of our great God and Saviour Christ Jesus will appear. He it is who sacrificed himself for us, to set us free from all wickedness and to make us his own people, pure and eager to do good.

> *Create in me a pure heart,*
> *so that, through the power of your spirit,*
> *I may inhale your salvation.*
>
> Joseph the Visionary, 8th century

Day 7

A Holy Priesthood

B E OBEDIENT to God your Father, and do not let your characters be shaped any longer by the desires you cherished in your days of ignorance. He who called you is holy; like him, be holy in all your conduct. Does not scripture say, 'You shall be holy, for I am holy'?

Now that you have purified your souls by obedience to the truth until you feel sincere affection towards your fellow-Christians, love one another whole-heartedly with all your strength. You have been born again, not of mortal but of immortal parentage, through the living and enduring word of God. As scripture says:

> All mortals are like grass;
> all their glory like the flower of the field;
> the grass withers, the flower falls;
> but the word of the Lord endures for evermore.

And this word is the gospel which was preached to you.

So come to him, to the living stone which was rejected by men but chosen by God and of great worth to him. You also, as living stones, must be built up into a spiritual temple, and form a holy priesthood to offer spiritual sacrifices acceptable to God through Jesus Christ.

Lord, I pray that you may be a lamp for me in the darkness. Touch my soul and kindle a fire within it, that it may burn brightly and give light to my life. Thus my body may truly become your temple, lit by your perpetual flame burning on the altar of my heart. And may the light within me shine on my brethren that it may drive away the darkness of ignorance and sin from them also. Thus together let us be light to the world, manifesting the bright beauty of your gospel to all around us.

Columbanus, c.350–615

Wisdom and Truth: I

Day 1

The Wisdom of God

~⊱ ⊰~

MY FRIENDS, think what sort of people you are, whom God has called. Few of you are wise by any human standard, few powerful or of noble birth. Yet, to shame the wise, God has chosen what the world counts folly, and to shame what is strong, God has chosen what the world counts weakness. He has chosen things without rank or standing in the world, mere nothings, to overthrow the existing order. So no place is left for any human pride in the presence of God.

> *Take from us, O God, all pride and vanity, all boasting and self-assertion, and give us the true courage that shows itself in gentleness, the true wisdom that shows itself in simplicity, and the true power that shows itself in modesty, through Jesus Christ our Lord.*
>
> Charles Kingsley, 1819–75

Day 2

God's Hidden Wisdom

B Y GOD'S ACT you are in Christ Jesus; God has made him our wisdom, and in him we have our righteousness, our holiness, our liberation. Therefore, in the words of scripture, 'If anyone must boast, let him boast of the Lord.'

So it was, my friends, that I came to you, without any pretensions to eloquence or wisdom in declaring the truth about God. I resolved that while I was with you I would not claim to know anything but Jesus Christ – Christ nailed to the cross. I came before you in weakness, in fear, in great trepidation. The word I spoke, the gospel I proclaimed, did not sway you with clever arguments; it carried conviction by spiritual power, so that your faith might be built not on human wisdom but on the power of God.

Among the mature I do speak words of wisdom, though not a wisdom belonging to this present age or to its governing powers, already in decline; I speak God's hidden wisdom, his secret purpose framed from the very beginning to bring us to our destined glory. None of the powers that rule the world has known that wisdom; if they had, they would not have crucified the Lord of glory.

> *God our Father, the contradiction of the cross*
> *proclaims your infinite wisdom.*
> *Help us to see that the glory of your Son*
> *is revealed in the suffering he freely accepted.*
> *Give us faith to claim as our only glory*
> *the cross of our Lord Jesus Christ,*
> *who lives with you and the Holy Spirit,*
> *one God, for ever and ever.*
>
> Liturgy of the Hours

Day 3

The Depths of God

S CRIPTURE SPEAKS OF things beyond our seeing, things beyond our hearing, things beyond our imagining, all prepared by God for those who love him; and these are what God has revealed to us through the Spirit. For the Spirit explores everything, even the depths of God's own nature. Who knows what a human being is but the human spirit within him? In the same way, only the Spirit of God knows what God is.

And we have received this Spirit from God, not the spirit of the world, so that we may know all that God has lavished on us; and, because we are interpreting spiritual truths to those who have the Spirit, we speak of these gifts of God in words taught us not by our human wisdom but by the Spirit. An unspiritual person refuses what belongs to the Spirit of God; it is folly to him; he cannot grasp it, because it needs to be judged in the light of the Spirit. But a spiritual person can judge the worth of everything, yet is not himself subject to judgement by others. Scripture indeed asks, 'Who can know the mind of the Lord or be his counsellor?' Yet we possess the mind of Christ.

> *Why, O my God, must this mortal structure put so great a separation between my soul and thee? I am surrounded with thy essence, yet I cannot perceive thee? I follow thee, and trace thy footsteps in heaven and earth, yet I cannot overtake thee; thou art before me, and I cannot reach thee, and behind me, and I perceive thee not.*
>
> *O thou, whom unseen, I love, by what powerful influence dost thou attract my soul? The eye has not seen, nor the ear heard, nor has it entered into the heart of man to conceive, what thou art; and yet I love thee beyond all that mine eye has seen, or my ear heard, beyond all that my heart can comprehend. thou dwellest in heights of glory, to which no human thought can soar, and yet thou are more near and intimate to my soul than any of the objects of sense.*
>
> Elizabeth Rowe, 1647–1737

Day 4

God's Secret Purpose

B LESSED BE the God and Father of our Lord Jesus Christ, who has conferred on us in Christ every spiritual blessing in the heavenly realms. In the richness of his grace God has lavished on us all wisdom and insight. He has made known to us his secret purpose, in accordance with the plan which he determined beforehand in Christ, to be put into effect when the time was ripe: namely, that the universe, everything in heaven and on earth, might be brought into a unity in Christ.

Bring us, O Lord God, at our last awakening, into the house of God and gate of heaven that we may dwell in that place where there is no cloud nor sun, no darkness nor dazzling, but one equal light, no noise nor silence but one equal music, no fears nor hopes, but one equal possession, no foes nor friends, but one equal communion and identity, no ends nor beginnings, but one equal eternity.

John Donne, 1571–1631

Day 5

A Prayer for Enlightenment

I PRAY THAT the God of our Lord Jesus Christ, the all-glorious Father, may confer on you the spiritual gifts of wisdom and vision, with the knowledge of him that they bring. I pray that your inward eyes may be enlightened, so that you may know what is the hope to which he calls you, how rich and glorious is the share he offers you among his people in their inheritance, and how vast are the resources of his power open to us who have faith. His mighty strength was seen at work when he raised Christ from the dead, and enthroned him at his right hand in the heavenly realms, far above all government and authority, all power and dominion, and any title of sovereignty that commands allegiance, not only in this age but also in the age to come. He put all things in subjection beneath his feet, and gave him as head over all things to the church which is his body, the fullness of him who is filling the universe in all its parts.

We thank you, O God, through your Child, Jesus Christ our Lord, because you have enlightened us and revealed to us the light that is incorruptible.

Through him the glory and power that are his and the honour that is the Holy Spirit's are also yours, as they will be throughout the unending succession of ages.

Hippolytus, c.170–236

Day 6

A Prayer for Insight

W E ASK GOD that you may receive from him full insight into his will, all wisdom and spiritual understanding, so that your manner of life may be worthy of the Lord and entirely pleasing to him. We pray that you may bear fruit in active goodness of every kind, and grow in knowledge of God. In his glorious might may he give you ample strength to meet with fortitude and patience whatever comes; and to give joyful thanks to the Father who has made you fit to share the heritage of God's people in the realm of light.

Just as in this earthly life thou causest the sun to shine on the world to give physical light, let thy Holy Spirit illumine my mind to guide me in the way of thy righteousness. Thus in everything I do, let my goal and intention always be to walk reverently and to honour and serve thee, relying only on thy blessing for my well-being, and undertaking only what is pleasing to thee.

Grant also, O Lord, that as I labour for my physical needs and for this present life, I may lift up my soul to that heavenly and blessed life which thou has promised to thy children.

John Calvin, 1509–1564

Day 7

In the Likeness of God

MAINTAIN THE TRUTH in a spirit of love; so shall we fully grow up into Christ. He is the head, and on him the whole body depends. Bonded and held together by every constituent joint, the whole frame grows through the proper functioning of each part, and builds itself up in love.

Were you not as Christians taught the truth as it is in Jesus? Renouncing your former way of life, you must lay aside the old human nature which, deluded by its desires, is in process of decay: you must be renewed in mind and spirit, and put on the new nature created in God's likeness, which shows itself in the upright and devout life called for by the truth.

Then have done with falsehood and speak the truth to each other, for we belong to one another as parts of one body.

Father in heaven,
form in us the likeness of your Son
and deepen his life within us.
Send us as witnesses of gospel joy
into a world of fragile peace and broken promises;
and touch the hearts of all with your love
that they in turn may love one another.

Roman Missal, adapted

WEEK 49

Wisdom and Truth: II

Day 1

Worthy of God's Approval

STOP DISPUTING ABOUT mere words; it does no good, and only ruins those who listen. Try hard to show yourself worthy of God's approval, as a worker with no cause for shame; keep strictly to the true gospel, avoiding empty and irreligious chatter; those who indulge in it will stray farther and farther into godless ways, and the infection of their teaching will spread like gangrene.

Turn from the wayward passions of youth, and pursue justice, integrity, love, and peace together with all who worship the Lord in singleness of mind; have nothing to do with foolish and wild speculations. You know they breed quarrels, and a servant of the Lord must not be quarrelsome; he must be kindly towards all.

Lord God, give us grace to set a good example to all amongst whom we live, to be just and true in all our dealings, to be strict and conscientious in the discharge of every duty, pure and temperate in all enjoyment, kind and charitable and courteous toward all men; so that the mind of Jesus Christ may be formed in us and all men take knowledge of us that we are his disciples; through the same Jesus Christ our Lord.

Richard William Church, 1815–90

Day 2

The Purpose of Scripture

BUT FOR YOUR PART, stand by the truths you have learned and are assured of. Remember from whom you learned them; remember that from early childhood you have been familiar with the sacred writings which have power to make you wise and lead you to salvation through faith in Christ Jesus. All inspired scripture has its use for teaching the truth and refuting error, or for reformation of manners and discipline in right living, so that the man of God may be capable and equipped for good work of every kind.

O God, the Father of lights, who by the entrance of thy word giveth light unto the soul: grant to us the spirit of wisdom and understanding; that, being taught of thee in holy scripture, we may receive with the faith the words of eternal life, and be made wise unto salvation; through Jesus Christ our Lord.

Book of Common Order, 1562

Day 3

Ask in Faith

M Y FRIENDS, whenever you have to face all sorts of trials, count your-selves supremely happy in the knowledge that such testing of your faith makes for strength to endure. Let endurance perfect its work in you that you may become perfected, sound throughout, lacking in nothing. If any of you lacks wisdom, he should ask God and it will be given him, for God is a gener-ous giver who neither grudges nor reproaches anyone. But he who asks must ask in faith, with never a doubt in his mind; for the doubter is like a wave of the sea tossed hither and thither by the wind. A man like that should not think he will receive anything from the Lord. He is always in two minds and unstable in all he does.

> *Save us, O Lord, from the snares of a double mind.*
> *Deliver us from all cowardly neutralities.*
> *Make us to go in the paths of your commandments,*
> *and to trust for our defence in your mighty arm alone,*
> *through Jesus Christ our Lord.*
>
> Richard Hurrell Froude, 1803–36

Day 4

Wisdom from Above

WHICH OF YOU is wise or learned? Let him give practical proof of it by his right conduct, with the modesty that comes of wisdom. But if you are harbouring bitter jealousy and the spirit of rivalry in your hearts, stop making false claims in defiance of the truth. This is not the wisdom that comes from above; it is earth-bound, sensual, demonic. For with jealousy and rivalry come disorder and the practice of every kind of evil. But the wisdom from above is in the first place pure; and then peace-loving, considerate, and open-minded; it is straightforward and sincere, rich in compassion and in deeds of kindness that are its fruit. Peace is the seed-bed of righteousness, and the peacemakers will reap its harvest.

> *God, you are peace everlasting,*
> *whose chosen reward is the gift of peace,*
> *and you have taught us that the peacemakers are your children.*
> *Pour your grace into our souls,*
> *that everything discordant may utterly vanish,*
> *and all that makes for peace be sweet to us for ever;*
> *through Jesus Christ our Lord.*
>
> Charles Kingsley, 1819–75

Day 5

True Religion

Gᴏᴅ'ꜱ ᴅɪᴠɪɴᴇ ᴘᴏᴡᴇʀ has bestowed on us everything that makes for life and true religion, through our knowledge of him who called us by his own glory and goodness. In this way he has given us his promises, great beyond all price, so that through them you may escape the corruption with which lust has infected the world, and may come to share in the very being of God.

It was not on tales, however cleverly concocted, that we relied when we told you about the power of our Lord Jesus Christ and his coming; rather with our own eyes we had witnessed his majesty. He was invested with honour and glory by God the Father, and there came to him from the sublime Presence a voice which said: 'This is my Son, my Beloved, on whom my favour rests.' We ourselves heard this voice when it came from heaven, for we were with him on the sacred mountain.

All this confirms for us the message of the prophets, to which you will do well to attend; it will go on shining like a lamp in a murky place, until day breaks and the morning star rises to illuminate your minds.

But note this: no prophetic writing is a matter for private interpretation. It was not on any human initiative that prophecy came; rather, it was under the compulsion of the Holy Spirit that people spoke as messengers of God.

O Lord, heavenly Father, in whom is the fullness of light and wisdom, enlighten our minds by thy Holy Spirit, and give us grace to receive thy word with reverence and humility, without which no man can understand thy truth, for Christ's sake.

John Calvin, 1509–64

Day 6

Knowing God

M Y CHILDREN, I am writing this to you so that you should not commit sin. But if anybody does, we have in Jesus Christ one who is acceptable to God and pleads our cause with the Father. He is himself a sacrifice to atone for our sins, and not ours only but the sins of the whole world.

It is by keeping God's commands that we can be sure we know him. Whoever says, I know him, but does not obey his commands, is a liar and the truth is not in him; but whoever is obedient to his word, in him the love of God is truly made perfect.

O God, the God of all goodness and of all grace, who is worthy of a greater love than we can either give or understand, fill our hearts, we beseech you, with such love towards you, that nothing may seem too hard for us to do or suffer in obedience to your will; and grant that thus loving you we may become daily more like unto you and finally obtain the crown of life, which you have promised to those that love you; through Jesus Christ our Lord.

Farnham Hostel Manual, 19th century

Day 7

Test the Spirits

My dear friends, do not trust every spirit, but test the spirits, to see whether they are from God; for there are many false prophets about in the world. The way to recognize the Spirit of God is this: every spirit which acknowledges that Jesus Christ has come in the flesh is from God, and no spirit is from God which does not acknowledge Jesus. This is the spirit of antichrist; you have been warned that it was to come, and now here it is, in the world already!

Children, you belong to God's family, and you have the mastery over these false prophets, because God who inspires you is greater than the one who inspires the world. They belong to that world, and so does their teaching; that is why the world listens to them. But we belong to God and whoever knows God listens to us, while whoever does not belong to God refuses to listen to us. That is how we can distinguish the spirit of truth from the spirit of error.

O Lord God of truth, we humbly beseech thee to enlighten our minds by thy Holy Spirit, that we may discern the true way to eternal salvation; and so free us from all prejudice and passion, from every corrupt affection and selfish interest, that may either blind or seduce us in our search after it. To thee, O Lord, to thy conduct and direction, depending upon thy mercy and goodness, we entirely resign ourselves, our souls and bodies. And if anything that concerns the worship and service of thee our God, and the everlasting happiness of our souls, we are in error and mistakes, we earnestly beg thee to convince us of them, to lead us into the way of truth, and to confirm and establish us in it more and more. Grant this for the sake of our blessed Redeemer.

Samuel Seabury, 1729–96

The Way of Love: I

Day 1

Love Sincerely

LOVE IN ALL SINCERITY, loathing evil and holding fast to the good. Let love of the Christian community show itself in mutual affection. Esteem others more highly than yourself.

With unflagging zeal, aglow with the Spirit, serve the Lord. Let hope keep you joyful; in trouble stand firm; persist in prayer; contribute to the needs of God's people, and practise hospitality. Call down blessings on your persecutors blessings, not curses. Rejoice with those who rejoice, weep with those who weep. Live in agreement with one another.

Bestow on me, O Lord, a genial spirit and unwearied forbearance, a mild, loving, patient heart, kindly looks, pleasant, cordial speech and manner, that I may give offence to none, but, as much as in me lies, live in charity with all.

Johann Arndt, 1555–1621

Day 2

The Fulfilment of the Law

D ISCHARGE YOUR OBLIGATIONS to everyone; pay tax and levy, reverence and respect, to those to whom they are due. Leave no debt outstanding, but remember the debt of love you owe one another. He who loves his neighbour has met every requirement of the law. The commandments, You shall not commit adultery, you shall not commit murder, you shall not steal, you shall not covet, and any other commandment there may be, are all summed up in the one rule, Love your neighbour as yourself. Love cannot wrong a neighbour; therefore love is the fulfilment of the law.

God of love, through your only-begotten Son you have given us a new commandment, that we should love one another in the same way as you loved us, the unworthy and wandering: give to us your servants, in all the time of our life on earth, a mind forgetful of past ill will, a pure conscience, and a heart to love our neighbours; through the same your Son our Saviour Jesus Christ.

Coptic Liturgy of St Cyril, 5th century

Day 3

The Greatest Gift

I MAY SPEAK IN the tongues of men or of angels, but if I have no love, I am a sounding gong or a clanging cymbal. I may have the gift of prophecy and the knowledge of every hidden truth; I may have faith enough to move mountains; but if I have no love, I am nothing. I may give all I possess to the needy, I may give my body to be burnt, but if I have no love, I gain nothing by it.

Love is patient and kind. Love envies no one, is never boastful, never conceited, never rude; love is never selfish, never quick to take offence. Love keeps no score of wrongs, takes no pleasure in the sins of others, but delights in the truth. There is nothing love cannot face; there is no limit to its faith, its hope, its endurance.

Love will never come to an end. Prophecies will cease; tongues of ecstasy will fall silent; knowledge will vanish. For our knowledge and our prophecy alike are partial, and the partial vanishes when wholeness comes. When I was a child I spoke like a child, thought like a child, reasoned like a child; but when I grew up I finished with childish things. At present we see only puzzling reflections in a mirror, but one day we shall see face to face. My knowledge now is partial; then it will be whole, like God's knowledge of me. There are three things that last for ever: faith, hope, and love; and the greatest of the three is love.

> *I pray for the gift of love;*
> *for if I have no love, I am nothing.*
> *Teach me, in love, to be patient and kind;*
> *not envious, boastful or conceited.*
> *Never let me be rude, selfish or quick to take offence;*
> *may I keep no score of wrongs.*
> *Never let me take pleasure in the sins of others;*
> *may I take delight in the truth.*
> *For then there will be nothing my love cannot face;*
> *no limit to its faith, its hope, its endurance.*
> *My love will never end.*
>
> 1 Corinthians 13.2, 4–8, adapted

Day 4

Love beyond Knowledge

I KNEEL IN PRAYER to the Father, from whom every family in heaven and on earth takes its name, that out of the treasures of his glory he may grant you inward strength and power through his Spirit, that through faith Christ may dwell in your hearts in love. With deep roots and firm foundations may you, in company with all God's people, be strong to grasp what is the breadth and length and height and depth of Christ's love, and to know it, though it is beyond knowledge. So may you be filled with the very fullness of God.

Now to him who is able through the power which is at work among us to do immeasurably more than all we can ask or conceive, to him be glory in the church and in Christ Jesus from generation to generation for evermore! Amen.

I am swallowed up, O God, I am willingly swallowed up in this bottomless abyss of thine infinite love: and there let me dwell, in a perpetual ravishment of spirit, till, being freed from this clog of earth and filled with the fulness of Christ, I shall be admitted to enjoy that, which I cannot now reach to wonder at, thine incomprehensible bliss and glory which thou hast laid up in the highest heavens for them that love thee.

Joseph Hall, 1574–1656

Day 5

Live in Love

I F YOU ARE ANGRY, do not be led into sin; do not let sunset find you nursing your anger; and give no foothold to the devil.

Let no offensive talk pass your lips, only what is good and helpful to the occasion, so that it brings a blessing to those who hear it. Do not grieve the Holy Spirit of God, for that Spirit is the seal with which you were marked for the day of final liberation. Have done with all spite and bad temper, with rage, insults, and slander, with evil of any kind. Be generous to one another, tender-hearted, forgiving one another as God in Christ forgave you.

In a word, as God's dear children, you must be like him. Live in love as Christ loved you and gave himself up on your behalf, an offering and sacrifice whose fragrance is pleasing to God.

Father, if I become angry, do not let my anger lead me into sin; let no offensive talk pass my lips, only what is good and helpful and brings a blessing to those who hear it; and never let me grieve your Holy Spirit. Help me to have done with all spite and bad temper; help me to be generous and tender-hearted; and help me to forgive as God in Christ forgave me.

Ephesians 4.26, 29–32, adapted

Day 6

The Same Love

I F THEN OUR common life in Christ yields anything to stir the heart, any consolation of love, any participation in the Spirit, any warmth of affection or compassion, fill up my cup of happiness by thinking and feeling alike, with the same love for one another and a common attitude of mind. Leave no room for selfish ambition and vanity, but humbly reckon others better than yourselves. Look to each others interests and not merely to your own.

Almighty God, and most merciful Father, who has given us a new com-
mandment that we should love one another, give us also grace that we may
fulfil it. Make us gentle, courteous and forbearing. Direct our lives so that
we may look each to the good of the other in word and deed. And hallow all
our friendships by the blessing of your Spirit, for his sake who loved us and
gave himself for us, Jesus Christ our Lord.

Brooke Foss Westcott, 1825–1901

Day 7

Unceasing Love

NEVER CEASE TO love your fellow-Christians. Do not neglect to show hospitality; by doing this, some have entertained angels unawares. Remember those in prison, as if you were there with them, and those who are being maltreated, for you are vulnerable too.

Jesus Christ is the same yesterday, today, and for ever. So do not be swept off your course by all sorts of outlandish teachings; it is good that we should gain inner strength from the grace of God, and not from rules about food, which have never benefited those who observed them.

Never neglect to show kindness and to share what you have with others; for such are the sacrifices which God approves.

Give us understanding and sympathy, and guard us from selfishness, that we may enter into the joys and sufferings of others. Use us to gladden and strengthen those who are weak and suffering; that by our lives we may help others to believe and serve thee.

Dick Sheppherd, 1880–1937

The Way of Love: II

Day 1

Love Is Impartial

M Y FRIENDS, you believe in our Lord Jesus Christ who reigns in glory and you must always be impartial. For instance, two visitors may enter your meeting, one a well-dressed man with gold rings, and the other a poor man in grimy clothes. Suppose you pay special attention to the well-dressed man and say to him, Please take this seat, while to the poor man you say, 'You stand over there, or sit here on the floor by my footstool,' do you not see that you are discriminating among your members and judging by wrong standards? Listen, my dear friends: has not God chosen those who are poor in the eyes of the world to be rich in faith and to possess the kingdom he has promised to those who love him? And yet you have humiliated the poor man.

Moreover, are not the rich your oppressors? Is it not they who drag you into court and pour contempt on the honoured name by which God has claimed you?

If, however, you are observing the sovereign law laid down in scripture, Love your neighbour as yourself, that is excellent. But if you show partiality, you are committing a sin and you stand convicted by the law as offenders.

> *O God of love, we pray thee to give us love:*
> *love in our thinking, love in our speaking,*
> *love in our doing, and love in the hidden places of our souls;*
> *love of our neighbours near and far;*
> *love of our friends old and new;*
> *love of those whom we might find hard to bear,*
> *and love of those who find it hard to bear with us;*
> *love of those with whom we work,*
> *and love of those with whom we take our ease;*
> *love in joy, love in sorrow;*
> *love in life and love in death;*
> *that so at length we may be worthy to dwell with thee,*
> *who art eternal love.*

William Temple, 1881–1944

Day 2

Love Cancels Sin

THE END OF all things is upon us; therefore to help you to pray you must lead self-controlled and sober lives. Above all, maintain the fervour of your love for one another, because love cancels a host of sins. Be hospitable to one another without grumbling. As good stewards of the varied gifts given you by God, let each use the gift he has received in service to others. Are you a speaker? Speak as one who utters God's oracles. Do you give service? Give it in the strength which God supplies. In all things let God be glorified through Jesus Christ; to him belong glory and power for ever and ever. Amen.

Teach me to kneel in spirit before all who it is my privilege to serve, because they are your children.

Come, Lord! Come with me: see with my eyes: hear with my ears: think with my mind: love with my heart – in all the situations of my life.

Work with my hands: my strength. Take, cleanse, possess, inhabit, my will, my understanding, my love.

Evelyn Underhill, 1875–1941

Day 3

Love Is Compassionate

T HE MESSAGE YOU have heard from the beginning is that we should love one another. Do not be like Cain, who was a child of the evil one and murdered his brother. And why did he murder him? Because his own actions were wrong, and his brother's were right.

Friends, do not be surprised if the world hates you. We know we have crossed over from death to life, because we love our fellow Christians. Anyone who does not love is still in the realm of death, for everyone who hates a fellow Christian is a murderer, and murderers, as you know, do not have eternal life dwelling within them. This is how we know what love is: Christ gave his life for us. And we in our turn must give our lives for our fellow Christians. But if someone who possesses the good things of this world sees a fellow Christian in need and withholds compassion from him, how can it be said that the love of God dwells in him?

> *O God, fountain of love, pour thy love into our souls, that we may love those whom thou lovest with the love thou givest us, and think and speak with the love thou givest us, and think and speak of them tenderly, meekly, lovingly; and so loving our brethren and sisters for thy sake, may grow in love, and dwelling in thy love may dwell in thee, for Jesus Christ's sake.*

Edward Bouverie Pusey, 1800–82

Day 4

True Christian Love

CHILDREN, love must not be a matter of theory or talk; it must be true love which shows itself in action. This is how we shall know that we belong to the realm of truth, and reassure ourselves in his sight where conscience condemns us; for God is greater than our conscience and knows all.

My dear friends, if our conscience does not condemn us, then we can approach God with confidence, and obtain from him whatever we ask, because we are keeping his commands and doing what he approves. His command is that we should give our allegiance to his Son Jesus Christ and love one another, as Christ commanded us. Those who keep his commands dwell in him and he dwells in them. And our certainty that he dwells in us comes from the Spirit he has given us.

O Lord Jesus Christ, the Lord whose ways are right, keep us in thy mercy from lip-service and empty forms; from having a name that we live in, but being dead. Help us to worship thee by righteous deeds and lives of holiness.

Christina Rossetti, 1830–94

Day 5

Love Banishes Fear

MY DEAR FRIENDS, let us love one another, because the source of love is God. Everyone who loves is a child of God and knows God, but the unloving know nothing of God, for God is love.

He who dwells in love is dwelling in God, and God in him. This is how love has reached its perfection among us, so that we may have confidence on the day of judgement; and this we can have, because in this world we are as he is. In love there is no room for fear; indeed perfect love banishes fear. For fear has to do with punishment, and anyone who is afraid has not attained to love in its perfection.

Teach us, O Lord, to fear thee without terror, and to trust thee without misgivings: to fear thee in love, until it please thee that we shall love thee without fear.

Christina Rossetti, 1830–94

Day 6

Love God's Children

W<small>E LOVE BECAUSE</small> he loved us. But if someone says, 'I love God,' while at the same time hating his fellow Christian, he is a liar. If he does not love a fellow Christian whom he has seen, he is incapable of loving God whom he has not seen. We have this command from Christ: whoever loves God must love his fellow Christian too.

Everyone who believes that Jesus is the Christ is a child of God. To love the parent means to love his child. It follows that when we love God and obey his commands we love his children too.

O God, we have known and believed the love that you have for us. May we, by dwelling in love, dwell in you, and you in us. Teach us, O heavenly Father, the love wherewith you have loved us; fashion us, O blessed Lord, after your own example of love; shed abroad, O you Holy Spirit of love, the love of God and man in our hearts. For your name's sake.

Henry Alford, 1810–71

Day 7

Love and Truth

D<small>O NOT THINK</small> I am sending a new command; I am recalling the one we have had from the beginning: I ask that we love one another. What love means is to live according to the commands of God. This is the command that was given you from the beginning, to be your rule of life.

Many deceivers have gone out into the world, people who do not acknowledge Jesus Christ as coming in the flesh. Any such person is the deceiver and antichrist. See to it that you do not lose what we have worked for, but receive your reward in full.

Above all I pray that things go well with you, and that you may enjoy good health: I know it is well with your soul. I was very glad when some fellow Christians arrived and told me of your faithfulness to the truth; indeed you live by the truth. Nothing gives me greater joy than to hear that my children are living by the truth.

To the invisible and only God, the true Father, who sent to us the Saviour and immortal Prince, through whom he revealed to us the truth and the life of heaven, to him be glory for ever and ever. Amen.

Clement of Rome, 1st century

WEEK 52

With God for Ever

Day 1

Hope of the Universe

I RECKON THAT THE sufferings we now endure bear no comparison with the glory, as yet unrevealed, which is in store for us. The created universe is waiting with eager expectation for God's sons to be revealed. It was made subject to frustration, not of its own choice but by the will of him who subjected it, yet with the hope that the universe itself is to be freed from the shackles of mortality and is to enter upon the glorious liberty of the children of God. Up to the present, as we know, the whole created universe in all its parts groans as if in the pangs of childbirth. What is more, we also, to whom the Spirit is given as the fruits of the harvest to come, are groaning inwardly while we look forward eagerly to our adoption, our liberation from mortality. It was with this hope that we were saved. Now to see something is no longer to hope: why hope for what is already seen? But if we hope for something we do not yet see, then we look forward to it eagerly and with patience.

O God, the author and fountain of hope, enable us to rely with confident expectation on thy promises, knowing that the trials and hindrances of the present time are not worthy to be compared with the glory that shall be revealed, and having our faces steadfastly set towards the light that shineth more and more to the perfect day; through Jesus Christ our Lord.

A Devotional Diary

Day 2

A Spiritual Body

You may ask, how are the dead raised? In what kind of body? What stupid questions! The seed you sow does not come to life unless it has died; and what you sow is not the body that shall be, but a bare grain, of wheat perhaps, or something else; and God gives it the body of his choice, each seed its own particular body. All flesh is not the same: there is human flesh, flesh of beasts, of birds, and of fishes all different. There are heavenly bodies and earthly bodies; and the splendour of the heavenly bodies is one thing, the splendour of the earthly another. The sun has a splendour of its own, the moon another splendour, and the stars yet another; and one star differs from another in brightness. So it is with the resurrection of the dead: what is sown as a perishable thing is raised imperishable. Sown in humiliation, it is raised in glory; sown in weakness, it is raised in power; sown a physical body, it is raised a spiritual body.

> *O Lord Jesus Christ, exalt me with thee so to know the mystery of life that I may use the earthly as the appointed expression and type of the heavenly; and by using to thy glory the natural body, I may be fit to be exalted to the use of the spiritual body.*
>
> Charles Kingsley, 1819–75

Day 3

The Second Adam

I F THERE IS such a thing as a physical body, there is also a spiritual body. It is in this sense that scripture says, The man, Adam, became a living creature, whereas the last Adam has become a life-giving spirit.

Observe, the spiritual does not come; the physical body comes, and then the spiritual. The man is from earth, made of dust: the second man is from heaven. The man made of dust is the pattern of all who are made of dust, and the heavenly man is the pattern of all the heavenly. As we have worn the likeness of the man made of dust, so we shall wear the likeness of the heavenly man.

Draw near, according to thy promise from the throne of thy glory: look down and hear our crying, we humbly beseech thee.

Come again, and dwell with us, O Lord Jesus Christ: abide with us for ever, we humbly beseech thee.

And when thou shalt appear with power and great glory: may we be made like unto thee in thy glorious kingdom.

Thanks be to thee, O Lord: Hallelujah.

Source unknown, 12th century

Day 4

A Heavenly Home

I N THIS PRESENT body we groan, yearning to be covered by our heavenly habitation put on over this one, in the hope that, being thus clothed, we shall not find ourselves naked. We groan indeed, we who are enclosed within this earthly frame; we are oppressed because we do not want to have the old body stripped off. What we want is to be covered by the new body put on over it, so that our mortality may be absorbed into life immortal. It is for this destiny that God himself has been shaping us; and as a pledge of it he has given us the Spirit.

Therefore we never cease to be confident. We know that so long as we are at home in the body we are exiles from the Lord; faith is our guide, not sight. We are confident, I say, and would rather be exiled from the body and make our home with the Lord. That is why it is our ambition, wherever we are, at home or in exile, to be acceptable to him. For we must all have our lives laid open before the tribunal of Christ, where each must receive what is due to him for his conduct in the body, good or bad.

> *Glory to the Father, who has woven garments of glory*
> *for the resurrection;*
>
> *worship to the Son, who was clothed in them at his rising;*
>
> *thanksgiving to the Spirit, who keeps them for all the saints;*
> *one nature in three, to him be praise.*
>
> Syrian Orthodox Church

Day 5

Citizens of Heaven

A s I HAVE often told you, and now tell you with tears, there are many whose way of life makes them enemies of the cross of Christ. They are heading for destruction, they make appetite their god, they take pride in what should bring shame; their minds are set on earthly things. We, by contrast, are citizens of heaven, and from heaven we expect our deliverer to come, the Lord Jesus Christ. He will transfigure our humble bodies, and give them a form like that of his own glorious body, by that power which enables him to make all things subject to himself.

> *Worship and praise belong to you,*
> *God our maker.*
> *In Christ your Son*
> *the life of heaven and earth were joined,*
> *sealing the promise of a new creation,*
> *given, yet still to come.*
>
> *Taught by your Spirit,*
> *we who bear your threefold likeness*
> *look for the City of Peace*
> *in whose light we are transfigured*
> *and the earth transformed.*
>
> Scottish Liturgy

Day 6

Life in the Son

WE ACCEPT HUMAN testimony, but surely the testimony of God is stronger, and the testimony of God is the witness he has borne to his Son. He who believes in the Son of God has the testimony in his own heart, but he who does not believe God makes him out to be a liar by refusing to accept God's witness to his Son. This is the witness: God has given us eternal life, and this life is found in his Son. He who possesses the Son possesses life; he who does not possess the Son of God does not possess life.

You have given your allegiance to the Son of God; this letter is to assure you that you have eternal life.

We thank thee, O God, the Father of our Lord Jesus Christ, that thou hast revealed thy Son to us, on whom we have believed, whom we have loved, and whom we worship.

O Lord Jesus Christ, we commend our souls to thee. O heavenly Father, we know that although we shall in thine own good time be taken away from this life, we shall live for ever with thee.

'God so loved the world, that he gave his only begotten Son, that whosoever believeth in him should not perish, but have everlasting life.' Father, into thy hands we commend our spirits; through Jesus Christ our Lord.

Martin Luther, 1483–1546

Day 7

The Heavenly City

I SAW A NEW HEAVEN and a new earth, for the heaven and the earth had vanished, and there was no longer any sea. I saw the Holy City, new Jerusalem, coming down out of heaven from God, made ready like a bride adorned for her husband. I heard a loud voice proclaiming from the throne: 'Now God has his dwelling with mankind! He will dwell among them and they shall be his people, and God himself will be with them. He will wipe every tear from their eyes. There shall be an end to death, and to mourning and crying and pain, for the old order has passed away!'

Thank you, Lord, for making all things beautiful in their time, and for putting eternity into our hearts.

O most high Almighty, good Lord God, creator of the universe, watch over us and keep us light in your presence.

May our praise continually blend with that of all creation, until we come together to the eternal joys which you promise in your love, through Jesus Christ our Lord. Amen.

Source unknown

INDEX OF AUTHORS AND SOURCES

INDEX OF THEMES AND BIBLE PASSAGES

Part Two: God with Us